THE POLITICS OF PEACE

THE
POLITICS OF PEACE

Brian Frost

with Introduction and Theological Reflections by
Donald W. Shriver, Junior

Foreword by the Most Revd Desmond Tutu
Archbishop of Cape Town

DARTON, LONGMAN AND TODD
LONDON

For three Methodists in Liverpool,
one, Ann, a Liverpudlian by birth, two,
John and Rachel, Liverpudlians by adoption.
Without them this book would never have been
completed.

First published in 1991 by
Darton, Longman and Todd Ltd
89 Lillie Road, London SW6 1UD
© 1991 Brian Frost
Theological Reflections © 1991 Donald W. Shriver, Junior

ISBN 0-232-51937-4

A catalogue record of this book is available from the British Library

Phototypeset by Intype, London
Printed and bound in Great Britain by
Courier International Limited, East Kilbride

CONTENTS

FOREWORD

ON 20 MARCH 1990 I was one of thousands in the Wind-hoek Stadium waiting for the clock to strike the midnight hour, when Namibia would become an independent nation. Just before this auspicious hour, the South African State President, Mr de Klerk, made a very good speech which was received with very warm applause. I thought then that he missed a golden opportunity to have made a speech that would have set the world agog. He failed to say two things which would have stamped his speech as outstanding and epoch-making. Had Mr de Klerk added something like, 'If we had caused you any pain in the past, I apologise and to help you celebrate your richly deserved independence we are giving you Walvis Bay', the stadium would have erupted ecstatically. (The port of Walvis Bay is a bone of contention between South Africa and Namibia, it is Namiba's only natural outlet to the outside world.) Mr de Klerk would have dealt with the horrible entail of the past, a legacy of potential hostility, anger, bitterness, and vengefulness that augured ill for future relations between the neighbour countries. He would have done so by repenting on behalf of his people and would have demonstrated his sincerity by the token reparation of abandoning South African claims to Walvis Bay.

On 6 August 1985 I was present in Hiroshima with many thousands as the Japanese commemorated the dropping of the atom bombs on Nagasaki and Hiroshima. As guests with other Nobel laureates of the City of Hiroshima we had been to the commemorative museum and seen the exhibits and the films recording the levels to which we are capable of sinking in our inhumanity to one another. We met with several disfigured survivors of that horrible obscenity perpetrated forty years earlier and we were devastated. I asked what purpose was being served by recalling such a traumatic experience and I was deeply touched when the Japanese said without bitterness or rancour that they commemorated it because this awful thing had happened to them and they did not want it ever to happen again to others. I found their willingness to forgive and their concern for humankind quite staggering.

I have no doubt that repentance and forgiveness are indispensable for setting right relationships between those who have been wronged and the wrongdoers within nations and between nations. Unless you deal with the past in a creative and positive manner then you run the terrible risk of having no future worth speaking about. The past can have a baleful or beneficent impact on the future. This is a fact that is absolutely crucial for us here in South Africa at the present time. We stand on the threshold of exciting possibilities of creating a new, democratic, non-racial, and non-sexist society largely because of the very courageous initiatives of the same Mr de Klerk who must be commended very warmly. And yet that possible future will be seriously undermined if those who benefited from the obnoxious apartheid system, perceived as the oppressors, will not ask for forgiveness for the awful things done under apartheid and if the victims, the oppressed, do not offer forgiveness.

Repentance and forgiveness do make new beginnings possible. They have an inner dynamic which can set off critical acts which then develop a momentum towards new possibilities. I have no doubt that the meetings that Mr de Klerk and his colleagues had with Nelson Mandela and other long-term political prisoners must have played an important role in the courageous decisions that Mr de Klerk subsequently made. Had they encountered embittered people hell-bent on revenge, looking to get their own back on those who had treated them so unjustly, it is doubtful whether Mr de Klerk would have risked releasing them and embarking on the course which makes the emergence of a democratic dispensation a strong probability.

Many believe that you cannot just let bygones be bygones when people have been subjected to the anguish of the injustices and atrocities of apartheid; as when three and a half million have been forcibly uprooted from their traditional homes and dumped, many of them in poverty-stricken bantustan homeland resettlement camps, or relocated in crowded ghetto townships many miles from their places of work when formerly they had lived in mixed residential areas near the cities where they worked; or the trauma that people experienced as they learned of the mysterious deaths in detention of loved ones. The pain of these searing experiences goes deep and the wounds are raw and open. Part of the soothing balm that can be poured over them to assuage the agony is without doubt the expression of regret and repentance at having been part of a community or a system that caused the hurts of oppression and inhumanity. Thus it was a poignant moment fraught with considerable significance for South Africa when the white Dutch Reformed Church, which had provided the theological justification for apartheid, confessed its part in that unholy alliance, and the blacks expressed their willingness to forgive them. These actions are almost certain to have crucial repercussions on developments in our country.

That is why many of us have tried to persuade Mr de Klerk to say, 'We are sorry for all the pain that apartheid has caused you, its victims'. I am deeply distressed that he appears to have a blind spot on this issue. He suggests that certain people have an unfortunate obsession with the past and spoke somewhat insensitively of what he called 'imagined hurts'. You cannot wipe out the past just like that, not even if you then have apparently normal and even warm and friendly relationships, without expressing regret over the past hurt. Even a quarrel between husband and wife cannot be swept under the carpet or be dealt with by being ignored. The hurt will fester and inexorably poison relationships. One of the couple must ultimately say the very difficult words, 'I am sorry', for any hope of reconciliation to emerge. Of course, if Mr de Klerk said he was sorry representatively that would not necessarily make up for all the injustice, but it would have a dramatic effect on human relations which are the basis of community. It would begin to turn enemies into friends. It would begin to draw the poison from the past and make possible new starts.

How I wish I had had a copy of Brian Frost's book because it would have provided me with so many examples of heads of State, political leaders, and others confessing – which would have helped in our discussions with Mr de Klerk and made him realize we were not asking him to blaze a trail that no one else had traversed before. That there were many noble examples in recent history, such as the President of West Germany going to apologize in Coventry cathedral, or Japanese political leaders confessing the Japanese iniquities to the American people, or the United States government paying compensation to native Americans for a violation of their land rights. Perhaps we should point to the fact that Africans seem to be inclined to forgive more readily than most, citing the examples of Kenya under Jomo Kenyatta, or the Zimbabweans under Mugabe where Ian Smith could remain a member of Parliament in post-independent Zimbabwe until he resigned; or the more recent example of Namibia, where we are seeing a remarkable example of efforts at national reconciliation after a bitter war in a country headed by a smiling Sam Nujoma, who returned without a trace of bitterness after over thirty years in exile.

Perhaps we should have told Mr de Klerk the story of the young black political activist, who after being banned with his wife and tortured in detention said of his white jailors to me, 'You know, Father, when they apply these third degree methods on you, you look on them and say, "By the way, these are God's children and they are behaving like animals"; they need us to help them recover the humanity they have lost'. There is hope in a country with such people that the past will not be a dead hand stifling movement to a new future.

This book makes a significant contribution to an indispensable process between and within nations – reconciliation. I hope many politicians will read it and save the world avoidable heartache. Otherwise what on earth is going to happen in places like Kampuchea, El Salvador, Ethiopia, Liberia – will the list ever end?

DESMOND TUTU

PREFACE

SOME TIME AGO I was discussing with a member of the staff of Darton, Longman and Todd what I might do with a wealth of material I had assembled from many parts of the world on the theme of forgiveness in political life. I suggested an anthology but she countered with the suggestion that I write a book, quoting the material but weaving it into a narrative.

The conceptual task was formidable: how could various pieces of history of which I had documentation be made into a chapter around a theme? I decided to provide a broad framework by selecting different parts of the world and, looking at the material in the light of history this century, try to discover how much forgiveness there had been in the political life of each of these areas.

Each of my readers is invited to share the experience I had and to wrestle with the material as I have done. How authentic an experience of forgiveness is being described? How effective is it? These are the questions with which I was left. Also I came to see that forgiveness is only one facet of a complex interplay of themes in many a political scenario.

Obviously much more work needs to be done, as Donald Shriver indicates here in his assessment. What has become clear to me is that, in each of the eleven areas of the world considered in this book, there is a search for peace, and that there can be no peace between groups or between nations unless the issue of forgiveness, whether in the context of group or nation, is faced. But saying this opens up a subject which is both obvious and at the same time irritatingly elusive. If I make readers aware of the importance of this theme, I will have done some useful spadework; I hope others may now be able to start to till the ground.

London, March 1991   BRIAN FROST

INTRODUCTION

CENTRAL TO THIS BOOK is a claim that forgiveness is a fact before it is a theory. This assumption strikes at the root of the popular and academic dogma that so antiseptically separates fact and value. In this book Brian Frost tells us something about his theory of what constitutes a fact; and in eleven of his chapters he often tells us implicitly how humans go about choosing some facts in their history as more important than others. He concentrates on a certain selection of facts in certain histories without worrying too much about the rule under which historians prefer to labour: 'Write the history, and make clear the distinction between the history and your interpretation of it.' Historians are being responsible intellectuals when they try to observe this rule; and doubtless Mr Frost, too, would be the first to agree to qualifications of his interest in forgiveness in the history of nations: politics is more complex than he always acknowledges; what he calls forgiveness may sometimes rightly be called by other names; all the participants to these events have not been heard from – *et cetera*. But I suspect the historians themselves would be the first to come to his defence here. Theirs, too, is a rather embattled science these days. Historians tell stories about the interactions of humans in the past. It is hard to tell such stories without imaginative identification with the lives of persons long dead; hard, too, to be a storyteller without insinuating into the story your own standpoint for telling it and your own participation in some aspect of its impact on the present. Few of us, least of all historians, can avoid the Uncertainty Principle.

Published at a time when war has added new animosities to old in the Middle East, this book is both sober and hopeful about the human future. It offers rich evidence for two generalizations about the political relations of humans on our planet. The first was stated succinctly by William Faulkner: 'The past is not dead and gone; it isn't even past.' The second comes close to being a truism, but it is heavy with wisdom for political change: getting past our past is a prerequisite for getting into our future. New justice in politics is often crippled because the agents and victims of old injustice cannot repair the breach between them. Forgiveness, in politics, is about the repair of that breach.

Here, in these pages, is enough record of actual occurrences of such repair in recent world human affairs to strengthen the hope that realism, not just idealism, is ultimately on the side of an emerging global human community. A political form of forgiveness may not guarantee that we humans can survive our sins against each other. But without it, we might not have survived this long; and we need it, as our capacity to harm or hurt each other grows, more than ever.

New York, March 1991   DONALD W. SHRIVER, JR
                                                                        President
                                                     Union Theological Seminary

1

THE THREAD OF
FORGIVENESS

TO LINK POLITICS and forgiveness is unusual, for they
are two words rarely used in the same context. Some would
say they can never be joined; yet, 'without forgiveness, hurts go
unchecked and we recycle failures, resentments, bitterness, and
mistrust in our lives . . . Without forgiveness, there can be no
real peace and no lasting reconciliation.'[1]

What is politics and what is the nature of forgiveness? 'Politics' is surely the way human beings organize themselves in
groups, either locally, nationally or internationally, to determine
and distribute the use of resources, often in short supply, and
how they handle the institutions they create for doing this.
'Forgiveness' is a word used to indicate that a wrong has been
committed which needs redressing. It is also a word which
implies both accepting a wrong and dealing with it in a constructive way.

'Without being forgiven, released from the consequences of
what we have done, our capacity to act would, as it were, be
confined to a single deed from which we could never recover;
we would remain the victims of its consequences for ever,' the
Jewish philosopher Hannah Arendt has argued.[2] But is there a
difference between individual forgiveness and its effects and
group forgiveness? That is the essence of the debate which the
American theologian, Reinhold Niebuhr, focused on in his book
Moral Man and Immoral Society, where he maintained that 'every
effort to transfer a pure morality of disinterestedness to group
relations has resulted in failure'.[3] Nevertheless Niebuhr did
recognize that forgiveness is a necessary feature of family life.[4]
Perhaps he should have gone on to argue that as we first learn

about the distribution of resources and about issues of justice, power, change and history in a family, it is here we have our first political experience. But he did not seem to link this primary experience of group life with a wider political understanding of forgiveness.

For Christians especially there should be no separating the personal from the corporate, for the Trinity – the doctrine of God at the heart of Christianity – points to a God who reaches us through both our individual and communal relationships. In the Old Testament the Jewish insight is that the covenant people are addressed by God both as a group and by name. In the New Testament this is further developed in the Lord's Prayer as Jesus teaches his followers to link both the horizontal and vertical aspect of relationships when he teaches about forgiveness (Matthew 6:12).

'Jesus once wrestled all night and sweat great drops of blood, only to rise to face his crucifixion with the power of forgiveness on his lips and the imminent finish of the drama of humanization on its way (Luke 22:39–46),' wrote Paul Lehmann in his study of Jesus Christ and the question of revolution. Here he considers that although the Gospel does not show itself fit to deal with 'the centrality and ambiguity of power in human affairs it shows itself in a hidden way fit . . . for dealing with the reality of power'.[5] This passage draws our attention to two forms of power: the power of Jesus' forgiveness made effective through the voluntary offering of his life, and the effect of his at-one-ment on the realities of power if people in authority are willing to seek a way to implement the consequences for politics of this Atonement.

This attitude to power is explored further by Alan Falconer when he writes that

> the distinctiveness of Christianity is not that it renounces the use of power, but that it calls for the integrative use of power. As Christians we experience the 'liberating power of Jesus'. In this we experience God standing alongside human beings, giving them the possibility to grow and develop.[6]

In the following chapters this maturity in handling specific situations is often evident. For example, in the African chapter in the person of Jomo Kenyatta, and in the American chapter through the work of Martin Luther King. There is also much evidence of the abuse of power, whether by Marxists who seek to bring in a new age, or by oppressed groups who wish to transfer power from one group to another. Perhaps the most glaring example of all is Nazi rule in Germany, but the aftermath of colonialism has, on occasions, the same ingredients as the politics which produced such atrocities in Europe.

Issues of peace and war occur continually, leading us to wonder whether there is much difference between the two: are the conflicts of day-to-day politics in 'peacetime' really warfare, only without the weapons of destruction? Several chapters raise the question of the relationship of forgiveness to violence, especially in the Russian context; to repentance, in the case of Germany; to charismatic personalities and the way they handle conflicts, as in the Indian chapter; and to long-standing and unsatisfactory histories between two countries, as in the chapter on Britain and Ireland.

In the two African chapters, where the issue of violence is also prominent, the relation of forgiveness to change is considered. In the narratives on the Middle East, Japan and India, the role of non-Christian faiths emerges strongly as one ingredient in politics and forgiveness, as does Christianity in the European chapter and those on the Americas. How can the oppressed be forgiving? – is the key question raised by the chapters on Latin America and on China's revolution.

Clearly then, as Bishop David Jenkins has argued,

> Forgiveness must not be seen in isolation from the broader theological issues or without any realization of the necessary mediating processes which have to go on in relating these personal categories to structures and institutions. I think that although one can't be satisfied with Niebuhr on the necessary separation between love and justice, nevertheless you can't go behind him.[7]

The relation of forgiveness and justice is thus the vital concept to consider, for much political action is based on the sense of an injustice which needs reversing. But maybe there is an elusive quality to justice, as metaphysical a concept as love, because in reality it is a word which represents hopes which we often cannot reach.

> Distributive justice can never take us beyond the norm of reparation; commutive justice can provide only due compensation, retributive justice has no means of repairing the damage save by punishment and expiation. Restorative justice, as it is revealed in the Bible, alone has positive power for overcoming sin.[8]

We seem, however much we seek to avoid it, to be driven back to the concept of forgiveness in politics again and again, however limited a tool for interpreting human existence it may be. The thread of forgiveness across the twentieth century, with which this book is concerned, shows that despite this difficulty men and women from many backgrounds have wrestled with the issue. Now here, now there, they have found themselves exploring forgiveness in relation to the great themes of political life – to justice, to history, to repentance and reparation, to reconciliation and to power. What is surprising is not that some initiatives failed, but that there have been these attempts to link forgiveness with the processes of politics, and that they can, at least in part, be documented.

The complexities of these topics are well demonstrated in a comment by an American theologian as he described an encounter between a Sri Lankan and a South African. The Sri Lankan, a priest, gave an account of Tamil–Singhalese conflicts there. 'A South African challenged his description because it did not identify a clear oppressor and clear oppressed. It was hard for him to understand a conflict where reconciliation is the first priority and justice a consequence of it.' Later, when visiting South Africa the writer found a further development of this theme; there the question was 'whether the oppressed can maintain Christian fellowship with even repentant fellow believers on the other side'.[9]

A politics of forgiveness must include a recognition of the suffering of the offended.

> In forgiveness the initiative lies with them. The suffering of the oppressed may weld them together into a force capable of breaking powerful regimes. But their real power

or powerlessness becomes apparent after their victory: is it the power to reconstruct or to make a society new? At that point, if those who have grievances cannot find it in themselves to forgive, they will never have the freedom of vision and action necessary to make a different society . . .[10]

Can politicians act in this way only if they have Christian faith? Or is forgiveness part of human experience and wisdom regardless of what faith politicians profess? Here is another complex question posed in this book: it raises the issue of the relation of Christ to the other world faiths and also Christianity's encounter with Marxism. Perhaps God's activity is to be found hidden in the life of the world, as well as within the Churches, that part of society which has recognized and responded to the significance and purpose of Jesus.

Yet there is an inevitable dichotomy. On the one hand is the Church as a corporate institution, 'the community which proves that it is worthy of the gospel of forgiveness by constantly and sincerely proclaiming *God's* forgiveness,' as Dietrich Bonhoeffer has suggested.[11] On the other, Christians are part of the political processes, working with people from many backgrounds to make policy and take decisions. Often they will find colleagues who seem to exemplify forgiveness in politics who do not subscribe to Christian belief, or who have a theological understanding different from their own.

This should make Christians wary of claiming a monopoly of insight and perception. Yet they must wrestle with the implications of their faith, especially as it urges them to shun self-righteousness. This is what the Indian theologian M.M. Thomas does when he talks about 'the real tragedy of Christian witness in politics'. For 'political justice necessitates a self-righteousness leading to definite political decisions,' yet this

> breaks to pieces as we expose ourselves to the Cross of Christ wherein all are seen in common guilt as crucifiers of Christ, needing forgiveness of God and one another. In politics, we are called upon to alternate between this shattering of self-righteousness and this gathering of the pieces of self-righteousness.[12]

M.M. Thomas felt this tension acutely over the issue of Indian independence, but many a politician must have experienced that tension in other contexts. However, the deepest conflict for Christians in politics is surely the tension between the relation of the insights found in communities where Christianity is not in evidence and those of Christian faith.

This is one of the as yet unsolved problems which raise the relation between Christ and culture, touched upon in the Indian and African chapters especially. It is here that the conflict between the Gospel which destroys the past for a new and different future and the Gospel which can penetrate a culture is highlighted. What we can know for certain, as we wrestle with the mystery of God's activity in history, is that the presence of God is known through 'forgiveness and renewal rather than through power and sovereignty, that is, in and through human freedom and not over it . . .'[13]

This is why forgiveness in politics is vital; it concerns our freedom. Yet we can espouse it, or not, as we see fit. It is always easier not to go to God for healing, for bread, for forgiveness, despite Dietrich Bonhoeffer's assertion in his poem 'Christians and Unbelievers' that all turn to God when in need of these.[14] It is always easier, too, to believe that God's mercy has definite boundaries and to build our politics on this conviction rather than act on a wider understanding of human community.

Thus the twentieth century has been a testing time, both for believers and non-believers. The following chapters give some indication of the countless deaths and tragedies in all continents that have resulted from political conflict. Surely this poses a question: If all this suffering is the outcome of the national and international policies pursued this century, is it not time we tried to find a new basis for political action in situations of conflict?

2

THE SOVIET UNION AND HER NEIGHBOURS

TOLSTOY WAS ASLEEP and dreaming he was in a court-room on trial. Yet he was also judge, Czar, and executioner too, of those who, on 1st March 1881, had murdered Alexander II. He woke up from his after-dinner nap in a sweat. He knew that if he were Alexander III, he would pardon the assassins; so he sent a letter to the new Czar urging clemency.

'Your position is a dreadful one,' he wrote, 'but the doctrine of Christ is necessary precisely in order to guide us through such moments of dire temptation which befall every man . . .' Aware of his daring he continued:

> If you do not pardon, but execute the murderers, you will have done away with three or four individuals out of hundreds; but evil breeds evil, and thirty or forty will spring up to replace those three or four . . . But forgive, return good for evil, and out of a hundred wrongdoers ten will be converted, not to your side but to the side of God . . .[1]

Tolstoy was not the only person to urge Alexander III to pursue the way of forgiveness. The writer Soloviev was giving a series of lectures. At his final lecture he startled everyone when he made a strong appeal to the new Czar

> to forgive the murderers of his father, and thus to show the whole world that Russia was a Christian country . . . After a moment of tense silence the crowd rose to its feet. There were shouts of 'Traitor' and 'Murderer' and equally vehement cries of approval.[2]

The next day Soloviev wrote to the Czar in a vein similar to

Tolstoy's letter and received both a rebuff and a restriction on lecturing in public. Tolstoy's plea was also rejected; the Czar was determined to avenge his father's death, and the six assassins were hanged.[3]

In other parts of Europe at that time revolutionary ideas of a very different kind were developing, though some early socialist thought seems to have included elements of forgiveness. For example, Lassalle, a German socialist, was writing:

> He who invokes the idea of the workers' estate as the governing principle of society ... utters a cry that is not calculated to split and separate the social classes. He utters a cry of reconciliation, which embraces the whole of society ... a cry of *love*, which from the very first moment when it rises from the heart of the people, will *remain for ever the true cry of the people* and continue by reason of its content to be essentially a *cry of love* even when it rings out as a battle-cry.[4]

Lassalle, in this statement with its implicit recognition of the possibility of forgiveness in politics, seems to demonstrate solidarity with the oppressed in a manner different from that of Karl Marx. For Marx, unlike his erstwhile colleague, such ideas of brotherhood come only when the classless society has been achieved. Until then the Communist must, if necessary, be as repressive as the capitalist. 'It is a serious misrepresentation of Marx to minimise the sadistic element in his writing,' argues Edmund Wilson.[5] In his address to the Communist League of April 1850, Marx even said that 'far from opposing so-called excesses, the vengeance of the people on hated individuals or attacks by the masses on buildings which arouse hateful memories, we must not only tolerate them, but even take the lead in them.'[6]

Despite this, however, the idealism espoused by Tolstoy was also present in Marx. For, although Marx readily saw the greed of the bourgeoisie, the proletariat, seemingly sinless in his eyes, would act in an exalted way as it flung off its chains in Germany and England. He saw it as the antithesis of the other classes and capable of bringing in a new world.

Here then is another dream, but it contains in it no concept of forgiveness, despite its sense of corporate sin. The way to deal with the past was not to forgive it but to overthrow it. History was seen to be not evolving, but punctuated by abrupt transitions and complete upheavals. Marx himself was sure an upheaval was due, but few expected it to occur in Russia, for to move from a peasant to an industrial society appeared too great a jump. However, the conditions in Russia were ripe for change.

> Was Russia just unlucky in the assassination of 1881, or were all the reforms in her history always too late? If either Alexander II or Alexander III had brought in some kind of representative constitution it would probably have been only a partial reform and would not have silenced the terrorists, but it would have started something which could have grown, if all other circumstances had continued favourable.[7]

This is a large conjecture: at any rate the fledgling social democracy which was emerging just before the First World War proved too weak to withstand the Bolshevik revolution.

But the Russian Revolution went sour. Lenin died, Trotsky was exiled, then murdered, and Stalin reigned supreme, increasingly paranoid and involved in such terror that to this day the Soviets have difficulty in coming to terms with it. A move toward this was made by Mikhail Gorbachev, speaking on the seventieth anniversary of the Revolution, when he described Stalin's crimes as 'enormous and unforgivable',[8] and called for an examination of 'painful points' in Soviet history as he announced the setting up of commissions to study the rehabilitation of Stalin's victims.[9]

In his famous speech to the Communist Party in 1956, Khrushchev too had admitted many of these 'errors' though a recent report has indicated he risked his own life in the process, as the majority of his colleagues were against his denunciation of Stalin.[10] This is hardly surprising, for Marxism, the one Western idea about which Western Europe had been most ambivalent, has a difficult world view mixing as it does nineteenth-century rationalism and Hegelian dialectic. With its essentially materialistic interpretation of reality, it fits uneasily with the holistic and ecological views of the universe now emerging.

Moreover for Marx, 'morality is and always has been "class morality" '.[11] Lesek Kolakowski, once a leading Polish theoretician, and author of a history of communism, seemed to confirm this view when he wrote, in connection with forgiveness in politics, 'I do not know of any Marxist literature dealing with the subject, and, in general, "forgiveness" is an entirely un-Marxist idea.'[12]

Marxists are, however, intensely aware of evil. 'There is no doubt that the leaders of contemporary Marxist societies are well aware of corporate sin: corruption, anti-social selfishness, and so on. The list is long. But the response is condemnation, not forgiveness.'[13]

This corporate sense is evident in a recent evaluation of Dostoyevsky by a Marxist critic. 'Of all Dostoyevsky's novels *Crime and Punishment* is the most socially significant. Here Dostoyevsky relates the "poisoned" mind and heart, the "poisoned" thoughts and feelings of his characters directly to society which is corrupt, which is itself "poisonable".'[14]

The matter is more complex than this, for, as Paul Tillich has observed when writing about the neo-collectivist:

> It is not his personal sin that produces anxiety or guilt but a real or possible sin against the collective ... To the collective he confesses, often in forms reminiscent of early Christianity or later sectarian groups. From the collective he accepts judgement and punishment. To it he directs his desire for forgiveness and his promise of self-transformation.[15]

This seems to be borne out by a letter in *The Guardian* in 1985 about the emigration of Jews from the Soviet Union to Israel. Writing from the Novosti Press Agency in Moscow, Sergei Snegov explained why there seemed to be a hold-up over certain Jews leaving the USSR. In the particular case of Dimitry Shapiro, he defended what had happened, but the point to note is not the defence but the language he uses: 'The article of the criminal code which is relevant to his crime envisions a prison term of up to three years, but in view of his sincere repentance the court rules to release him from detention and to suspend his sentence.'[16]

Behind such a statement, for Western readers, there lies the spectre of show trials. The story of the arrest and treatment under pressure of Cardinal Mindszenty of Hungary, who con-

fessed to nonsensical crimes and was sentenced to life imprisonment, indicates that such methods lasted well into the 1950s.

The Marxist solution to evil in society – revolution – seems
almost always to lead to tyranny, sometimes even greater than
the oppression which has been overthrown. Moreover, how can
one speak about ethical ideals if, as Marxism has maintained,
history is dialectical, and wrong interpretations are inevitably
going to be overcome in due time? The 1960s edition of the
Soviet Encyclopaedia made an attempt when it condemned
Vishinsky, Stalin's chief prosecutor, for taking 'an erroneous
view of the law and the state'. About the same period the Soviet
Encyclopaedia of History, reproducing Lenin's 'testament'
which criticized Stalin, gives credit for his early revolutionary
work, then adds: 'Extreme measures were taken and mistakes
made in carrying out collectivization, the responsibility for which
Stalin must bear.'[17]

The same issue, of how to forgive the events of history when
all possibility of a politics of forgiveness seems to have been
excluded, occurs in the Soviet Union's relations with its Eastern
bloc partners. And it works both ways. If the Soviet Union has
difficulty forgiving Germany (over 20 million USSR citizens
died in the great 'patriotic war', as they call the Second World
War), the Hungarians cannot forgive the Soviet Union its role
in history.

> In Hungary a great effect was produced by the charming
> little story, about the Ambassador of the Mongolian Peo-
> ple's Republic who, in his first official note after taking up
> his duties here, apologized in the name of his government
> for Ghenghis Khan's cruel invasion of 1241, which half
> destroyed our country.[18]

Maybe this was a small incident, safely in the past, but:

> Oppression's most powerful enemy is the memory of the
> survivors and their descendants. We Hungarians have long
> felt ashamed because we occupied part of the Ukraine for
> two or three years during World War II. Now they ought
> to start being ashamed for having kept us under occupation
> for nearly forty years.

Perhaps the first critical exhibition of Stalinism and the move to multi-party politics in Hungary will be a decisive step in this direction.[19]

Yet co-existence with the Soviet Union is difficult, not only because of its fear (twice in two centuries West Europeans have reached the heartland of Russia), but because it has a distinct sense of mission, stemming in part from the idea of Moscow as the 'Third Rome' as well as the messianic claims of Marxist theory.

For example, when the Czechoslovaks tried to create a new form of socialism in the 1960s, the Soviet government was unable to accept these developments. The 'Prague Spring', as it was called, came to focus on Alexander Dubcek who became First Secretary of the Czechoslovak Communist Party in January 1968. Dubcek, married in church, had already demonstrated unusual qualities as a Communist, and was elected to the Communist Party Presidium in 1962. He had been a member of a commission set up by the Party (with pressure from Khrushchev) to investigate the justice or injustice of politics between 1949 and 1954. Since 1960 he had been concerned about the validity of earlier trials, especially those of bourgeois nationalists, and whether they had violated socialist legality.

This commission reported in February 1963 that during 'the cult of personality' injustice had occurred, many good communists had been victims and the leadership of the time was to blame.[20] Once in office Dubcek 'only then began to realize the appalling things done by the Party in the fifties'. He wept 'when people told him of the cruelties of the past ... "How is it possible for Communists to behave like this?" '[21] he asked.

The commission led to changes in policy, and it was these which alarmed the Soviet leadership. Eventually there was a confrontation at Cierna involving most of the Politbureau of the USSR and their Czech opposite numbers, when for four hours Brezhnev recounted the crimes the Czechs were said to have committed, including a number of articles in the press (Dubcek had allowed considerable press freedom). Brezhnev also abused some of Dubcek's colleagues for their views.

Here was a twofold irony: Dubcek had been a loyal ally of

the USSR and had not considered such treatment possible; nor did he believe that Warsaw Pact forces would invade. Yet he remained penitent, if that is the right word, for the way the Czechoslovak Communist Party had behaved, and thereby lost popular support. On 22 February 1968, the twentieth anniversary of the communist take-over of power, in the presence of East European and Soviet leaders, he asked all Czechs and Slovaks to help him lead the country away from apathy. He wanted workers to co-operate and he stressed the need for full rehabilitation of former political prisoners, those who had suffered under the old regime and especially all who had 'worked for the Republic in the First and Second World Wars'. He criticized the nationality clauses in the 1960 constitution and said that a new arrangement for both Slovaks and Czechs must be created.

At that time Dubcek also talked of the Party not ruling society by force, but having to defend its leading position in public discussion. He argued that 'authority must be renewed, it's never given to anyone once and for all'.[22] He expected greater freedom for artists and also a new type of 'socialist democracy'. This was heady stuff, and inevitably some found it difficult when political prisoners were exonerated. 'A former investigator and his victim live at a small summer resort near Prague. One of them has retired, and the other has been rehabilitated,' one writer has recorded. 'Both are mentally and physically broken. On sunny days they meet for lunch at a garden restaurant. Such amity is not general.'[23]

Dubcek's socialism with a human face ended after the invasion by Warsaw Pact forces, and Dr Gustav Husak took his place. With it ended also the formal aspects of the Christian-Marxist dialogue of the 1960s, which had flourished, especially in Prague, as the two ideologies and some of their leading intellectuals began to view each other more sympathetically, perhaps even with forgiveness.

However, history is full of surprises, and recently the director of the Institute of Marxism-Leninism in Moscow has said he felt the 1968 military invasion of Czechoslovakia would be included in Mr Gorbachev's broad reassessment of Soviet history,[24] an assessment which led to an official condemnation of the intervention.[25] More dramatic, because more personal, was the 'pilgrimage' of retired Colonel-General Ivan Dimitrivich Yershov, the Soviet general who, as deputy commander of the Warsaw Pact forces, had master-minded the invasion. Now a private citizen, in the autumn of 1990 he went to Prague to see Alexander Dubcek and to visit the shrine to Jan Palach (the student who burnt himself for freedom) in Wenceslas Square. It had been expected that Dubcek would accept his apology for the invasion. The historic encounter lasted more than an hour, but Dubcek offered no forgiveness; the best response he could make was that the general's second visit to Prague was 'better late than never'.[26]

The Soviet Union's use of its power has been viewed with alarm by Alexander Solzhenitsyn. He maintains that states cannot be exempted from the 'laws and demands which constitute the aim and meaning of individual lives'.[27] Solzhenitsyn considers that, amongst the Russian intelligentsia of the nineteenth century, there was a mood of repentance which had incalculable consequences. 'Not for nothing,' he writes, 'was the "day of forgiveness" such a high point in our calendar.'[28] One nineteenth-century historian studying earlier documents even found many cases of Russians moved by repentance to forgive debts, cancel debt-slavery or set bondsmen free, actions which did much to soften cruel laws. In the present century such attitudes have declined, and often the guilty ones are seen to be other groups, anyone except ourselves.

Yet evil, on a massive scale, perpetrated by Russians, has been 'in our own country, not abroad, not to *others*. No one has borne so much of the suffering as the Russians, Ukrainians and Byelorussians.'[29] Only through the repentance of a multitude of people can 'the air and soil of Russia be cleansed so that a new, healthy national life can grow up'.[30]

Solzhenitsyn believes that, once national repentance occurs, Russians may then turn to acknowledge their *external* sins. If for example you take the Russo-Polish theme, there is 'an endless tangle of crimes'.[31] There has been the suppression of the 1830 and 1863 risings, Russification, and more recently the Katyn massacre, as well as Russian immobility as Warsaw burned, and the stab in the back to Poland in September 1939.

Not that the Poles are innocent either, for theirs is a long history of anti-Russian activity. How can we possibly rise 'above all this, except by mutual repentance?' Solzhenitsyn thunders. If there is mutual guilt, perhaps the repentance is that much easier. But the Russians must do more than cry. Indeed, 'repentance opens up the path to a new relationship, between nations as between individuals'.[32] Solzhenitsyn then makes a critical observation when he maintains:

> The repentance of a nation, like any other kind, assumes the possibility of *forgiveness* on the part of the injured. But it is impossible to expect forgiveness before you yourself have made up your mind to forgive. The path of mutual repentance and mutual forgiveness is one and the same.[33]

Stemming from this, Solzhenitsyn sees a second most important activity – self-limitation. We are always willing to limit others; now the task is painfully to learn to limit ourselves. For Russians especially, this means developing the north-east areas of the USSR, not Africa, or the Mediterranean, or Asia!

Some will make of this argument yet another example of Solzhenitsyn's unrealistic messianic vision. Yet they could be wrong, for in the Russian experience there is this feeling for, and hope of, forgiveness. It is a fact, for example, that the Beatitudes of Christ are regularly intoned in the Orthodox liturgy, and over the centuries this exaltation of the Sermon on the Mount must have influenced the lives of the Russian peoples greatly.

This Christian background may well be also a source of the characteristic outgoingness of Russians. For, while their rulers have tended to follow an urge to crush and overpower, among the people can often be seen a splendid generosity. It comes out in Yevtushenko's biography as he describes how his mother took him back to Moscow in 1941, and he saw German war prisoners being marched through Moscow's streets. 'There I saw our enemies for the first time. If my memory is right nearly 20,000,' he records. The watching crowd were mostly women, their hands rough from hard work. 'Every one of them must have had a father or a husband, a brother or a son killed by the Germans.' They were, therefore, gazing with hatred as the column of prisoners approached. Now 'they saw the German soldiers, thin, unshaven, wearing dirty bloodstained bandages, hobbling on crutches or leaning on the shoulders of their comrades; the soldiers walked.with their heads down.' There was silence in the street, the sound only of shuffling of boots and crutches hitting the ground. 'Then,' writes Yevtushenko:

> I saw an elderly woman in broken-down boots push herself forward and touch a policeman's shoulder, saying, 'Let me through.' . . . She went up to the column, took from inside her coat something wrapped in a coloured handkerchief and unfolded it. It was a crust of black bread. She pushed it awkwardly into the pocket of a soldier, so exhausted that he was tottering on his feet. And now suddenly from every side women were running towards the soldiers pushing into their hands bread, cigarettes, whatever they had . . . The soldiers were no longer enemies. They were people.[34]

We catch an echo of this spirit in the words of Archbishop Pitrim, as he maintains that 'the only real enemies are sin and death', and these combine in war, the common enemy of all. We have to overcome, he argues, 'the images which reduce one another to an enemy, for such an enemy as war often comes from perceptions or misperceptions of others, from our enemy images'. In conversation with his New Testament class at Zagorsk he concluded, 'We have come to realize that the early Christians did not search for the enemy in others but rather in themselves, and in this way they transformed the whole world.'[35]

So, although it may be hard to find in the USSR spoken evidence of forgiveness at the level of national and international politics, there is often at the personal level a declared willingness to forgive. Henry Metelmann, a member of the German army unit which had fought in the USSR, experienced this spirit in the Russian people. Haunted for many years by the kindness of those he met at the time of the battle of Stalingrad – people who had every reason to hate him – in later life he came to repent of his actions as a soldier then and sought out Russians to ask their forgiveness.

In 1985 an English magazine devoted to fostering British-

Soviet friendship reprinted a letter by Valentina Chekunoya, which had originally appeared in *Pravda*. It recounted the sufferings of her small village when the Germans invaded. Metelmann wrote her a letter telling of his own part in similar incidents. Accepting that he had no right simply to say he was sorry or to ask for forgiveness, he yet wanted to stretch out his hand to Valentina Chekunoya. He said he hoped that Russian people would take it, for he wanted to be their friend.[36]

Klaus Krance had a similar encounter when he visited the Soviet Union with a group. He has recorded how he was

> deeply moved by an old woman we met while travelling along a country road. . . . As soon as she heard that we were German, on our way to the memorial at Katyn, where German soldiers had locked the inhabitants of a whole village, 149 people in all, 76 of them children, the youngest only a few weeks old, in a barn and set it on fire, she started giving us flowers and apples as gifts, having tears in her eyes.

He came away from his Russian visit convinced that he found there people who had learned their history well, yet 'were willing to forgive'.[37]

How have the churches in the USSR handled issues of forgiveness? The continual evocation of the Beatitudes in the Russian Orthodox liturgy has been noted already. But the churches are also political institutions, with a dynamic which interacts with other groups.

For many decades Christians in the Soviet Union were perceived in the West as either too conformist to the demands of the state or as martyrs, needing the prayers and concern of Western Christians. Certainly this was one aspect of Russian life – with some alleviation for the churches during the Second World War. Now, under Mr Gorbachev's policy of *perestroika* (re-structuring), the situation has changed dramatically and the churches have much greater freedom. During the millennium celebrations of the Russian Orthodox Church, for example, the Orthodox Liturgy was seen on television.

Equally significant has been the appearance of works like

Pasternak's formerly banned *Dr Zhivago*, also of a remarkable film *Repentance* (*Pokayaniye*), which has been shown all over the Soviet Union. This film is about a dictator called Varlaam who, even after death, has an awful presence when he reappears, propped up in the garden of the family villa.

A night watch on the cemetery reveals that the daughter of two of his victims, who were artists, has dug up the corpse. On trial she maintains that Varlaam should not be buried, for that implies he is forgiven; instead, he should be thrown to the vultures. His family are appalled, especially Varlaam's grandson who finds it difficult to believe in the tyrant as revealed by the trial. Eventually convinced, he asks forgiveness of the woman on trial, and then, with a gun given him by Varlaam, he shoots himself. His father too sees the stark truth and is finally seen throwing the remains of his father to the vultures.

'More than anything else', writes a reviewer,

> this is a religious film. The daughter of the artists has survived. By the time of Varlaam's death she is a baker making cakes modelled as churches . . . in the final scene an old lady asks her: 'Does this street go to the church?' 'No, it is Varlaam Street – a street named after Varlaam can't lead to a church.' 'What good,' asks the lady, 'is a street that doesn't take you to a church?'[38]

'The conflict in the socialist countries again and again centres around the social consequences of religious freedom,'[39] observed Gunter Krusche. Herein lies the painful dilemma for Christians in the Soviet Union, for Christianity is social, influencing all life. A key aspect of this fact is the relation of repentance and history which has led some to see the rise of Marxism in eastern Europe as a judgement of God on the churches there for having been linked too closely in previous centuries to structures of injustice and privilege.

Bishop Berecksy in Hungary writes:

> One day I saw in front of our church a naked corpse which was flung on the pavement, and all I had to say to my family was that when our corpses will lie in that manner, there will be nothing else to say but this: 'Lord God Almighty, true and righteous are thy judgments.' My fare-

well to the congregation was this word: 'There shall not
be left one stone upon another.'

But instead, Bishop Berecksy continues, God chose to spare his
Church and the Hungarian people. The bishop realized this
when the first Soviet soldiers broke in on his family. He
expected to be killed outright, but instead the soldiers smiled
and started to play with his grandchildren. 'In that very moment
a new reality began to dawn on me . . . It was the kindness of
these Soviet soldiers to my grandchildren which brought hope
into my consciousness. Perhaps, after all this destruction, there
will still be a church, a nation, a future.'[40]
Yet does not such identification of the new order with God's
actions in history contain a weakness? The same question may
be applied to concepts of repentance as developed by Professor
Hromadka in Prague, despite the truth in his attack 'on the
disquieting self-assurance of too many "Western" churchmen
and theologians that they are free of any self-imposed prejudice
and that only "the other side" might be a victim of propaganda
pressure, a police supervision, and a systematic indoctrination.'[41]
For Hromadka's and Berecksy's own repentance, with all its
biblical ring, follows too closely the requirements of adjustment
to the power of Communism to be wholly convincing. It is
repentance for *past* sins. This is, of course, valid, but these
spokesmen for Christians in eastern Europe fail to face the
problem of repentance for more immediate sins.[42]
This will not do, nor the too easy alignment of Christianity
and capitalism in the West. Certainly the Soviet Union is right
to be proud of its collective identity and its often startling
economic achievements since 1917. But the *sobornost* (together-
ness) of the Church and nation did not allow sufficient disconti-
nuity between Christ and society. It was not, therefore, only the
state's refusal to allow Christians to contribute to society which
was wrong, but also the way many Christians in eastern Europe
often saw their way of relating.
It may be that the recent agreement between Mother Teresa
and the Soviet authorities, which allows her order both to bring
succour to destitute Armenians and also subsequently to open
a house to serve Russians in distress, points to an alternative
way for Russia's Christians. Certainly the USSR now seems

ready to allow its churches to play a constructive role in helping in the social affairs of people, especially those in acute need, and sees its curb on religious activity to have been a serious error.

A significant contribution has also been made by Andrei Sakharov. His plea for peaceful co-existence will surely, in the long perspective of history, help towards a greater sympathy between peoples. Solzhenitsyn, as he nominated Sakharov for the Nobel Peace prize, said the Nobel Committee ought not to have doubts because of Sakharov's earlier work in the field of weapons nor feel that this was a contradiction. 'For when man's spirit acknowledges earlier errors, it is cleansed and freed from them: and herein lies the highest value of man's existence on earth.'[43]

There can be no doubt that Mr Gorbachev too has made a powerful impact with his policies, not least in admitting difficulties due to the Soviet Union's 'own shortcomings and deficiencies'. Moreover, in relation to the USA, his conviction that 'we must not allow things to go so far as confrontation between our two countries,'[44] indicated a readiness for co-operation between the USSR and the USA, the fruits of which can be seen already in many parts of the world, as well as in arms-limitation agreements.

One of the main aspects of forgiveness in politics is here acknowledged: the willingness of politicians to allow systems to coexist and live side by side, even though there is disagreement about aims and goals. We need to see that utopianism can often become dogmatic and cause much suffering. Therefore 'the task for contemporary man is to accept the reality that society is unperfect, but also to understand that humanist, humanitarian dreams and visions are necessary in order to reform society, in order to improve and advance it'.[45]

Perhaps it is the task of the churches, with vision and a strong sense both of the personal and corporate wrong of which human beings are capable, to help politicians understand this and to play an interpreting role so that the twin responses of apathy (because the task of politics is too difficult) and utopianism (which is a flight from reality) can be transcended.

Such a role seems possible, especially in the context of Russian Christianity.

... the Russian soul has, perhaps, a greater capacity for asserting its will to achieve the miracle of religious transfiguration, ... the will of the Russian people has need of purification and tempering; and our people has a great expiation in store for it. Only then will its will to transfigure life give it the right to determine its mission in the world,

wrote the Russian philosopher, Nicolas Berdyaev, pointing to a crucial area of religious experience.[46] For if Marxism needs the spirituality of the churches, they in turn need a more dynamic sociality. So Dostoyevsky's conviction that Christ 'can forgive everything, all and for all, because he gave his innocent blood for all and everything,'[47] can be seen as helpful both to church and society.

Moreover, we are *all* to blame. It is significant that when the jury system was instituted in Russia in the 1860s it was found extremely difficult to secure convictions. Dostoyevsky seized on this as he tried to picture a jury's state of mind:

We sit in the juror's box and perhaps we think: 'Are we ourselves better than the defendant? Here we are, rich and secure; but if we were to find ourselves in the same position as he, perhaps we should do even worse than he – so we will acquit.' Perhaps it is good that we should feel thus; it is sincere mercifulness. It is perhaps the pledge for some sort of higher Christianity which the world has not yet known.[48]

Dostoyevsky was also aware of the essential freedom human beings have. Indeed, yearning for a new world can end up in despotism (as in the Soviet Union in the 1930s). ' "Oh," says Father Zossima, "there are some who remain proud and fierce even in hell in spite of this certain knowledge and contemplation of the absolute truth ... They refuse forgiveness, they curse God who calls them ..." '[49]

Perhaps the Rumanian writer Petru Dumitriu has written more clearly than anyone else of this vision of living by forgiveness. He, a believer, in the sense that Marxists are believers, came to see the essential frailty of all political power and explored this as the narrator in a novel. Had he not found hatred and fear in the way he had lived and must he not therefore try something else? Through suffering, he realized, he was being impelled towards love and forgiveness.

> But since I was part of the world, with everything that I was and did, then my love and forgiveness were the world's own love and forgiveness, which it was teaching me in this harsh fashion, the only one I was capable of understanding. And if to love and forgive the world could bring me comfort and joy, was this not the proof of its own love and forgiveness? Whence did I acquire the power to love and forgive except from the world, from life itself, which had bestowed it on me, ready for my own use when I was ready to use it?[50]

It is a strength of Mikhail Gorbachev's policies that east European countries are now finding a new place for themselves in Europe, as well as new relationships with the USSR itself. Already these new policies from Moscow have enabled the East Germans to apologize to Prague for the part they played in the Warsaw Pact invasion of Czechoslovakia in 1968.

Inside the USSR *perestroika* has allowed a new and unprecedented candour, both in terms of multi-party politics and in a willingness to admit the mistakes of the past. But it has also unleashed forces of nationalism and economic discontent, which impede processes of gradual reform and provoke the reactionary forces of hard-line Communism. Within this crisis are the seeds of change and a challenge to the Soviet Union to come to terms with its past and to create a different future. It remains to be seen whether that future will contain within it the possibility of forgiveness of the kind Dumitriu has described.

3

GERMANY'S ROLE IN EUROPE

DURING THE SECOND WORLD WAR France, like Russia, was devastated by the German invasion. It was significant, therefore, when President Mitterand and Chancellor Kohl clasped hands at Verdun on 24th September 1984, thus setting the seal on a long process of German–French reconciliation.[1] Indeed, it can be argued that seeds of the Second World War lay in the settlements concluding the First World War.

That war was savage in its disregard of life. Apart from the Christmas truce, when German and English soldiers at the front fraternized, sang carols, shared food together and were allowed to bury their dead, few incidents are now recalled which transcend the 'enemy images' of which Archbishop Pitrim spoke. During the war there were, however, a few people in Britain who drew attention to the situation which led up to the conflict, and to human sinfulness. Amongst these was Studdert Kennedy, an army chaplain with the troops in France. 'I see *John Bull* says you're saints. Well, all I can say is "eyes right" and look at your neighbour,'[2] he declared. He was part of a National Mission of Repentance and Hope which the Church of England had sponsored; but it had little effect, for there were few who echoed the words of Mrs E.K. Paget, wife of the Bishop of Stepney: 'Motherhood, womanhood, has reached her Calvary. Then let the words on our lips be the words of forgiveness and hope.'[3]

When the Peace Treaty was signed on 28th June 1919 many in Britain, like Bishop Moule, considered that Germany 'must not go without some retributory pains and penalties as will mark her awful wrongdoings with a brand of solemn condemnation,' an opinion echoed by Bishop Chevasse who argued that 'the evil-doers must be punished and reparation made'.[4] On the other hand, 'A sore, bitter and hostile Germany will be of no benefit to the community of European nations,' wrote a correspondent to *The Manchester Guardian* in November 1918,[5] but such a view was seldom expressed.

The Versailles Peace Conference, which opened in January 1919, set up the League of Nations and a mandatory system whereby the victorious powers were to govern the German colonies and the Turkish areas now under their control. Provision was also made for a Court of International Justice. Some German territories and boundaries had to be settled; Poland and Czechoslovakia were the immediate gainers, Austria a loser. German forces were to be severely curtailed, Germany demilitarized, all German state property in her former colonies confiscated and her trading privileges abrogated. France, with devastated areas and desolated cities, wanted the highest indemnities, her memory indeed going back to 1871. With this lack of generosity on the part of the victors toward their defeated enemies, the seeds were sown for further tragedy in Europe.

Many things caused Germany to smart, especially the French occupation of the Ruhr and the high cost of reparations leading to economic hardship and unemployment. Even as late as 1931 France forced Austria to abandon her idea of a customs union with Germany. This did, however, lead to intervention by Britain and America which produced first a moratorium, then a final liquidation of Germany's debts.

It was too late. In 1924 Adolf Hitler had written *Mein Kampf,* sketching the programme he was eventually to put into practice. Slowly Germany moved to the Right and Hitler was appointed Chancellor. At the core of his vision was a political system in which a superior master-race obeyed a leader in whom all authority was vested. This set the course for all that came after – persecution of the weak and glorification of the Aryan race. The Jews and the Marxists became the scapegoats for Germany's problems as German nationalism became the virtue most admired.

By the middle of the 1930s Hitler was firmly entrenched in power, merging the office of President with that of Chancellor on the death of President Hindenberg. On 7 March 1936, Hitler announced his intention to reoccupy the Rhineland, a demilitarized zone under the Versailles Treaty. German troops entered the Rhineland the same night. Hitler justified his action by arguing that the Versailles Treaty had been violated by the recently forged Franco–Soviet Pact of 2 May 1935.

By 1936 Hitler had committed himself to regaining German colonies, showed his contempt for the League of Nations and made a move to the east. Slowly countries fell to the German armies. After the Rhineland came Austria, then the Sudetenland, then the rest of Czechoslovakia. Italy joined Germany in the Axis Pact. On 25 November 1936 Japan and Germany signed a pact against Communism to which Italy later acceded.

International politics were tortuous, with France and Russia joined for some purposes and Britain pledged to defend France. It was clear that the Munich Agreement only postponed war. Growing Polish-German tension led to a widening breach between Germany and Britain. Hitler declared that the Anglo-Polish Declaration of 6 April 1939 broke the German-Polish Treaty of January 1934, but the Poles denied this.

On 1 September 1939, despite all efforts to stop him, Hitler invaded Poland. First Britain, then France, gave Germany an ultimatum; on 3 September war was declared.

This brief summary of interactions between various states of Europe serves to illustrate how situations get out of hand and war ensues. It is commonly thought that war solves problems; in effect it only suspends the problem and makes forgiveness in politics more difficult. When a war is over, then societies have to revert to the problems of fallible corporate life with the added complications which the war has brought to already complex histories.

So it proved after the Second World War. Russia was determined that never again would western Europe, in particular Germany, attack her. Hence she needed secure boundaries, and to ensure this Germany must be divided in two. There were other immense changes: Lithuania, Latvia and Estonia became part of the USSR; Poland's boundaries were once again altered; and during the next few years the USSR helped communist elites to take power in countries on her western borders – in Bulgaria, Rumania, Czechoslovakia and Hungary. The war had altered the balance of power in Europe and left her with a 'civil war' at her heart between the rival ways of seeing reality.

The immediate effects of the Second World War were disastrous also for Germany. Its economy and many of its cities were shattered, and the difficulties it faced in rebuilding relations with the rest of Europe were compounded when the full horror of the persecution of the Jews and their fate in Buchenwald, Belsen, Ravensbrück and other concentration camps became known.

The German Churches had immediate post-war difficulties, too. How were they to relate to the world-wide fellowship of Churches now emerging? Since the 1930s there had been a split within German Protestantism between the members of the Confessing Church (Christians who had opposed Hitler entirely) and those members of the official Churches who had compromised with the Nazi state. It was the confessing Christians, amongst whom were Martin Niemöller and Hans Lilje (Dietrich Bonhoeffer had been hung at Flossenberg as a result of the attempted bomb plot on Hitler's life), who met together with other church leaders soon after the end of the war to consider the situation of the Churches now the war had ended. 'Guilt for the past rests on us,' said Niemöller, 'a guilt that is terrible in the eyes of men, terrible also and enormous in the eyes of God.'[6]

These church leaders then met, in October 1945, with representatives of the World Council of Churches, at that time in process of formation. They issued what became known as the Stuttgart Declaration of Guilt, which repudiated all efforts to vaporize German guilt or to make repentance a matter between Germany and God rather than between Germany and the offended nations. It admitted that through Germany endless suffering had been brought to many peoples and countries, and went on to speak of a new beginning which was to be made with other Churches across the world. It was signed by nearly a dozen leaders some of whom, like Bishop Dibelius and Dr Heinemann, were destined to play an important role in the post-war Churches of both East and West Germany.[7]

The Stuttgart Declaration has to be understood in the context of the debate then ensuing in Germany about guilt for the Second World War. Some people outside the country were trying to make Germany solely responsible for what had happened. This raised the spectre of a charge that had been levied against Germany after the First World War of 'sole war guilt'. Now it was seen as 'collective guilt' on the part of the German people. The indictments were only half true, for though it *was* true that the German people were collectively responsible for the rise of Nazism, this did not make all Germans equally guilty of each of Hitler's crimes.

Professor Helmut Thielicke, in particular, felt that the 'historic guilt' of a whole people was never unilateral and that the 'Dictate of Versailles' had laid the groundwork for the current situation. Moreover, the subsequent recognition of the Nazi regime by other states made them as guilty of collaboration as ordinary Germans.

His argument did not carry the day. As early as Whit Sunday 1945, when the Church of Frankfurt spoke its first official word to the congregation, it sternly repudiated evasion of guilt: 'Certainly the war was rooted in the sins of *all* nations, but at this moment it is not for us to blame this punishment on others, but on ourselves.' Others, like Pastor Hans Asmussen in Nuremburg, did the same.[8]

Reaction to the Stuttgart Declaration outside Germany was positive; inside Germany the bald statement handed out to the press with little explanation of its background raised hostility. Some even felt it opened the way to another Versailles; others that the obliteration of Dresden and other bombing atrocities cast doubt on the righteousness of other countries. Yet more felt they had expressed repentance before and no notice had been taken of it; indeed the repentance had been misinterpreted. Some even felt the occupation forces themselves were behaving like the Nazis.

The Protestant church leaders met these attacks directly, encouraging pastors and people to adopt the Declaration spirit of *public* contrition as their own. Hans Lilje hammered home the need for repentance by relating how, during the war, the Anglican Bishop of Chichester had protested frequently in the House of Lords about Britain's indiscriminate bombing of residential areas and how Pastor Pierre Maury of France had admitted at Stuttgart his own personal feelings of guilt, despite the occupation of his country and the fact that only twelve out of the forty of his parishioners who went to concentration camps survived.

In November 1945, a few weeks after the Declaration, there was held the first post-war Day of Repentance and Prayer, a Christian festival the Nazis had tried to suppress. At a great public service Martin Niemöller listed the countries that had suffered at the hands of Germany: 'Poland! Greece! Norway! Holland! We must resolve that this never happens again,' he declared.[9]

What was the significance of the Stuttgart Declaration? It was threefold: it enabled the German Protestant Churches to face the churches of other countries with frankness, and opened the way to a new relationship; it enabled the German Churches themselves to go ahead and help in the task of rebuilding Germany; and it had an effect on other countries, like Japan, who issued their own confessions of guilt in the early 1960s. Indeed its influence was still felt in the 1980s, for Christians in South Africa have been well aware of the Stuttgart Declaration when making their statements and confessions about the sin of *apartheid*.

The issue of corporate responsibility for Nazism lingered on, as seen, for example, in the furore which occurred when the West German government announced in November 1964 that it would not extend the statute of limitations for Nazi war criminals.

The immediate issue was whether enough Nazi war criminals had been traced by the special department set up for this purpose by the West German government. Since 1945, 5,445 war criminals had been convicted and sentenced, and the department had information on 7,000 further suspects whose cases would eventually come before German courts. However, many believed that perhaps 6,000 more were living under assumed names.

The issue of the statute of limitations itself was settled, temporarily at least, when the West German Parliament voted on March 25th, 1965, to extend the limitations until December 31st, 1969, twenty years after the new West

German Republic was given its first measure of sovereignty
by the Allied Occupation Powers . . .[10]

But the question the statute raises is this: When does a nation
become free of its past, especially in relation to other nations?
'Twenty years is enough,' said Willi Brandt, 'the time for repentance is over.'[11]

But there were many who were not ready to forgive or forget.
The failure of West Germany to extend diplomatic recognition
to most East European nations in the 1950–60 period, due to
unresolved territorial disputes and the recognition given to these
states by East Germany, was branded by some critics of West
Germany as *Unbussfertigkeit* (unwillingness to repent). Against
this, however, signs of repentance may be seen in the treaty
between Germany and Israel agreed in 1952, whereby Israel
received from West Germany payments in the form of goods
worth three billion deutschmark, to be made within twelve years.
The formal basis for this treaty was the fact that during the
Hitler period hundreds of thousands of refugees from Germany
had arrived in Palestine deprived of their possessions. But
behind the treaty, it had been said, 'was the determination not
to atone for – that was impossible – the worst crime in Europe's
long and bloody history, but to make a gesture in that direction'.[12] Moreover the Federal Republic paid the surviving Jews,
those who returned to Germany and those who did not, compensation which amounted to some $11,000 million.

Some critics did not regard this as sufficient, nor other forms
of reparation to European states, considering that only a complete change in the economic structure of Germany, such as
changes forced on Japan by the USA, would be enough. West
Germany began to feel it was being punished for the sins of the
fathers which should not be visited on the children. 'West
Germans recoil from the repetitive trials today because they feel
that the new Germany is being made to pay for the sins of the
old,' observed an American press report.[13]

One thing is clear from these arguments: guilt must be turned
into responsibility. 'What *does* the family of nations want Germany to *do* now about its guilty past?' asks one commentator.
'Certainly we do not want Germans to forget their past. That
is why we should be sure that the Nazi period is adequately

dealt with in textbooks, history courses, and literature . . .' But also some word of 'forgiveness and restoration must be spoken to Germans, both individually and collectively. This word will have to be spoken, when it is spoken, by those who were most seriously hurt by the Nazis . . .'[14]

In 1985, the fortieth anniversary of the Second World War, the issue surfaced again, over the decision by President Reagan to visit Bitberg cemetery in West Germany where both ordinary and SS soldiers were buried. In Jerusalem the decision aroused anger over all the unresolved problems concerning forgiveness by Jews of Germans, and consternation in the USA led to a visit to Bergen-Belsen being inserted into the President's schedule.

But it was in Germany that the memories brought up by the anniversary were the most difficult, arousing again the issues of corporate responsibility and guilt, of trying to heal the past by forgetting rather than by forgiving and being forgiven for it. Chancellor Kohl spoke to Jewish concentration camp survivors in a ceremony at Bergen-Belsen where some 100,000 had died. He said of the German people that 'there is no time limit on the shame they must bear for the crimes committed in their name by the Nazis'.[15] It was his most forthright statement on the Nazis' past since taking office in 1982.

Still more significant was the speech in the Bundestag on 8 May, the anniversary day, by President Richard von Weizsäcker. He argued that the more honesty shown that day, the more free Germans would become to face the consequences with responsibility. There was every reason 'for us to perceive May 8th, 1945, as the end of an aberration in German history, an end bearing seeds of hope for a better future'. He went on to commemorate all the nations and individuals who suffered, especially the six million Jews who were murdered, and continued:

> The vast majority of today's population were either children then or had not been born. They cannot profess a guilt of their own for crimes that they did not commit. No discerning person can expect them to wear a penitential robe simply because they are Germans. But their forefathers

have left them a grave legacy. All of us, whether guilty or not, whether young or old, must accept the past . . .

The President then paid tribute to former enemies, to how they 'set out on the road to reconciliation with us'. He praised the work of the Churches in promoting reconciliation: the *Aktion Suhnezeichen*, a campaign in which young Germans carried out atonement activity in Poland and Israel, was one example of such practical efforts to promote understanding.

The speech recalled the reconciliation which had been effected between France and Germany. (No doubt some listeners remembered President de Gaulle's important visit to Bonn earlier when he had said, 'We will forgive but we will not forget.' That was part of the long process which had led to the Franco-German Treaty of 22 January 1963, followed shortly after by a service in Rheims Cathedral attended by both President de Gaulle and Chancellor Adenauer.)

Finally, the President urged his fellow citizens not to be 'arrogant and self-righteous'. 'If we think what our Eastern neighbours had to suffer during the war, we will find it easier to understand that accommodation and peaceful neighbourly relations with these countries remain central tasks of [West] German foreign policy . . .'[16]

Foremost in this work of reconciliation with eastern Europe has been the policy of Willi Brandt – first as a member of a coalition government and then as Chancellor. Brandt's work as Mayor of Berlin had made him world famous and he was highly respected for his active resistance to the Nazis and for his courage. Deeply concerned about relations with eastern Europe, he developed a policy of *Ostpolitik*; this included a step-by-step progress towards East-West understanding, and especially better relations with Czechoslovakia and Poland. The Germans had to make it clear to the Czechs that the Federal Republic rejected the 1938 Munich agreement, and to the Poles that the question of Germany's eastern frontier could be settled in a free agreement with Bonn.

Subsequently, as Chancellor, Brandt took his *Ostpolitik* further, especially in recognizing the Oder-Neisse Line as the boundary between Germany and Poland. A Russo-German Treaty was signed during August 1970, and on 6 December that same year Brandt signed in Warsaw a treaty between the Federal Republic and Poland, which he saw as 'a historic act', parallel to the reconciliation with France a decade earlier. As the treaty was signed Brandt gave a message to the people of West Germany, 'Names like Auschwitz will be in the minds of both nations for a long time to come, and will remind us that Hell on earth is possible . . . I therefore say, to subscribe to this treaty, to reconciliation, to peace, is to accept German history in its entirety.'[17] In a dramatic gesture the following year he knelt at the Warsaw Ghetto Memorial.

During these years the Churches in both Germany and Poland had been trying to help toward reconciliation. The Council of the German Evangelical Church, in October 1965, had issued a memorandum exhorting the Bonn Government to reconsider its position on the Oder-Neisse frontier question and to make a fundamental change in the Federal Republic's *Ostpolitik*. In Rome the Roman Catholic Polish and West German bishops had met for the first time during the Second Vatican Council. Now, perhaps stimulated by the October memorandum of the Evangelical Church, a message, in German and signed by the thirty-six Polish bishops, was delivered to their counterparts during the fourth session of the Vatican Council. The German bishops replied on 5 December 1965.

Because of the political nature of much of the content of the Polish message, it precipitated criticism in Poland. Some of it was considered to be at variance with the principles of Poland's foreign policy. 'The Polish bishops were taxed with raising the problem of Polish-German relations but failing to press their partners (whom they forgave for all sins against Poland) for recognition of the Oder-Neisse frontier as final . . . ,' wrote one Polish commentator.[18]

Although Cardinal Wyszynski, one of the authors of the bishops' message, and his fellow bishops stood by the original letter, Archbishop Boleslaw Kominesk subsequently began to speak sceptically of the West German episcopate's attitude and appealed to it, in vain, to explain that it was in fact sympathetic to Poland's right to all the lands east of the Oder and Neisse rivers. Mr Gomulka, the Polish Prime Minister, took note of the Archbishop's second thoughts, as he wrote:

> Now let us consider the question of reconciliation and forgiveness. Archbishop Kominek has pointed out that these are Christian concepts, transcending politics, connected with the concept of sin. The sins of the German people against the Polish people are great, continues the Archbishop. Reconciliation and forgiveness apply only to those who are prepared to do penance. Without contrition there is no forgiveness.
>
> If this had been written in the Polish bishops' message, the Polish people would probably have applauded. But the whole point is that neither in the message nor in the communiqué is there a word about penance.[19]

Another attempt to approach the West German bishops was made by the Polish Cardinal in October 1970, when he had a meeting in Rome with Cardinal Dopfner of West Germany. It was followed by a letter from Cardinal Wyszynski in November 1971, explaining how the Poles had been disappointed by the German bishops' earlier response, made

> all the sadder in that German Protestants are approaching Catholic Poland with a far more evangelical outlook and that it is they who are with increasing frequency demonstrating signs of contrition for all that we have suffered during the war and a will for reconciliation in the Name of Our Saviour . . .

Cardinal Wyszynski went on to explain his present position on forgiveness.

> To 'forgive' does not, I am afraid, mean 'to forget', and the increasingly exhaustive studies and documents being published in Poland remind the young generation also of wounds which have not yet healed, of the losses suffered by every Polish family.

He spelled out the mass executions, the children's skeletons he had seen.

> Things like that cannot be forgotten, but they can be for-

given in the Name of Our Saviour. But those who, before the law of nations and before the law of God, bear part of the responsibility for them must help us to forgive and, it may be, eventually to forget.[20]

Cardinal Dopfner's replies, suitably timed to relate to treaties then being signed, were cautious. Relations between the two episcopates remained static for some time until in 1978 Cardinal Wyszynski decided to take up an offer to visit the Federal Republic. The six-day visit, an event considered one of great psychological and symbolic significance for West German–Polish relations, included visits to Cologne, Munich and Mainz by the Cardinal and his eight colleagues. The delegation also attended 'a memorial service at Dachau, the Nazi concentration camp near Munich, where 868 Polish priests were killed during the war'.[21]

It is difficult to assess the effect of such a visit on public opinion, especially in West Germany, but seen in a long process of reciprocal relations, it was part of an attempt by both countries to come to terms with recent history. The sending of money to help Christians in Poland to build churches and the participation by a number of Germans in the public commemoration of Maximilian Kolbe, when he was beatified by Pope John Paul II in 1982, were among a number of small steps towards forgiveness and reconciliation.

On the German-British side similar attempts have been made to deal with some of the consequences of the Second World War. Bishop Bell, of Chichester, stood out as a friend of the German people. During the 1930s he met with Bonhoeffer in Sweden and, on his return, presented Churchill with a plan for dealing with Germany if Hitler could be removed. Later, during the war, Bell spoke out:

> 'When a Minister of the Government speaks in exulting terms of a ruthless and destructive bombing of the German people; or quarters, supposed to be authoritative, contemplate the subjection of fifty German cities to the same terror as Hamburg (or Coventry) has suffered . . . then we have a real cause to grieve for a lowering of moral tone . . .'[22]

Bishop Bell was one of the British church leaders at Stuttgart in 1945, and his tour of the town brought comfort to many, including the family of Bonhoeffer, his close friend in the Confessing Church. On 28 October in the *Marienkirche* in the Russian sector of Berlin, he spoke to some 2,000 people about the sick man in the gospel story who was carried by his four friends to the feet of Jesus. 'Within this church, his words brought a sense of hope and reconciliation at a time when the whole atmosphere was one of hatred, bitterness and despair,' reported one who was present.[23]

'Recovery came', Bell argued elsewhere, 'not through retribution but through the reaching out of the offended and the wronged in forgiveness and charity to the author of the wrong.'[24] His misgivings about the trials of war criminals supplemented Pope Pius's broadcast on Christmas Eve 1945, when he warned the Allies to be wary of committing crimes themselves.[25] Later, in the House of Lords, Bell expressed his opinion that the trials raised issues of justice, humanity and political wisdom.

George Bell touched on a sore point when he spoke of British wrongs; it took until 1977 for one such wrong to come to light. This concerned the forcible repatriation to Russia of numerous Soviet citizens (and others) by Britain at the end of the war.[26] In 1978 *The Times* published a letter signed by a number of people in political life and headed *'Monument to the victims of Yalta'*:

> As an act of remembrance and expiation it is proposed to erect a monument to those hundreds of innocent and helpless prisoners of war and civilians who found themselves in British hands and were then forcibly repatriated to the Soviet Union between 1944 and 1947.[27]

A memorial was erected, but one night it was mutilated beyond repair. A second memorial was built in 1986 and stands in Thurloe Place, Kensington, London.

If the story of these Soviet victims shows Britain at its worst, the work of Coventry Cathedral reveals it at its best. On 14 November 1940 Coventry Cathedral collapsed in flames as the city experienced the first ever act of obliteration bombing. 'The choice was to take the road of vengeance and hatred, or to take the road to forgiveness and renewal,' wrote the Provost of

Coventry.[28] Out of the ruins the cathedral's stonemason made a charred cross and planted it on the mound of destruction, and a local priest fastened three nails into the form of a cross. Two months later an altar was erected and the charred cross set behind it with the words 'Father, forgive,' at the Provost's request, and with the cross of nails on it. So began the cathedral's ministry of forgiveness, which has been taken to many parts of the world, including Dresden, Cape Town and Shefer Amer in Galilee.

On 14 November 1990 a memorial service was held in the cathedral to commemorate the fiftieth anniversary of the blitz on Coventry. The German President, Richard von Weizsäcker, was present and he asked those gathered for their forgiveness for injustice done in the course of the Second World War,[29] thereby setting a seal on the work at Coventry Cathedral for reconciliation between Britain and Germany.

Forgiveness by individuals, as well as by groups both known and unknown, often occurs after hostilities have ended. Irene Laure, for example, was a leader in the French resistance, whose son was tortured by the Gestapo. After the war she went to a Moral Rearmament Conference at Caux in Switzerland, burning with hatred. She spoke at a meeting where Germans and French were together, in a tense atmosphere. 'Can you think what it meant for me to go there?' she asked later.

> In my heart I had willed the ruins of World War II . . . I am a socialist and all my life I have talked about fraternity, yet I had longed for a whole people to be destroyed. I had to ask forgiveness for my hatred from those people who were living in the ruins, I had to ask forgiveness from 50,000 women whom I saw, grey with fatigue, clearing the rubble in Berlin . . .[30]

Corrie ten Boom tells another story of forgiveness. Her father and sister died at the hands of the Nazis (the family had succoured Jews in Holland). She herself had been with her sister in Ravensbrück. After the war, at a church service in Munich where she had been preaching, she saw a former SS man who had guarded the shower room door in the camp. This man told her how grateful he had been for her message. 'To think, as you say, He has washed my sins away,' he said. At first she recoiled but as she prayed for forgiveness she felt able to take his hand and allow God's love to reach him.[31]

Time, too, often calms memories and helps old enemies to forgive. As a German band played the French national anthem at a 70th anniversary of the Battle of the Somme, two ninety-year-old veterans – one German, the other French – stood together alongside young soldiers from France and Germany.[32]

Or old enmities may be healed by friendship in a later generation. According to a newspaper report in 1984, Manfred Rommel, son of the general who commanded the German armies in North Africa during the Second World War, 'was in Blackpool as the guest of honour with Field-Marshal Montgomery's son, David, for an annual El Alamein reunion ... Viscount Montgomery ... said: "It is a tragedy that my father and Rommel never met. Now history has rectified that and their sons have met." '[33] But behind that encounter lay the remorse of Field-Marshal Montgomery: ' "I couldn't sleep last night," he confided to a friend, "I had great difficulty. I can't have long to go now. I've to meet God – and explain all those men killed at Alamein ..." '[34]

Ventures in Europe to overcome the results of the two world wars have included the setting up of many bilateral and multilateral organizations, some more successful than others. Most dramatic of all has been the effect on Europe of Mr Gorbachev's policies which have opened the way for the rapid reunification of Germany, a new relation between Germany and the Soviet Union, including a treaty of friendship signed in 1990, as well as the dramatic emergence in eastern Europe of states freed from undue influence from Moscow.

Fifty-one years after Hitler invaded Czechoslovakia President von Weizsäcker of Germany stood in Prague Castle, where Hitler had announced the country's takeover, and said, 'We ask your pardon for this memory and we need your forgiveness.'[35]

Once again a unified Germany has been thrust into the centre of European politics and policies, hopefully now a bridge country between East and West and no longer a cockpit of war.

4

ISRAEL

O Lord,
Remember not only the men and women of good will,
But all those of ill will.
But do not remember all the suffering
They have inflicted upon us;
Remember the fruits we have bought
Thanks to this suffering –
Our comradeship, our loyalty, our humility,
Our courage, our generosity, the greatness of heart
Which has grown out of all this;
And when they come to judgement,
Let all the fruits we have borne
Be their forgiveness.

THIS PRAYER was found written on brown wrapping paper beside the body of a dead child at the Ravensbrück concentration camp, where ninety-two thousand women and children died. No one knows who wrote it. It highlights the immense human, political and theological issues which stem from the core of Germany's actions in the Second World War and before it, as Hitler's attempt to find a 'final solution' to the Jewish question attacked not only Judaism but Christianity too, for surely there is no Christianity without Jesus the Jew?

To visit *Yad Va-Shem* in Jerusalem, the memorial to the six million Jews killed by the Nazis, is to be reminded of the depth of the evil with which the Jews grapple today as they ask, 'Where was our God?' Though it is true that German reparations helped to keep the Israeli state going for many years,[1] nothing can remove the memory of the Holocaust, nor the fear of another.

Should the Jews stop perpetuating the memory of the Holocaust? Some argue they should forget because they have been able to find a way to forgive Germany for their past experiences under the Nazis.[2] For, as Rabbi Albert Friedlander has written: ' "Let us forgive and forget" is a central thought within our society . . .', and he adds, 'Jews mourn their dead without requiring the outside world to share in their grief.' They remember the goodness, the victims rather than the villains, the few who helped (there is a Street of the Righteous Gentiles in the Memorial) instead of the many who killed. 'But they cannot forget. Once the mind dwells on the Holocaust, can anyone really forget the event?' And forgiveness? 'Who are we to take over God's role?' the rabbi asks.[3]

The issue of forgiveness emerged strongly in 1985, when President Reagan proposed a visit to Bitberg and its cemetery, as we saw in chapter 2. 'Even death cannot blur the difference between those buried as murderers and those buried as their victims,' Prime Minister Peres said when addressing the Knesset at that time. 'Conciliation between peoples is possible,' he continued, 'but not conciliation with regard to the past . . .'[4] Gideon Hausner, the former Attorney-General and Chief State Prosecutor at Eichmann's trial, was more astringent:

> The air is so contaminated that it can never be cleansed.
> I admit that it [the trial] did help to bring about a better understanding between the Germans and the Jews. It sort of established our positions. But normal relations will never be established in our lifetime. The wound is too deep, too sensitive, too aching . . .[5]

Can declarations of repentance help towards the healing that Jews seek for the Holocaust experience of their friends and relations? In April 1990 the German Democratic Republic declared, 'We ask the Jews of the world to forgive us for the hypocrisy and hostility of official East German policies toward Israel and for the persecution and degradation of Jewish citizens also after 1945 in our country.' It is to be hoped that the declaration of East Germany's politicians of a willingness to contribute towards the healing of the sufferings of Holocaust survivors, if necessary with financial compensation, will be honoured by the now united Germany,[6] and that this will be yet another step towards Israel's capacity to create a new and different future.

Attempts by individuals and groups to bridge the divide between Germans and Jews include the reconciling work of Rabbi Friedlander, through his lectures and writings. In 1985, for example, he spoke at a meeting with the West German Chancellor on Germans and Jews since 1945. Martin Buber also crossed that divide when, in 1953, he received the Peace Prize of the German book trade. In his speech he referred to the diverse types of Germans, their responses to Hitler and the shades of grey they reflected. Of those who opposed the Nazis, or killed themselves, he said: 'I see these men very near before me in the special intimacy which binds us at times to the dead and to them alone. Reverence and love for these Germans fills my heart.'[7]

In May 1985 a group of former Jewish residents of Oldenburg visited their town at the mayor's invitation. Here on Kristallnacht, 9 November 1938, the synagogue had been set alight, Jewish shops vandalized, the male Jewish population arrested and sent to Sachsenhausen concentration camp. Once there had been four hundred Jews living in the town; in 1985 there were only two. The visit was organized by a local group, the Association of Christian and Jewish Co-operation, which for many years had kept alive the memory of Jews in Oldenburg and had collected more than £100,000 for the event. Former residents came from Israel, Holland, America, England and South America; some spoke no German. A service of remembrance was led by the last rabbi of Oldenburg on the site of the former synagogue, now a small park with an impressive memorial stone in Hebrew and Greek. The group received much hospitality and one of them, Joe de Haas, addressed three hundred teen-age students:

> I tried to make them understand that for nearly twenty years I intentionally never spoke or read a word of German. My theme song was that it is the duty of the survivors to tell the tale of the Holocaust. I mentioned that the philosopher Santayana put it very clearly when he said: 'Those who cannot remember the past are condemned to repeat it.'[8]

The group, in return for the kindness of the Association, presented certificates showing how money had been collected to honour it by planting trees in the Freedom Forest in Jerusalem. On the Sabbath a morning service was held in a large church, led by a rabbi, at which clergy gave sermons, accepting the wrong that had been done and the neglect by the Christians who had forgotten 'the teaching of the Jew, Jesus Christ'. It was a moving experience. 'Inge, the survivor from Auschwitz, was in tears . . . "I am glad I came, now I can grasp the outstretched hand of reconciliation," she said.'9

Earlier, in the 1960s, Rabbi Marmur of London, together with Pastor Schoenich from West Germany, organized joint meetings in London which received much publicity. 'Jews forget their bitterness to welcome Germans,' was one headline in a Sunday paper.10 'History is made at a local synagogue,' wrote another journalist as the pastor answered press questions about the visit of seventeen young people from West Berlin. Rabbi Marmur considered the visit to have been of great benefit to all, the Germans meeting in London a Jewish community self-confident in its Judaism, and 'at the same time the hosts were helped to free themselves from the destructive feeling of universal hatred'. As a result, a group called European Action was formed in London to promote similar work and a group in the Sinai Synagogue, Leeds, organized a youth visit.11

Some of the most compassionate work was done by the British Jew, Victor Gollancz, who had run an organization helping Jewish refugees out of pre-war Germany. In 1945 he published an anthology of acts of kindness done to enemies. Included in it was a story from a book of his own about a pious Jew who, on the Day of Atonement, had been taken by the Nazis and whipped. They led him into the yard and said:

'Now, Jew, preach to us on this Day of Atonement about the Jewish religion.' It may be that he heard an echo of those other words, 'Now prophesy'; or it may be that he found in his own nature and strength to do what he did. For he said: 'Meine Freunde' – my friends, to the SS men who had tormented him – 'My friends, the fundamental principle of the Jewish religion, as of all the other great religions of the world is: Love thy neighbour as thyself.'12

For all this wrestling with problems arising from the Holocaust, the event itself still remains a mystery for Jews. To the question, 'Has God forsaken us?' they have found only two answers. One impinges directly on their perception of the Middle East where, after two thousand years, they have now a permanent home. They see Israel as an act of God, as powerful for Judaism as the Exodus, despite the controversy surrounding its birth.

A symbol of the second answer is to be found in a book by Elie Wiesel, himself a survivor of the Holocaust. There he describes how a group of prisoners came back to base at the end of a hard day and saw three gallows had been erected in the assembly place. There was a roll call and all were brought to see the three victims in chains hung. One was a boy. As the SS guards tipped over the chairs on which the victims stood the boy was seen to be still alive; the noose had failed to break his neck. Someone asked 'Where is God?' Half an hour later, as the boy still hung, alive, he asked again, 'Where is God now?' Elie Wiesel says he heard a voice within himself say, 'He is hanging on this gallows.'[13]

It has been these two convictions – that God was in their sufferings and had vindicated them – which have convinced Jews that they will never again be made to wander.

The state of Israel was founded in 1948. At that time 600,000 Jews lived within its boundaries; now there are well over 3 million as Jews continue to migrate from many countries, including large numbers from the USSR. But can Israel be totally Jewish? For within the territory live over three-quarters of a million Palestinians who are Israeli citizens, and also a small number of Christians.

Though often bitterly divided among themselves, these Christians form the gateway to Christian sites in Jerusalem, Bethlehem, Nazareth and Galilee, and raise for Israel its vexed and complex relationships with Christianity. On the one hand is the refusal of the Vatican to recognize Israel at present; on the other the world-wide fundamentalist movement acutely sensitive to biblical prophecy about the Holy Land.

An indication of relations with the Roman Catholic Church is given by the former Israeli Prime Minister, Golda Meir. She describes first a delicate encounter in 1904 between Pope Pius X and the Zionist leader Theodor Herzel and then her own meeting with Pope Paul VI.

'We cannot prevent Jews from going to Jerusalem,' [the Pope] said, 'but we could never sanction it . . . the Jews have not recognized our Lord: we cannot recognize the Jews.' Now, in 1973, Pope Paul VI was gracious in manner and simplicity, but started by telling me he found it hard to accept the fact that the Jews – who, of all people, should have been capable of mercy towards others because they had suffered so terribly themselves – had behaved so harshly in their own country.

Golda Meir found this difficult. She argued that Jews had not mistreated Arabs in the administrative territories, though she conceded they had put terrorists in jail and blown up Arab houses which sheltered them. Her response to the Pope indicated the depth of Jewish feeling and experience:

'Your Holiness, do you know what my own very earliest memory is? It is waiting for a pogrom in Kiev. Let me assure you that my people know all about real "harshness" and also that we learned about real mercy when we were being led to the gas chambers of the Nazis.'[14]

Behind that encounter lies a long troubled history of Jewish and Christian interaction. Indeed, some thinkers see the origin of the Holocaust centuries ago, as Christians in their liturgies (especially in Holy Week) were taught that the Jews were deicides.

The Christian needs to hear the truth from Jews. And the truth is that the organized Christian forces will find it easiest to drop the ancient charge of deicide, harder to recognize the roots of Christian antisemitism in the New Testament, and hardest of all to admit that both Jews and Judaism are alive . . .[15]

Some Christians now recognize this, as biblical scholarship since 1945 has come increasingly to understand that Jesus was primarily a Jew and that Christianity without its Jewish roots, as Dietrich Bonhoeffer discovered, is null and void. Indeed, many Jewish scholars have helped Christian scholars unravel some parts of the Bible which had previously been difficult to understand.

There is also a changed attitude within the Roman Catholic Church. A priest, who served as a ghost writer for Pope John XXIII, wrote in a report on Vatican II that Pope John had composed a prayer about the Jews which asked for forgiveness for the church for crucifying Christ a second time through its treatment of them in history.[16] 'While this prayer is apocryphal,' Irving Greenberg has commented, 'as no trace of it has been found in John's papers, widespread acceptance of its attribution reflects John's known regret and concern.'[17]

The Second Vatican Council's declaration on Judaism in 1965, *Nostra Aetate*, stated that, as it searched into the mystery of the Church, it remembered 'the bond that spiritually ties the people of the New Covenant to Abraham's stock'; it was the most important paragraph in the Document. Later, in 1974, the Vatican itself issued guidelines to the conciliar declaration urging Christians 'to strive to learn by what essential traits the Jews define themselves'. But although these steps show a great improvement in Roman Catholic attitudes, some who are concerned with Jewish–Christian relations feel that much remains to be redressed.

> One might have expected German bishops to condemn explicitly the general silence of the Church on the extermination policy of Hitler and their frequent collaboration with the Nazis. Some former statements of the past (1945, 1961) are referred to but there is no open admission of guilt on the part of many Catholics, priests and bishops included.

However, this writer does consider the statement of the Synod of the Protestant Church of the Rhineland (1980) an improvement, beginning as it does with a clear recognition of Christian 'co-responsibility and guilt for the Holocaust', and continuing with the view that the election and covenant of the Jewish people are of 'permanent validity'.[18]

The World Council of Churches has emphasized in one of its reports the importance of the land and the state of Israel as elements in Jewish self-awareness, asking Christians to re-examine their theological views on the bond between people, faith and one particular country, even though the Christian faith is not linked to any one land. However, they add, the country where Jesus was born and lived holds a special significance for Christians also. They express, too, a wish that a just solution may be found for the Arabs who lay claim to the country they call Palestine.[19]

The Roman Catholic document, *Notes on the Correct Way to Present the Jews and Judaism in Preaching and Catechesis* – following as it does, *Nostra Aetate*, the Guidelines of 1974, and a significant discourse by Pope John Paul II on 6 March 1982 – is important. It was, *The Times* considered, of note because it contained the doctrine, based on Romans 2:28–9, that the Covenant between God and the Jews had not been abrogated but still applied. If the concept of the 'Chosen People' was still valid in Catholic teaching, why not also the concept of the 'Promised Land', the editorial suggested.[20]

These are heady waters, for what would be the implications of such a policy for Muslims in the Middle East, let alone the effect on the Christian Arabs who have to share the terrain with a Muslim majority? A very different view is that 'the religious interpretation of Israel, as the Promised Land given by God and as a land whose restoration was regarded as a messianic event, impedes the search for that pluralism that is necessary for peaceful co-existence with indigenous Arab peoples, both Muslim and Christian',[21] although this writer does admit that the collapse of Christendom and the founding of Israel provide both Christians and Jews with a new context within which to think again about their relationship.

'There is finally only one genuinely ecumenical question: our relations with the Jewish people,' maintained Karl Barth,[22] when he was invited to address the Secretariat for Christian Unity in the Vatican. 'If Barth was right,' adds Van Buren,

> and I believe he was, then that could only be because the Jewish people are the very foundation of the life and meaning of the Church of Jesus Christ... if the Church were ever to confess with full conviction what it has done to Jesus and to his fellow Jews, it is conceivable that it could be forgiven, but that would still not undo that history.[23]

For Jews, too, there is need for new approaches. The work

of Geza Vermes points in this direction as he attempts to claim back Jesus for the Jewish community. As he has observed:

> The positive and constant testimony of the earliest Gospel tradition, considered against its natural background of first-century Galilean charismatic religion, leads not to a Jesus as unrecognizable within the framework of Judaism as by the standard of his own verifiable words and intentions, but to another figure: Jesus the just man, the *zaddik*, Jesus the helper and healer, Jesus teacher and leader, venerated by his intimate and less committed admirers alike as prophet, lord and *son of God*.[24]

There are signs that new approaches are happening also at less exalted levels, whether it be the *Kaddish for Terezin*,[25] first performed in Canterbury Cathedral in June 1986, or the work of Nes Ammim, a Christian community in Israel, established in 1960, which the Kibbutz 'Ayelet Hashachar' in Upper Galilee asked one of its members to help. Nes Ammim's industrial enterprises, together with its decision to educate its children in Israeli schools, all help to build up good relationships, as does its study of the Jewish tradition.

For the Jews to come to terms with Christians in the post-Holocaust world is a difficult enough task, but how are they to relate to Islam? For the immigration of Jews to the Middle East caused an Arab exodus in 1946–8 and involved them eventually in a situation they had never before experienced: rule over more than two million Arabs, some of them Israeli citizens, some not.

Add to this the pressures of the super-powers in the region, the presence in the north of an unstable Lebanon and a growing Syrian influence, and to the south Saudi Arabia, the custodian not only of Islam's holiest shrines, but rich with oil (a commodity the West needs) and there is a political scenario of unparalleled complexity. In the centre of this is Israel's nearest neighbour, the kingdom of Jordan, where over one million Palestinians live.

Also complicated is the inter-state situation within the Arab and Islamic world. On the one hand are those within Islam who consider *jihád* (holy war) justified to remove Israel (with its backer America) from the area. On the other are more moderate states who would like some compromise with Israel and the emergence of a Palestinian body inter-relating with Jordan and Israel.

Given all these pressures it is not surprising to find in Israel a politics of pathologies in evidence: the frustrations of the Palestinians (especially those in camps since the early 1950s); the intractability of the extreme Zionists (who seem to think that even the three-quarters of a million Muslim Israeli citizens ought not to be there); and the actions of the Israeli military as it tries to contain the Palestinian *Intifada*, a situation often erupting into violence.

What can Muslims contribute to forgiveness in such a complex political situation? Certainly the Koran encourages forgiveness, for Muhammad, once victorious, showed mercy to those who had ill-treated him. And in the Arab and Muslim *soulah* (whereby the families from two villages may be brought together to deal with their members who have done wrong to each other) is a method for resolving disputes between groups which is not found either among Jews or Western Christians. Two Christian–Arab–Moslem gatherings held in Jerusalem in 1983 and 1984 indicate a desire by Muslims and Christians to get to know each other, and their encouragement of both groups to read the others' Holy Book, study the changes in Palestinian society and teach students to understand the two faiths, illustrates the depth of this dialogue.

Within Islam there are unresolved tensions which make the path difficult. These were brought out dramatically when President Sadat of Egypt visited Israel in 1978. Sadat sought to break down the long-standing wall of suspicion between Israel and the Arab world. Did Israel want peace? he wondered, and asked this question of the President of Rumania, whom he was visiting. Having been assured that Menachim Begin, then Prime Minister of Israel, also wanted peace, Sadat decided to visit Jerusalem 'to perform the *Bairam* prayers at al-Aqsa Mosque in fulfilment of my claim that I was ready to go to the end of the earth to achieve peace'.[26] This initiative, announced at a new session of the Egyptian People's Assembly, startled the world.

While in Israel President Sadat addressed the Knesset. He spoke there of the risk he knew he was taking, but said that he felt before God it was his responsibility to Jew and Arab and the world. Then he referred to his speech at his own People's Assembly, where he had called for an international conference to establish a just and lasting peace. It could be neither a peace between Egypt and Israel alone, nor even a disengagement from Sinai, the Golan Heights and the West Bank. It had to be long-term. As tension in the Knesset rose, he admitted faults on the Arab side. One barrier, Israel's invincibility, had collapsed in 1973; another remained – 'a psychological barrier between us'. In order for this barrier to go, said Sadat, the Israelis had to do their part, 'to give up, once and for all, the dreams of conquest, and give up the belief that force is the best method of dealing with the Arabs'. A complete withdrawal from all the occupied territories was necessary, including Arab Jerusalem.

General Ezer Weizmann, the Defence Minister, apparently leaned over towards the Foreign Minister Moshe Dayan and passed a note: 'We've got to prepare for war.' Begin said in a whisper which could be heard that Sadat had given an ultimatum.

Menachim Begin's reply to Sadat demonstrated the conflicting theocracies which are part of the Arab-Israeli conflict. 'No, sir,' he said, 'We did not take a foreign country. We came back to our homeland. The link between ourselves and this country is eternal . . .'[27]

'What is a Palestinian?' Golda Meir had once asked, 'Such a thing does not exist.'[28] This remark indicates the measure of the gulf separating the Israelis and the Arabs in the Middle East and the courage of President Sadat in beginning to attack the problem head on. His dramatic visit to Jerusalem had included the mosque where in 1951 a Palestinian assassin had murdered King Abdullah, grandfather of King Hussein (for dealing secretly with the new-born state of Israel) and the Church of the Holy Sepulchre, where demonstrators indicated their opposition to him. Syria went into mourning the day of his arrival and in Iraq al'Adha celebrations were cancelled. In Beirut Sadat's name was linked with Kerzel, Balfour, Weizmann, Ben-Gurion and others perceived as enemies to Arab interests.

Sadat went from Muslim and Christian shrines to *Yad Va-Shem*, the memorial to Jews who died in the Holocaust, walking barefoot through its rooms. He wrote in the visitors' book: 'Let us put an end to all the sufferings of the human race'.[29]

It was President Sadat's initiative that led to the hammering out of the Camp David Agreement with the help of President Carter, an agreement that divided the Arab world when announced and isolated Egypt for many years. However, it did stabilize Egypt's relations with Israel, and these have held through all the subsequent ups and downs, including the Gulf War. In the agreement Israel abandoned its claims to Sinai, which it had conquered in the 1967 war (hoping thereby to neutralize Egypt) but retained control of its other occupied territories – the Golan Heights, the Gaza Strip and the West Bank including Arab Jerusalem. Nearly all sides of Israeli opinion greeted the 1979 agreement with enthusiasm, partly no doubt because there was no deal envisaged as yet with the Palestinians.

The accord offered the Palestinians, according to one journalist writing soon afterwards, nothing more tangible than 'an assurance that, if they are co-operative now and go along with the terms of the agreement which they have had no hand in shaping, at the end of the "transitional period" of five years they will have their reward'.[30] It was never stated what that reward might be. Indeed the agreement only mentioned talking with 'representatives of the West Bank and Gaza', thereby seeming to exclude any future negotiations with Palestinians living in exile.

The Palestine Liberation Organization was not mentioned. Had the offer implied a mini-state for Palestinians, perhaps it could have been taken up, but on his return from Camp David Mr Begin made it clear that Israel would veto that suggestion. Indeed he sanctioned more Jewish homes in the West Bank and affirmed the indivisibility of Jerusalem. Sadat had thus agreed to a scheme which would leave the core question of the Palestinians and their future to be settled at a later date, if at all. His peace was a half-peace, valuable for that but only a step on the way.

The role of Israel in Lebanon with its massacres and disasters, extreme Palestinian terrorism, the growth of fundamentalism in Egypt after Sadat's murder, have all made peace work arduous. Yet there have also been some hopeful signs – President Mubarak, Sadat's successor, though under pressure, has continued to be open to the possibility of progress, however slow, and in 1984 Jordan transformed the landscape of Arab diplomacy by restoring relations with Egypt.

There are within the Israeli-Arab world a number of groups and individuals wanting to live out a politics of forgiveness, and exhibiting the spirit in which a future peace in the Middle East may be constructed. For example, there was Ghassibe Kayrouth, a twenty-two-year-old theology student from Jamhou near Beirut, who left there on 20 December 1975 to spend Christmas with his family in a village where Maronite Christians and Metoualo Muslims lived together. On his way there, he was murdered. His testament, in Arabic, was found afterwards in his room. 'These days everyone who is Lebanese is in danger,' he had written, urging his family not to be sad if he died.

> I have only one thing to ask of you: Forgive those who killed me with all your heart . . . and to my country I say: People who live in the same house can hold different opinions without hating each other; they can be angry with each other without becoming enemies; they can quarrel without killing each other.[31]

A striking contribution to Christian-Muslim and Christian-Jewish reconciliation has been made by Father Elias Chacour. This Melkite priest, from a village destroyed by the Israelis when Israel was founded, came to realize that 'the first step towards reconciling Jews and Palestinians was the restoration of human dignity . . . If I were really committing my life to carry God's message to my people, I would have to lift up, as Jesus had, the men and women who had been degraded and beaten down.'[32] So he set about doing good works in his village, including raising money to rebuild the local mosque and establishing community centres. As Jerusalem prepared to welcome President Sadat, he showed the film of *The Diary of Anne Frank* in the centres, so that young Palestinians could begin to understand what the Jews had suffered, and perhaps to forgive. He also intended it as a warning to the Palestinians not to turn to violence.[33]

The strength of his witness stems from his own inner searchings. Pondering on the Sermon on the Mount he was forced to wrestle with forgiveness, and as he contemplated the death of Christ and found forgiveness himself, his new strength enabled him to confront his congregation with their feelings of hate.

In one family the brothers had refused to be reconciled, even when their mother died. But then, 'After a long silence one brother, a hard-bitten policeman, stood up. "I am sorry. I am the worst of all," he said. "I've hated my own brothers. Hated them so much I wanted to kill them. More than any of you I need forgiveness." ' He then turned to Father Chacour who gave him the kiss of peace and urged him to greet his family. 'Before he was halfway down the aisle the three brothers had rushed to him. They held each other in a long embrace, each one seeking forgiveness of the others. In an instant,' Father Chacour concluded, 'the church was a chaos of embracing and repentance. Cousins, who had not spoken to each other in years, wept openly together. Women asked forgiveness for malicious gossip; men confessed to passing damaging lies about each other . . .'[34] Here was a group forgiveness of great power with consequences for the whole community.

It is that kind of spirit which at a broader level, lies behind the statement by Amos Kenan, a radical Israeli: 'We already no longer live in a Jewish state but, *de facto*, in a bi-national one.'[35] He has looked at earlier Israeli attitudes and seen them to be false. The Jewish peace group Oz veShalom and the only Palestinian–Jewish village in Israel, Neve Shalom/Wahat al-Salam, with its educational programmes designed to encourage tolerance and understanding, also seek a new approach to Israel's complex political existence. Though at the moment the outlook for such approaches is bleak, in the long run some form of new arrangement in the Middle East is inevitable. Can the Palestinians, who have suffered so much as a result of the catapulting of Europe's conflicts into the region, find a form of *soulah* extending beyond Arab society, and help create a state for Jews which gives them security after their two thousand years of wanderings? This is the key question in Middle East politics. The PLO's recent recognition of the state of Israel and its renunciation of terrorism has helped at one level, but the growing credibility of the PLO in the eyes of the West has been severely damaged by its support of Iraq in the Gulf War.

The new approaches to the Middle East by the Soviet government have been particularly helpful, for there can be no peace in the area without both super-powers being in co-operation. However, the Gulf War has drastically affected all configurations, changing alliances and perceptions, though it does seem to have made the international community, acting through a stronger United Nations, more determined that the Palestinian issue cannot be allowed much longer to poison the politics of the Middle East.

Creative developments toward peace in the Middle East, however, depend on there being more of the quality of forgiveness as displayed by the Iranian bishop who prayed after the murder of his son:

> O God,
> We remember not only Bahram
>   but also his murderers.
> So when his murderers stand before Thee
>   on the day of judgement
> Remember the fruit of the Spirit by which
> They have enriched our lives,
> And forgive.[36]

and of the kind of honesty of the Jew who tracked down a Nazi war criminal in Bolivia. Faced with the opportunity of killing him, he turned away. 'Actually,' he wrote later,

> I had just inflicted a defeat on myself. It was the first, in the area most important to me and probably the only one in which I was vulnerable. Was it more important to make myself tougher or to cure me?[37]

5

JAPAN AND THE WEST

'WE JAPANESE are a hundred million brothers,' said a Japanese industrialist. It was not a joke, for he was trying to describe the way in which the Japanese people have a single consciousness. Indeed, they have a well-known proverb which indicates that group consensus is the order of the day: 'The nail that sticks up gets pounded down.' This does not mean, however, that there have been no groups within Japan opposed to its handling of relations with other nations.

One opposition group, the Oomoto organization, started in Ayabe in 1892. A spiritual movement, led by powerful individuals like Nao Deguchi and Onisaburo Deguchi, it spread rapidly in the 1920s across Japan. Many influential Japanese were followers, or friends and supporters. It tended to deny organized politics, saying there was a world transcending these and the social mores of the day. Onisaburo Deguchi's prophecy that there would be a world war involving Japan and America, that Japan would be occupied and many cities devastated, led to a trial which began in 1921 and ended only in 1927 at the start of the reign of Emperor Hirohito.

Though once again active, Oomoto remained under government surveillance. In December 1935 a second Oomoto incident occurred, following which the government gave orders to dissolve Oomoto completely. The headquarters in Ayabe and Makeoka were dynamited and burned. Shrines were destroyed and meetings forbidden. Some 3,000 people were arrested and many tortured in detention; some committed suicide.

Oomoto's present leader, Kyatoro Deguchi, has summed up the result of its trial, held in September 1945: 'Oomoto was found innocent; therefore Onisaburo and Oomoto obtained complete freedom.' After the trial, the advocates of Oomoto began to estimate the compensation due to Onisaburo, but Onisaburo laughed, saying that the amount of money was incalculable. He felt that as the government had acknowledged its wrong, it was unfair to blame people who knew what they had done. 'Onisaburo and Oomoto decided that they wanted to participate in reconstructing a peaceful country without receiving any government aid.' They felt animated by this spirit and that history would remember their commitment as a milestone in creating peace.[1]

Behind the earlier conflict had been an ideological disagreement. 'Oomoto doctrine has an idea that is similar to the Kingdom of Millenium,' says Mr Deguchi.

> In Buddhism, there is the Kingdom of Buddha (Hotoke), *Miroku no yo*, and in old Shinto there was *Matsu no yo*, all of which are very close in meaning. This way of thought plays a central role in Oomoto. In the early 1900s, Japanese Imperial Rule did not accept these ideas, but rather, they felt that Japanese Imperial Rule lasts for ever throughout Japan and all of Asia. As a result, Oomoto and the Japanese officials were in disagreement . . .[2]

Japan's militarism had already led her to dominance of Korea and increasing control over Manchuria and parts of China by 1940. Allying herself with Nazi Germany she entered the Second World War, overrunning most of South-East Asia during 1942. However the war proved devastating for Japan, and her place in the world since 1945 has for three decades been dominated by it, even though she has prospered economically.

The Second World War was brought to an end by the dropping of two atom bombs – the first on Hiroshima, the second on Nagasaki. With his military cabinet equally divided for and against surrender, the Emperor cast the key vote to end the war.

'By their own standards,' Kosuke Koyama considers, 'the Japanese had created chaos in Asia.'[3]

> The day General MacArthur arrived in Tokyo [30 August 1945] the Prime Minister, Prince Higashikuni, gave his first post-war press conference. 'All one hundred million Japanese must repent (*ichioku so zange*),' he said, in order

to start a new national life. In the confusion and emptiness of Tokyo, I welcomed gladly the suggestion of national repentance. My Christian sentiment told me that the suggestion was right and timely. We had committed a crime against humanity, as the Americans had put it.[4]

But to whom could the Japanese repent? Certainly not to the spirits of their ancestors because they had been invoked at the start of the war. 'Should we not acknowledge our guilt to living persons?' asks Koyama, 'to the Koreans, Indonesians, Singaporeans and Burmese?'[5] To apologize to the Americans was perhaps too much to expect, when it was they who had destroyed the Japanese cities in a way unique in history. Indeed, an American chaplain had prayed before the bombing of Nagasaki:

> Almighty God, Father of all mercies, we pray Thee to be gracious to those who fly this night . . . Keep them both in body and soul and bring them back to us. Give to us all the courage and strength for the hours that are ahead . . .

Here was no sense of repentance. In fact there was little horror among the Western nations at what had been done – only relief the war had ended. Even many decades later Group Captain Leonard Cheshire was defending the bombing as justified, though the rise of the peace movements in the West from the 1950s to protest at the development of atomic weapons and their use in a politics of mutual deterrence between East and West suggests that some were determined that never again should such weapons of mass destruction be used.

For the Japanese there was, and perhaps always will be, the ache of Hiroshima. Yet they had to come to terms with the American occupation and go on living. Moreover, their situation was exceptionally complex, for they had both to endure American rule and sort out their relationships with the Asian countries whom they had invaded.

A somewhat surprising source of help came to them in the person of Frank Buchman, the founder of what came to be known as Moral Re-Armament (MRA). Buchman, an American Lutheran, had undergone a dramatic experience of Christ, after which he wrote to those he had injured asking their forgiveness. From that moment he travelled round the world enjoining his four absolutes: absolute purity, honesty, truthfulness and commitment to a God who was to be waited on in prayer for guidance each day. The movement he founded (originally called the Oxford Group) had considerable success in transforming individual lives, as well as making an impact on political leaders.

Buchman took the view that MRA, though based in the Christian faith, was an ideology around which all could unite: 'Catholic, Jew and Protestant, Hindu, Moslem, Buddhist and Confucianist – all find they can change, where needed, and travel along this road together,' he maintained.[6]

As early as the 1930s Buchman had contacts with leading Japanese, and after the war a number of them were allowed to attend a Buchman Conference in California in June 1948; they were among the first Japanese to leave the country following its surrender. The next summer a further Japanese party went to Caux, the MRA conference centre outside Geneva, including a delegation centred around the Socialist Prime Minister, Tetsu Katayama. After a month at Caux, Katayama's party was received by the German, French and British governments and by Socialist parties.

One MRA member, Basil Entwistle, went to live in Japan. Much of his work there was dealing with conflicts that occurred among supporters, between those who wanted moral standards to be Christian and applied only to personal matters, and others who saw MRA as 'a moral and spiritual force to reshape Japan into a united, democratic responsible nation'.[7] Also important were Entwistle's contacts with the subsequent Prime Minister, Shigeru Yoshida, the Governor of the Bank of Japan and the President of Mainichi communications conglomerate, among others. From this came a plan for seventy-six Japanese to go to Caux in summer 1950. They included members of the Diet, representing all the main parties, seven governors of prefectures, the mayors of Hiroshima and Nagasaki and leaders of finance, industry and labour. The Prime Minister said on their departure: 'In 1870 a group of Japanese travelled to the West. On their return they changed the course of Japanese life. I believe that when this delegation returns you too will open up a new page in our history.'[8]

During their stay in Europe the Japanese heard French and German people promising to rebuild Europe together, both sides of industry saying they would help meet people's needs, and rivals seeking ways to unite their countries. The gathering had a considerable effect on the Japanese. For example, 'the Governor of Nagano province and the Mayor of its capital publicly forsook their well-known antagonism to each other; and a militant labour leader Katsuji Nakajima, and his "public enemy number one", the regional chief police, Eiji Suzuki, were reconciled'.[9]

Yashuhiru Nakasone, later Prime Minister of Japan but then the youngest of the six Diet members present, wrote from Caux to a Japanese paper: ' . . . the ice in the Japanese hearts was melted by the international harmony that transcends race and class in this great current of world history moving through the continents of America and Europe'.[10]

The Japanese were deeply impressed. Mayor Hamai of Hiroshima, speaking on US television on the anniversary of the dropping of the atomic bomb, said: 'Dr Buchman has said, "Peace is people becoming different." This hits the nail on the head. I for one intend to start this effort from Hiroshima . . .' When they visited the US senate the senior Japanese representative, Chorojuo Kurijama, said: 'We are sincerely sorry for Japan's big mistake. We broke almost a century-old friendship between the two countries. We ask your forgiveness and help.' One member of the delegation, Kitamuru, said to Trygve Lie, the United Nations' General Secretary: 'The Japanese people here present are very deeply convicted by a sense of responsibility and shame for the troubles they have created in the Far East.'[11]

Seemingly the ice had been broken by these visits, but rebuilding Japan and its relations with former enemies was bound to be difficult. Prime Minister Yoshida, speaking to the Diet in October 1951, referred to the various difficulties being experienced in peace-making. The reparation burdens he said would be 'undeniably heavy', but Japan would not refuse to shoulder its treaty obligations. The Peace Treaty had been signed with forty-eight nations in San Francisco on 8 September 1951, but did not represent an overall peace settlement. The Soviet Union, Poland and Czechoslovakia refused to sign. The Philippines would not ratify it until a solution had been found for its reparations claims; and Indonesia would not ratify it even after the reparations problem had been dealt with, preferring to sign a bilateral treaty in January 1958. Neither China nor Taiwan were invited to sign the treaty and India, Burma and Yugoslavia chose to disassociate themselves from it, making their own bilateral arrangements.

The Soviet Union and other socialist countries of Europe normalized relations with Japan in 1956, but a peace treaty between Russia and Japan was not concluded because of a dipute over the Kurile Islands. In January 1986 it was reported in the press that 'Moscow and Tokyo agree to resume peace talks'.[12]

Japan's relations with China were not normalized until September 1972, when the Japan-Taiwan Peace Treaty of April 1952 was declared null and void and China waived war reparations. An accommodation was reached with South Vietnam in 1959, but relations with North Vietnam could be normalized only in October 1975, when Japan extended an aid grant of 8,500 million yen. Peace negotiations with Korea proved especially difficult. Korea had been split in two as a result of the Korean War in the early 1950s, and relations with North Korea still await normalization. A Treaty of Basic Relations with South Korea was concluded after lengthy negotiations in 1965, and only after Japan agreed to give South Korea $300 million in outright grants, $200 million long-term, low-interest credits.

At the Potsdam agreement in 1945 the leaders of the USA, USSR and Britain had prescribed the demilitarization, disarmament and deconcentration of the economic powers of Japan. Twenty-eight major war criminals were tried in November 1948, and 160 million dollars reparation was exacted under the Far Eastern Commission. But in 1948 American policy changed and the emphasis in its dealings with Japan, because of the growing cold war with the Soviet Union, came to stress rearmament as well as reform and rehabilitation. Indeed, the Johnston report of 26 April 1948 recommended an end to reparations.

John Foster Dulles (then special adviser to the US Secretary of State with responsibility for peace negotiations with Japan) regarded the Peace Treaty of 1951 as 'the most broadly based peace treaty in all history'. According to one observer, Dulles also considered the treaty to be 'an outstanding example of foreign policy according to the Moral Law', and that in the treaty

> the principle of forgiveness overcame that of vengeance. The victor powers renounced the rights to which retributive justice would have entitled them, and welcomed Japan once more as a partner (*The Christian Century*, 19 March 1952).
> Nothing could make clearer the delusions of this kind of conservative moralism operating in the name of the Christian faith. Perhaps it was God's will that the Japanese Peace Treaty be signed as it was. But the motives behind it were at least ambiguous: the fear of Russia, the desire to shift the cost of defence more on to Japanese shoulders, the hope of engaging Japanese nationalism in our cause: these mixed with the purer Christian motives Dulles described . . .[13]

This view seems to be borne out by the signing on the same day (8 September 1951) of the US-Japan Treaty, considered at the time to be a severe diplomatic defeat for the Soviet Union.

The real weakness of the Peace Treaty, however, was that no Asian power signed it. As the aggrieved Asian countries negotiated reparations, Japan was involved in a network of intricate politics and continual pressure; it experienced its nemesis. However, this aspect did not seem to trouble Tsutomu Nishiyama, the Japanese Ambassador-designate to India, who said (in September 1952) that the Peace Treaty had been 'the most liberal treaty ever concluded by victorious powers with a vanquished country', but added that the Indo-Japanese Treaty signed in June and ratified in August 1952, 'goes much further'. The Japanese greatly appreciated India's 'unparalleled magnanimity'. In waiving all claims to war reparations and agreeing to return, or restore, all Japanese property in India, she had set 'a new pattern of international reconciliation after a war'.[14]

However, the calls for reparation would not go away, whatever the US government might wish. In the Peace Treaty itself, Japan was ordered to pay $12,500,000 to members of the allied forces who had suffered undue hardship as prisoners of war. And, as far as economic reparations can help to ease relationships between states, Japan's total of $1,012 million (compared with the West German and Italian figures – $830 million and $360 million respectively) is not insignificant.

As a result of the Pacific War, Japan was stripped of 44 per cent of its overseas assets, 80 per cent of its merchant marine and large parts of industrial equipment, losing in all some 36 per cent of its national wealth. And the stationing of American forces in Japan became the 'unavoidable *quid pro quo* for the non-punitive peace settlement'.[15]

Whatever the true history of the events leading up to the 1947 constitution, implemented by Japan's only Socialist government, Japan *did* renounce war as an instrument of national policy, the only major power to have done so.

Japan made further acknowledgement of its wartime actions when, in autumn 1957, the prime minister at that time, Nobusuke Kishi, visited many countries that had suffered from Japanese aggression. A London newspaper reported that

> Premier Kishi is now back in Tokyo after having completed one of the most unusual missions ever undertaken by a statesman of his rank. All told, over the past three weeks, he has visited no fewer than nine nations that Japan occupied or threatened with conquest after the attack on Pearl Harbour sixteen years ago. And in each of these lands – including New Zealand, Australia, Indonesia and the Philippines – he has publicly apologized for his country's actions during the war.[16]

An attempt to put aside historic animosities between Japan and South Korea was made by Prime Minister Yashuhiru Nakasone when he visited Seoul in 1983. Relations between the two countries were still strained, due in part to the presence in Japan of a Korean minority living as second-class citizens.

Emperor Hirohito also expressed some regret to South Korea, during a visit to Japan by President Chun in 1984. According to a newspaper report, the Emperor's words were: 'It is regrettable that there was an unfortunate past between us for a period this century and I believe that it should not be repeated.' But, the report continued,

> The Emperor's long-awaited statement, regarded as the crucial point of the visit, fell some way short of the apology sought by many Koreans who have painful memories of the harsh subjugation of their country by Japan between 1910 and 1945. The wording, the fruit of much agonizing by aides to the Japanese Prime Minister, Mr Nakasone, and foreign ministry officials, resembled the mild regret expressed when Hirohito received the Chinese leader, Mr Deng Xiaoping in 1978.

In his response President Chun said he had 'listened solemnly' to the Emperor's remarks about the 'unfortunate past' and he quoted an old Korean proverb that the 'ground hardens after rainfall,' meaning that 'close friends, after a quarrel, become more friendly than ever before'. 'It was not known if the Emperor's public expression of regret corresponded with exchange at a private audience in the palace earlier in the day, shortly after the President arrived for his three-day visit,' the report concluded.[17]

The meeting, as students and religious and political dissidents in Seoul protested, did little to change the emotional climate between Japan and Korea, with its residue of rancour, guilt and pride.

Contrasting the postwar attitudes of the Japanese and German governments, a writer in *The Times* has pointed out that it took the Japanese 'thirty-nine years before it gave any hint of official regret to the Chinese for having laid waste to their country in the 1930s. And then it was in something less than fulsome terms.' He went on to notice dangerous trends in Japanese society – for example, officially approved textbooks which fudged the real import of the war.[18]

'I thought,' wrote Sir Laurens van der Post,

> that the only hope for the future lay in an all-embracing attitude of fogiveness of the peoples who had been our enemies. Forgiveness, my prison experience had taught me,

was not mere religious sentimentality; it was a fundamental law of the human spirit as the law of gravity. If one broke the law of gravity one broke one's neck; if one broke this law of forgiveness one inflicted a mortal wound on one's spirit and became again a member of a chain-gang of mere cause and effect from which life has laboured so long and painfully to escape.[19]

It is this theme, after the initial repentance and apology, which many Japanese and their victims have been exploring since 1945. Even during the war, some prisoners of war discovered this spirit of forgiveness. Ernest Gordon, for example, tells how a group of allied prisoners attended a Good Friday service of the Stations of the Cross. 'In my contemplation,' he wrote,

> I recognized that it was no easy thing to call that figure on the cross, 'Lord'. I heard again his words, 'Father, forgive them, for they know not what they do.' I could not say what he said, for he was innocent, whereas I was not. Humbly, I had to ask, 'Forgive me *and* my enemies, for we know not what we do.'[20]

Difficult as it was to follow this Jesus, slowly a new spirit began to grasp that group of prisoners which affected their attitude to their enemies.[21] A similar change occurred in some other camps. 'Captors were spared by their captives. When the liberating allied soldiers found the situation the prisoners were in, they wanted to shoot the Japanese guards on the spot. But "Let mercy take the place of bloodshed," said these exhausted but forgiving men.'[22]

John Leonard Wilson (later Bishop of Birmingham) tells a similar story. He was severely tortured by the Japanese; on one occasion he fainted and, on reviving, received 300 lashes. Finally he was taken to the cells and thrown on the floor with no medical help, only care from a fellow prisoner who subsequently died.

Three years later, in October 1946, he preached at a Sunday service broadcast by the BBC. 'In the middle of the torture they asked me if I still believed in God,' he recounted.

When, by God's help, I said, 'I do,' they asked me why

God did not save me, and by the help of his Holy Spirit, I said, 'God does save me. He does not save me by freeing me from pain and punishment, but he saves me by giving me the spirit to bear it.' And when they asked me why I did not curse them, I told them it was because I was a follower of Jesus Christ, who taught us that we were all brothers . . .[23]

There was a striking sequel to the story. In 1947 the Bishop was taking services in Singapore. He obtained permission for those in prison to attend.

Among those that I baptised and confirmed was one of the men of the military police who had been responsible, four years earlier, for taking part in my own torturing. I have seldom seen so great a change in a man. He looked gentle and peaceful, even though he was going back to serve a ten-year sentence, and later he received communion at my hands in prison.[24]

Years after that passion experienced by Leonard Wilson, it bore fruit at the time of the Emperor of Japan's state visit to London. The fact that Emperor Hirohito came to Britain was not perhaps understood as the profound act of humility it was towards those the Japanese had fought, for the Emperor seldom leaves Japan. The visit revived many unhealed memories, particularly in the minds of ex-servicemen. 'But at our annual conference held at Buxton last May,' wrote the deputy chairman of the National Federation of Far Eastern Prisoners of War Clubs, E.J. Coffey, 'it was agreed that we would take no action. This was mainly due to the conference being reminded of the teachings we had so often heard the bishop tell us.'[25]

'Forty years after the battle, a unique reconciliation,' was the newspaper headline in 1984 above a picture of Bill Gallop and Alan Cowell, two former British soldiers, with Susumi Nishida, sharing a pint of beer in a pub.

The last time they met face to face, they shared one thought – to kill each other.

Yesterday, in an historic act of reconciliation, the old soldiers met in a London hotel and shook hands. They

were joined by ten other Japanese and fifteen British survivors of one of the decisive battles of World War II.

It was the first meeting of its kind. Long after British
and German veterans buried the hatchet the bitterness
between British and Japanese lingered on.[26]

Such reconciliation is never easy. The following year a BBC
television news item reported that survivors of the Burma railway
were returning on a 'pilgrimage' to where many of their colleagues had died. (At least 13,000 lay buried in cemeteries by
the railway.) One survivor, when interviewed and asked if he
could forgive, said, 'Never, never'. But another considered that
since the end of the war 'as I've grown older, I've come to the
conclusion that I just can't go on hating'.[27]

In 1989 the issue of forgiveness came up again, when Buck-
ingham Palace announced that the Duke of Edinburgh would
attend Emperor Hirohito's funeral and there were many protests, especially from British ex-servicemen. The news media
found itself discussing the pros and cons of forgiveness in politics, almost despite itself. One ex-serviceman stopped a fast to
death only after he had received a letter from the Queen asking
him to do so.

Among those who have attempted to heal the bitter memories
of the war in the Far East is Nagasake Takashi. When he
received half a million yen royalties for translating a book about
the Second World War into Japanese, this prompted in him the
idea of erecting a Buddhist temple in memory of the hundred
thousand people who died building the rail link for Japan's
imperial army. It was while working as an interpreter for the
Allied Commission after the war, seeking out and identifying
the graves and makeshift cemeteries along the railway, that he
realized the horror of what the Japanese military had done. He
is reported as saying, 'The Japanese government wants everyone
in the world to forget what happened [in World War II], but I
do not want to forget.'

In 1976 he organized the first formal reunion of former
Japanese soldiers and allied prisoners of war; together they
walked across the bridge over the River Kwai. Later, there was
a consecration ceremony of a Buddhist statue for the planned

temple, involving also other Japanese concerned with the project and twelve Thai Buddhist priests.[28]

It is surely deeper responses like these which will allow healing. An Oomoto presentation of the Japanese Noh plays in Canterbury Cathedral chapter house a few years ago offered a symbolic exorcism. More such actions are needed if we are ever to move beyond remembered anguish, as we recall that even Kagawa, the Japanese social reformer who wrote:

> Like Christ who bore our sins upon the Cross,
> I, too, must bear my country's sins and dross,[29]

was nearly purged by the occupation forces for his anti-American talks as the war ended.

Yet, whatever Japanese war crimes were committed, the crime of a bomb brighter than a thousand suns also calls for expiation. The event which stands out above all others is the dropping of the first atomic bomb on an unsuspecting Hiroshima on 6 August 1945.

> On that day I saw dead bodies which looked like shreds of rags being loaded on the trucks. There were men and women looking like ghosts walking in search of help. All night long the city continued to burn like a ball of fire. The following day I walked on the hot ground looking for my parents and my brother.

Two years after the experience Fukimo Amano describes above, she became a teacher in an elementary school near the hypocentre of the bomb.

> At this school I taught children who suffered from keloids, malnutrition, leprosy, and other diseases caused by radiation. There were children caring for their sick parents and orphans who survived by stealing. Back then I realized that the greatest victims of war were the innocent children. So I decided to educate these children in good human values and the truth about Japanese military aggression in neighbouring countries.

But this was not the only effect on Fukimo Amano, for she

saw the building of a church where an American missionary preached the love of God. Fukimo could not accept his teaching because of the bomb. However, as she read the Bible, the words 'God is love' and Jesus' death convinced her. She realized that her hate and unforgiving heart were the same sins that had caused the bomb to be made. As she started to teach children to love instead of hate she found her own heart began to change, too.[30]

It was surely no coincidence that the first atom bomb was dropped on 6 August, the day many Christians, particularly in the East, celebrate the Feast of the Transfiguration, when all nature, and people, are seen as changed by the power of Christ. Even more blasphemous was naming the first atomic test, *Trinity*.

Contrast this raw approach with how the Japanese have treated their atomic experience, and it is evident the West has much to learn from their suffering. 'It was not so much something nasty done to them (which would justify, if not revenge, then self-pity on a grand scale) as a fearful portent of universal significance.'[31]

The Most Venerable Nichidatsu Fujii, the Buddhist leader who has planted peace pagodas in many parts of the world, sees things in a similar way: 'There is no longer a soul who visits the graves of MacArthur or Truman. However, year after year, thousands and tens of thousands of pilgrims gather at Hiroshima and Nagasaki to repose the souls of those who were sacrificed.'[32] And in his view there 'will be no one in the future who will rejoice at the victory of the people who dropped the atomic bombs. This is the power of the spiritual civilization.'[33]

One person whose life has been changed dramatically is Albert Bigelow, the captain of a US destroyer escort in Pearl Harbour at the time of Hiroshima; he resigned his commission in the American Naval Reserve in 1952. One experience that had an especially dramatic effect on him was when he received in his home two of the Hiroshima victims who had been injured and disfigured in the bombing and had come to America for plastic surgery. 'They harboured no resentment against us or other Americans,' he remarked. 'How are you going to respond to that kind of attitude?'

Albert Bigelow's answer was to become involved in protests

against nuclear war. On 7 August 1957, he sat with others before dawn in the Nevada desert protesting outside the entrance to the Camp Mercury testing grounds. The day before, with ten others, he had tried to enter a restricted area to protest against the summer-long tests.[34]

Whether it has been the work of Kiyoshi Tanimoto, chief director of the Hiroshima Peace Centre, who himself suffered atomic radiation, yet has been 'able to transcend his anguish, hate, sadness and misfortune through his religious inspiration' and 'through his devoted spirituality he has forgiven,'[35] or the peace pagodas across the world (one of which now stands in Battersea Park, London) a stream of healing *from* Japan, with its implication of forgiveness, has drawn many thousands of Westerners, like Albert Bigelow, into friendships with Japanese people and some understanding of the impact the Second World War has had on their country. A living example of the many friendships created in Britain is the link forged by Mukashi University in Tokyo with the University of Kent.

Perhaps the erection of the peace pagoda in Milton Keynes was the most startling symbol. 'A Buddha image has now arrived in England,' said the Most Venerable Nichidatsu Fujii at a gathering at Atami Dōjō in July 1979. 'It was not secretly brought at the private level, but publicly handed to Her Majesty the Queen of England. Her Majesty kindly wrote a letter of acknowledgment after her return to the Palace . . .'[36]

Ichiro Moritaki, President of the Japanese Congress against the Atomic and Hydrogen Bombs, in an assessment of the Venerable Fujii's contribution, has drawn attention to the likeness of his teaching to that of Albert Schweitzer and of Gandhi: in Schweitzer's commemorative lecture upon receiving the Nobel Peace Prize, 'the doctor appealed for the recovery of the "power of man's spirit". This is equivalent to Gandhi's teaching of soul force, as well as the Buddha's teaching of "the awakening of Buddha-nature" that the Venerable Fujii emphasized.'[37]

In 1946, soon after the two atomic bombs had been dropped, a Japanese theologian, Kazoh Kitamori, wrote:

> My prayer night and day is that the gospel of love rooted in the pain of God may become real to all men. All human emptiness will be filled if this gospel is known to every

creature, since the answer to every human problem lies in the gospel. Therefore I pray 'May thou, O Lord, make known to all men thy love rooted in the pain of God.'[38]

Perhaps a combination of the Buddhist reverence for all life and the Christian sense of God being involved in the pain of the world through the crucifixion will be the only way we can make sense of Hiroshima and Nagasaki, and this will stem from Japan's encounter with the West.

6

CHINA'S REVOLUTION

'ALWAYS REMEMBER two things about our country,' said a Chinese student to a newspaper correspondent in Beijing in 1980, 'One billion people and three thousand years of feudalism.'[1] 'We are trying to compress,' said Ying Ruocheng, Vice-Minister of Culture, 'the Renaissance, the Reformation and the Industrial Revolution into a single decade.'[2]

The essential point to consider when evaluating Chinese history, whether Confucian, Maoist or Marxist-Leninist, is that 'the Chinese do not separate people into a "private and public domain," psychologically'.[3] To be human is to be part of the group, and especially the family group. Indeed, Chinese life, whatever the current political style, has a continuity difficult either to avoid or evade and reaching back to Confucius and his disciple Mencius.[4] To understand contemporary China it is necessary to realize that past traditions live on. Indeed, in the mid-1980s a national society was set up for the study of Confucius.[5]

Also at the heart of the modern Chinese experience is another ingredient: a determination to overthrow centuries of serfdom and foreign rule. Their most recent experience of foreign domination, by the Japanese after they invaded China in the 1930s, has etched itself deeply into the Chinese imagination, perhaps even more deeply than the legacy of the nineteenth-century Opium Wars which left Hong Kong and Kowloon a British possession, with the New Territories leased to Britain, until 1997.

The wish to overcome China's internal poverty has been one thing; to accomplish it has been quite another. The 'Long March' of Mao Zedong and his followers is the symbol both of that pain, as they fought a bitter and protracted civil war, and of that determination to liberate China from its tortured past. The Chinese people recognized in Mao and his followers a Chinese nationalism which enabled the Communists in 1949 to gain advantage over Chiang Kai-shek's regime,[6] which had been propped up by foreign powers.

It was their sensitivity to injustice and their determination to alter it that turned Mao Zedong, Zhou Enlai and the other communist leaders to Marxist-Leninism, which they then proceeded to mould to a Chinese form. They saw early on, in the 1920s (the first meeting of the Chinese Communist Party was held in Shanghai in 1921), that it was not so much a 'lumpen proletariat' with whom they had to deal but landless and suffering peasants. Chinese Marxism therefore had to take a unique form. Perhaps they drew on their Confucian traditions more than they knew when, like all politicians, the Chinese Communists discovered they had to come to terms both with the pluralism of politics and also with their own mistakes.

Mao Zedong found he had to wrestle with this issue in connection with enemy troops captured during the Second World War. 'Our policy towards prisoners captured from the Japanese, puppet, and anti-communist troops', he wrote, 'is to set them all free, except for those who have incurred the bitter hatred of the masses . . .'[7] The latter were to be killed once the death sentence had been approved. Here Mao is not, of course, urging a practice of forgiveness in the Western, Christian sense; he is essentially dealing with the fact that politics is always, even in China, the art of the possible. And that involves inevitable compromise and pragmatism, even for utopian leaders.

It was this awareness of the subtleties of existence which also led him to change his own position as he came to feel that intellectuals, in contrast to workers and peasants, needed to be remoulded.[8]

Mao recognized the need for economic changes, but saw that *mental* change was even more essential if China was to experience liberation. Such change involved a struggle which would be a continuing process. Always aware of the contradictions of reality, he now added to this idea an emphasis on continual struggle: ' . . . genuine revolutionaries deeply understand that to revolutionize themselves is by no means an extra burden but it is intended to emancipate themselves thoroughly from the sludge and foul water of the old world,'[9] he wrote. Here surely, expressed in secular language, is a man repenting, showing *metanoia* in the biblical sense. Yet *his* repentance was to enable him to struggle more rather than to love more. 'We cannot love enemies, we cannot love social evils, our aim is to destroy them,'[10] he argued. A commentator on Mao elaborates:

> Mao's thought does not reject love for the sake of hatred but for the sake of justice . . . When the power of the enemies has been broken they can be dealt with 'on the basis of equality and mutual benefit' and transformed into useful citizens.[11]

But what if the revolutionary is a sinner, too? Here is the nub of the problem for Marxists. In chapter 1 we saw this as a key issue in the Soviet Union, and we see it again in China, because love – expression of which implies the possibility of handling mistakes creatively – is put aside until after the desired changes have occurred, or the revolution won. Strangely, there is one legacy from Mao Zedong which could help the Chinese handle this contradiction in their revolution, a legacy of difficult questions raised by Mao.

> 'May bureaucratic and political power be as real a source of exploitation, oppression and corruption as power based on property? Are there any political institutions – including the Communist Party – immune from corruption and error?' As new leadership attempts to create stable institutional bases in China these questions will remain to haunt them.[12]

Much of what Mao Zedong urged was implemented in the early days of the People's Republic of China, before the civil war had ended. It has been documented in *Fanshen*, a documentary account of revolution in a Chinese village. 'There are districts in which the position of the rural population is that of a man standing permanently up to the neck in water,' wrote R.H. Tawney.[13] Such was the village of Long Bow observed in *Fanshen*.

With the liberation of the area from the old Chinese power structures, the Communists and those who supported them gradually took over, distributing money and land more equitably.

They had then to deal with those whose power they had over-turned. But before that, party members themselves had to be corrected, if felt to be in error. This involved self-criticism in front of colleagues, which could last for hours, and admission of wrong-doing. One comrade, Chang Ch'Un-Hei, knew he could be suspended from the party for five months for taking too much grain and being too proud. If he failed to correct his mistakes he could be thrown out of the party and sent to the People's Court for punishment. He said that if his colleagues pardoned his crime he would try to turn over a new leaf.[14]

Is such action a secular form of repentance and forgiveness, forgiving oneself and receiving forgiveness from colleagues? The word forgiveness was never used in Long Bow, but the Chinese were certainly trying to deal with mistakes they felt people had made, some of them grave. Surely therefore, when individuals and families admitted error in this way, they were repenting, and in being pardoned of the error were forgiven?

However, this form of self-criticism led in the 1950s to a continuous period of purges – inevitable so long as the political process was focused on correct thought and interpretations. The purges were no respecter of persons. Deng Xiaoping, who had been with Mao on the Long March of 1934–5, was twice purged; others, who were considered counter-revolutionary, lost their lives. There were periods of less orthodoxy, as during the 'Hundred Flowers' movement of the 1950s when more diverse views were welcomed for a while, though always within a firm framework. Then disaster fell between 1966 and 1976 as the Cultural Revolution was unleashed by Mao himself. Through-out this period, under pressure from the Red Guards, who were mostly in their teens, people began to suspect each other. Only correct thought was applauded, and intellectuals and others were sent to rural areas to work in the fields with the peasants.

A nemesis was inevitable. In the mid-1970s, while Mao was dying, his wife and others, known afterwards as the Gang of Four, gained control of the body politic (they had already been active in the Cultural Revolution and then its leaders) and would brook no argument. Even the distinguished colleague of Mao, Premier Zhou Enlai, had to move with discretion and wisdom, though he did manage to save many lives.[15]

Mao, his speech limited by a stroke, designated Hua Guofeng

as his successor. Soon after Mao's death he and other leaders of the Chinese Communist Party acted swiftly and the Gang of Four were arrested. 'The Gang of Four are, of course, in confinement,' Hua stated. 'Like everyone else they eat and they sleep. We won't mistreat them in the way they tortured countless cadres. They will have to account for their towering crimes against the Chinese people.'[16]

The figures for what happened during the Cultural Revolution are contradictory. The *People's Daily* once suggested that one hundred million people were affected by the Cultural Revolution. According to a New China News Agency report in December 1980, during one period of forty days '1,700 people were beaten to death, 33,600 households were searched and ransacked, and 85,000 were driven out of the capital'.[17] In a speech that same year Deng Xiaoping stated that 2.9 million people had been rehabilitated since the end of the Cultural Revolution, and 'many more whose cases were not put on file,' he added ambiguously. Whatever the correct figures, the scale of suffering among the Chinese people was comparable to that under Chiang Kai-shek's rule in the 1930s and at times perhaps worse.

In a speech to the Military Commission of the Central Committee of the Chinese Communist Party in December 1977, Deng Xiaoping (reinstated earlier that year by a resolution of the Party's Tenth Central Committee, which restored him to all his former posts) tried to deal with the vexing problem of unity. 'We should not bear grudges against people who were once "out to get us",' he said. 'Instead of harbouring resentment against comrades, we should forgive old wrongs. People like us can't be faultless, and we should allow others to criticize our shortcomings. We veteran cadres should set a good example in this respect . . .'[18] He returned to the theme a year later, in an address to the conference preparing for the Third Plenary Session of the Eleventh Central Committee. 'Our principle', he stated, 'is that every wrong should be righted. All wrongs done in the past should be corrected. Some questions that cannot be settled right now should be settled after this conference . . .'[19]

From 1978 Deng Xiaoping consolidated his position and was able to step down and promote people sympathetic to his view, withdrawing into the background, though retaining his role in

the Political Bureau and as Chairman of the Military Commission. Hu Yeobang became General Secretary of the Party,
Zhao Ziyang the Premier and Li Xian the President. However,
in late 1986 the situation became fluid again with the dismissal
of Hu Yeobang and a power struggle seemed to be in evidence.
By 1988 Zhao Ziyang appeared to be the heir-apparent to Deng
Xiaoping, but in 1989 it seemed his role as General Secretary
of the Chinese Communist Party was in jeopardy. In Chinese
politics it is always possible that a new figure will emerge representing another wing of the Party.

A new party constitution had been brought in in 1978. This
dropped references to Mao Zedong's 'Thoughts' (inserted in
1945) and included a statement that 'no political party or person
can be free from shortcomings and mistakes'. China was trying
to grapple with a more collective style of leadership as well as
living with the consequences of the impending trial of the Gang
of Four and the tragic results of the Cultural Revolution.

Deng Xiaoping addressed himself to this problem again in
February 1980 in another speech.[20] He referred to a resolution
on the rehabilitation of a particular member who, like the party
itself, had made mistakes before the Cultural Revolution. He
agreed with the tenor of this, but urged the gathering not to
give the impression one person alone was in error, whilst others
were correct. Even he had made mistakes, he admitted: in the
anti-rightist struggle of 1957 he had, as General Secretary of
the Central Committee, shared responsibility for widening the
scope of the struggle. He and others were also carried away in
the Great Leap Forward of 1958.[21]

He drove home this point in 1981 in remarks on drafts of
the 'Resolution of Certain Questions in the History of the
Chinese Communist Party': 'When the Central Committee
makes a mistake, it is the collective rather than a particular
individual that bears the responsibility.' The resolution was
adopted at the sixth Plenary Session of the Eleventh Central
Committee of the Party. It admitted that the Party had made
mistakes, due to lack of experience and human error and understanding of Chinese conditions. These had included enlarging
the scope of class struggle and rashness in economic construction before the Cultural Revoluion. It had been a 'grave blun-
der'. Mao Zedong should be held chiefly responsible for it, but

not alone. A combination of his theoretical and practical mistakes about class struggle in a socialist society became serious and his personal arbitrariness had undermined 'democratic centralism in Party life'.[22] The resolution went on to praise Mao Zedong and said that, 'If we judge his activities as a whole, his contribution to the Chinese revolution far outweighs his mistakes. His merits are primary and his errors secondary.' It ended, 'Our party has both the courage to acknowledge and correct its mistakes of the past . . .'[23]

Parallel to these developments at a constitutional and structural level were the more human activities. In April 1978, in its first attempts at a general rehabilitation, the Party Central Committee ordered a case-by-case review of all the people pursued in the 1957 anti-rightist campaign. Those found wrongly convicted were to be compensated, the document stated, and where age and health permitted, given new work by the State Planning Commission. Where original verdicts were upheld the victims' bourgeois labels were simply to be removed and their political rights restored. Many of those brought back were unknown outside China. Yet once they had governed provinces as large as France, or Britain, and would perhaps do so again.

These rehabilitated veterans accounted for half of the ninety-one new Central Committee members appointed by the Congress. Their return to power was portrayed as part of a much broader united-front policy, aimed to mobilize all sections of Chinese society, Communist and non-Communist, behind the new regime. But the veterans were the key because of their experience.

To mark the anniversary of the Party's fifty-seventh year all newspapers printed a previously unpublished speech given by Mao Zedong in 1962 and dealing with errors during the Great Leap Forward. It admitted that in socialist construction they were still acting blindly to some extent and that there had been shortcomings and mistakes. Responsibility for these lay with the Central Committee and primarily with Mao himself.[24]

This line of thought gradually allowed a relaxation in the role of the Chairman Mao image and the renaming of the Red Guards as Young Pioneers. At the end of 1978 Deng Xiaoping left for a week's visit to Japan, the first senior Chinese leader to visit that country since the Sino-Japanese war. His journey symbolized the two countries' recognition of reconciliation after the brutality of the Japanese occupation.

The next eighteen months saw the reopening of temples, mosques and churches, and elaboration of a view on religion which placed believers on the same footing as everyone else. The former Maoist policy of assimilation towards minority nationalities had ended. In Guangzhou three men who compromised the Li Yi-che group and were spiritual fathers of the 'Beijing Spring' were released at the request of the Central Committee and were publicly exonerated. Provincial leaders declared that the poster which had led to their imprisonment had contained 'many correct views'.[25]

The Cultural Revolution was denounced as a 'ten-year holocaust'. Did this mean that China was reverting to capitalism? No: as Xu Wenli put it in Beijing in 1979, 'The majority of young people in China don't want a private redistribution of capital and the return of private ownership of land. But neither do they want a new bureaucratic class to rule over them.'[26]

The trial of the Gang of Four began on 20 November 1980, and involved Mao's widow, Jiang Qing, and three others, plus five military officers. Jiang Qing defended herself by saying she had been implementing Mao's programme, the most difficult thing which had to be handled. The trial stirred up immense bitterness. The death sentence was pronounced on the Four, but was suspended for two years and then commuted to life imprisonment. (The officers each received a nine years' sentence.)

The Communist Party has also had to deal with problems of ethnic minorities. Though only around 6 per cent of the total population, these minorities involve over sixty million people living in regions which cover half the land area of China, some of it strategically vital.

From this fact stems some of the Chinese paradoxes, especially in relation to the Tibetans. Before the age of nation-states, boundaries and borders were not so significant and the Tibetans had sat loose to political arrangements though they were within the Chinese sphere of influence. Indeed, prior to the 1949 revolution, it was only under the strongest dynasties that they were conscious of being part of China. Other countries had never formally recognized Tibet as an independent country but several dealt with it as one.

The 1931 constitution, promulgated by Chiang Kai-shek's government, stated categorically that Tibet was part of China. Tibetan delegates participated in the Nationalist constituent assembly which approved the 1946 constitution and also sat in the Chinese Nationalist Assembly in 1948. So when, after the Communist revolution, the People's Liberation Army started to move into Tibet they were pursuing the historic claim of Chinese governments that Tibet was part of China.

Whatever the pros and cons of Chinese involvement in Tibet the facts are plain: since 1949, despite protestations to the contrary, it appears that official Chinese policy, especially during the Cultural Revolution, was to sinocize Tibet. There were some improvements in health, education and even in wealth, but although Beijing did set up a Tibetan Autonomous Region, little self-government emerged. The highest levels of the party and administration were dominated by Chinese officials who often failed to learn local languages or respect local customs.

Between 1967 and 1979 religious and cultural relics were systematically destroyed. The Chinese commune system was introduced, nomadic peoples forcibly settled and the local economy damaged by the replacement of barley, the Tibetans' staple food, by wheat. Moreover, teaching in secondary classes had to be in Chinese. All this suppression led at one point to armed rebellion.

Can the death of thousands of Tibetans and the destruction of their culture (including priceless historical books – a fire of documents from the monasteries took four days to burn itself out) be justified? Certainly not, say the 100,000 Tibetans who, with their leader, the Dalai Lama, fled to India and elsewhere after the 1959 uprising had been crushed. Even the Panchen Lama, second in line to the Dalai Lama, who had supported the Communists on many occasions and urged the Dalai Lama to return, said shortly before his death (in January 1989) that the price paid by Tibet under Beijing's rule outweighed the gains.[27]

The pressures of the Tibetan struggle fell heavily on the Chinese leadership, which has since attempted to make some amends. In May 1980 a number of requirements for Tibet were laid down. These included: regional autonomy for minority nationalities; exemption from taxes and quotas for some years to allow Tibet to recover; economic policies which would take Tibet's particular situation into account; and vigorous attempts to revive and develop Tibetan culture and science. In addition, the complaints against the Chinese over neglect of Tibetan barley were admitted as legitimate.[28] There are reports also of language training for Chinese cadres in Lhasa to help them to govern better.[29]

During 1983 and 1984 the Chinese tried to encourage the Dalai Lama to return. 'If the Dalai Lama returns to work for China's unification and national unity, he can go and visit wherever he likes and his safety will be fully guaranteed,'[30] Yang Jingren, head of the United Front Work Department of the Central Committee said when speaking to three representatives sent to Beijing by the Dalai Lama. He reaffirmed the policy towards the Dalai Lama earlier advanced by Hu Yaobang in 1981 about letting the past be forgotten.

Was Chinese regret genuine? Had the policy, which had evolved through several stages really changed? Tibetans asked. Certainly compensation was paid to Tibetans who had been wrongly convicted, and in 1981 thirty books in the Tibetan language were published, an increase on the previous year. 'The damage to monasteries was serious. Many losses are irretrievable,' one Chinese writer considered, 'but we are making efforts to correct this and are striving to restore the monasteries.'[31] So far, so good, it seems. But the fact that Hu Yaobang was removed from office in January 1987, in part due to conservative resentment at his apology to Tibet for Chinese misrule, made the Tibetans wonder which of the rival factions was in control in Beijing.

What does the Dalai Lama himself think of the situation? In 1963 he drew up a draft constitution for Tibet on the basis of which his government in exile has been functioning. He considered that 'original Marxism and Mahayana Buddhism' had points in common, and that Buddhist theory was not sufficient of itself – it could learn about economics from socialist and democratic systems. Similarly these systems could learn from Buddhist theory.[32] If the six million Tibetans were happy he would be prepared to return with whatever status the majority granted.[33] In June 1988 he put forward an idea for a self-governing Tibet, giving Beijing the right to station troops there and be in charge of Tibet's foreign policy. He also offered to exclude himself from future office if this would contribute to a settlement.[34]

Parallel to the Dalai Lama's thinking was a Chinese reappraisal of the role of religion in different communities. At the end of 1985, for example, it was admitted at a propaganda department forum for cadres that:

> On the issue of religion we have lacked sufficient understanding of long-term, complex and mass nature of religious work; we have taken many preventive measures regarding this work, but have provided little positive guidance. We have even criticized religious belief as spiritual pollution. This is extremely wrong.[35]

This was a dramatic change from the days of the Cultural Revolution and indeed earlier. It exemplified what Wu Jinhua, Secretary of the Regional Committee, had said in a speech marking the twentieth anniversary of the founding of the Tibetan Autonomous Region:

> Freedom of religious belief is our Party's basic, long-term policy regarding religion . . . This question is one on which citizens have freedom of choice: it is their private business. Hence, far from banning it, we must respect and protect it.[36]

However, attempts by the Dalai Lama and the Chinese government to find an accommodation were set back in the spring of 1989 when the Chinese Premier, Li Peng, declared martial law and another uprising occurred in Tibet, thirty years after the initial revolt in 1959.

The Chinese handling of the Tibetans has a far-reaching effect on other minority groups, like Muslims and Christians. The Christians in particular are divided by some contradictions, especially how to cope with one another when they have taken different views of the Communist revolution. Liu Qingfen's comment is instructive:

> The reason why so many Christian believers are not willing to go to church lies in the fact that they were, to some degree, criticized or punished in the various political movements after liberation in 1949, and they were persecuted particularly in the Cultural Revolution. So they fear that those unhappy things could happen to them again some day . . .[37]

Some others are quite clear where they stand. 'Our point of departure', Chen Zemin considers, 'is to opt for the people, to opt for the welfare of our country, and to opt for a social system that is more just and humane than anything the Chinese people have witnessed over four thousand years . . .'[38] Bishop K.H. Ting adds to this: 'For a poverty-stricken people deprived of their rights for thousands of years, to have made mistakes in their first attempt at governing a vast country is only natural. But mistakes cannot stifle the wisdom and character of the people . . .'[39] And Jiang Wenhan writes: 'I know of no other political party in the world that has the courage to admit and correct its own mistakes. We are now on the road of rehabilitation and reconstruction,'[40] 'Our theological task', concludes Professor Chen, 'is not liberation in the Latin American sense, but reconciliation – reconciliation to and identification with the Chinese people as a whole, from whom we had long been alienated. At the same time, our task is to be reconciled to God, from whom the human race has been alienated . . .'[41]

So, relations between the government and religious believers remain complex. It is interesting to note that Muslims in the north successfully demanded an end to the above-ground testing of nuclear weapons.

There are also unresolved problems over Hong Kong, Taiwan and Macao: Hong Kong, the legacy of the last century; Taiwan the unresolved issue of the 1949 Revolution itself, for it was there that Chiang Kai-shek fled to when defeated by the Red Army.

The *Beijing Review* had this to say about the agreement

between Britain and China over Hong Kong, Kowloon and the New Territories

> The formula 'one country, two systems', which forms the basis of the Hong Kong accord is not someone's whims. It is solidly grounded on a theoretical understanding of the extended duration of the socialist transition period. When this is appreciated, lingering doubts about the durability of the present arrangements will disappear.[42]

Certainly the Chinese on the mainland have been very patient considering the painful memories of the Opium War and of how Britain gained this part of Asia. But will they be as patient with the way of life of Hong Kong?

The Chinese constitution states, 'Citizens enjoy freedom to believe in religion and freedom not to believe in religion and to propagate atheism.' By not permitting citizens to propagate religion this seems to legitimize the suppression of any activity which can be construed as furthering religious belief. Hong Kong, with its open religious life, will therefore pose a problem for the Marxist. The Chinese, perhaps one of the most pragmatic of people, will surely have to come to terms with the religious issue, not only in Tibet and Hong Kong but also in China itself.

Will the people of Hong Kong be able to explore with mainland China a politics of forgiveness? Perhaps so; perhaps not. Much depends on the way Chinese Marxism, with its differing strands vying for the supreme positions of state, develops.

Regarding the conflict with Taiwan, the most bitter and long-standing problem of the Chinese mainland, the *Beijing Review*, in 1984, suggested a way to resolve it:

> To our brothers and sisters across the Taiwan Straits we say: 'If such a complex issue like Hong Kong can be settled through peaceful negotiations with the British, why can't we Chinese sit down and talk and put an end to the separation before the year 2,000? Do not hesitate, lest we lose a golden opportunity.'[43]

From this it appears that the concept of one Chinese people is more important to the politicians than one monochrome system of belief. But will it be enough to overcome the last fifty years of bitterness and the lack of a clear human rights obligation entrenched in the constitution? Since 1980 a whole complex of economic and civil laws has been introduced and many books are being published drawing attention to the need for a more satisfactory legal system for China, but something in the Confucian tradition still lingers, making the Chinese in part suspicious of these more detailed approaches to legislation.

Undoubtedly there is something unique in the Chinese understanding of the relation of the person to the group. The attempts made by members of a neighbourhood committee to heal a conflict in a marriage as in-laws, brothers and sisters, as well as the official appointed to attempt a reconciliation, was impressive when shown on BBC television in 1985, though the attempt by the group to enable husband and wife to forgive one another appeared perhaps too pressurizing. Certainly the programme showed a complex interaction between individuals and the group which implied a different way of handling marriage conflict.

The pressures a group can bring to bear on an individual may make a situation worse. An indication of the spirit in which Chinese people may handle the suffering caused is seen in the following extract from a letter sent by Chen Ming to the writer Ding Ling, both of whom had been banished:

> Dark nights pass and dawn comes. Bitter cold days will turn to spring breezes. If wild winds and rains didn't beat down on soft shoots, how would the mighty trees ever grow? . . . We are seeds of grain on the ocean and we mustn't grieve too much.[44]

The same spirit can be seen in Zhou Enlai as he apologized to the British Charge d'Affaires for the fire which burned offices during the Cultural Revolution and his promise that the Chinese would pay for their rebuilding. A similar spirit breathes through his meeting with the former Emperor of China after the latter had received a special pardon (December 1959), and his measured assessment of the Soviet leadership when it tore up its contracts with China, withdrawing its experts. He always evaluated their assistance to China in the 1950s objectively.[45]

There is something intensely moving, too, about Deng Xiaoping's son. During the Cultural Revolution he was flung from a third-floor window and left for days on the ground below because of who he was; now, from his wheelchair, he quietly plays a leading role in the China Welfare Fund for the Handicapped. Moving, too, is a story of She Zui, a former high-ranking official in Chiang Kai-shek's government. Granted a special pardon in September 1959, after some eleven years in detention, he met Zhou Enlai along with others who had also been pardoned.[46] 'When Premier Zhou talked with me the first thing I did was to beg his forgiveness because when he was working in Shanghai, Chongque, Nanjing and other places, I had personally led or ordered secret agents to spy on him, tail him or watch his movements.'[47] She Zui is now a member of the National Committee of the Chinese People's Political Consultative Conference.

This struggle to forgive has been described in Dai Houying's novel, *Stones of the Wall*,[48] where a group of university teachers in Shanghai in the late 1970s is trying to forget the past and where former bitter enemies have to work as colleagues. All the main characters tell their own story of deprivation and forgiveness in a world of mass politics. It is like a symbol of current Chinese history – seeking a politics of forgiveness, yet not knowing how to make it happen. Perhaps some encounter with the Buddhist world and reconnection with China's own Buddhist traditions, may help the Chinese people through their impasse, or maybe a new *Chinese* experience of the forgiving Christ will help them found the new society they seek.

'Out of my experience,' wrote the Dalai Lama,

> I tell my friends, wherever I go, about the importance of love and compassion. Though the words are not elegant, they are meaningful and valuable. Further, it is easy to talk about love, compassion and kindness, but the mere words are not effective. If you develop these attitudes and experience them, you will know their real value; so, it is worthwhile to try to develop them. If you agree, please try. If not, leave it.[49]

The contradictions of China remain, with capital punishment

still a strong instrument of policy. 'The constitution gives the people the right to criticize their leaders because they are human beings and not deities. Only through criticism and supervision by the people can they reduce their errors,' says one document. Yet when Wei Jingsheng edited a periodical, *Explorations*, with a friend and sold it at Democracy Wall in May 1979 he was arrested and imprisoned. Contradictions indeed!

The *Ta Chuan* (The Great Treatise), which dates from the time of Confucius, contains an insight about the nature of Tao, the principle often thought by the Chinese to be at the root of all life:

> The kind man discovers it and calls it kind
> The wise man discovers it and calls it wise
> The common people use it every day
> And are not aware of it.[50]

It is only the strong who can admit a fault and be humble; it is only the strong who are able to forgive, and only the strong who laugh, even when that laughter is on the verge of tears, wrote the Russian author Herzen in *A Family Drama*. In an interview with the distinguished author, Ba Jin, the interviewer chose to refer to this passage because it reminded her of this great writer whose fourteen volumes had been banned during the Cultural Revolution.[51] Had he found the Tao? Is Ba Jin's capacity to transcend personal suffering and his ability to be generous being discovered by others in China? If so, then, though they do not use those words, they are exploring forgiveness in politics, especially where it relates to repentance and to change.

Perhaps it is too early to say this, in view of the contradictions within the Chinese Communist Party during the late 1980s. For by 1989 Zhao Ziyang, Deng Xiaoping's heir-apparent, had been removed from office as General Secretary of the Party, and some of the leaders who had supported the pro-democracy movement in June that year were in exile or on trial, after the military crack-down on the peaceful demonstrations in Tiananmen Square. The fear of internal chaos was too great for the conservative leaders in Beijing to contemplate – and so Beijing's 'Prague Spring' was brutally crushed.

7

INDIA'S STRUGGLE FOR INDEPENDENCE

AS IN CHINA, India's struggle for independence was focused in one person. Deeply rooted in Indian history, as Mao was in China's, Gandhi strode across the plains of India and gave the people a will to change and shake off British rule.

As a boy of fifteen Gandhi once stole some gold from his brother to repay a debt of some twenty-five rupees. Regretting the action, he decided to write a letter to his father who was ill, asking his forgiveness. His father cried as he read his son's note; so did Gandhi for he had thought his father would be angry.[1] It was, Gandhi later considered, an 'object lesson in *ahimsā*'.[2]

Also influencing Gandhi's later political life was his contact with Christians like Andrew Murray and C.F. Andrews. During his time in South Africa he attended a convention in Pretoria. He had difficulties with the Christian doctrine he heard expounded there, finding it hard to accept Jesus as the sole incarnate son of God, alone giving, to those who believed, everlasting life. 'If God could have sons,' he wrote, 'all of us were his sons. If Jesus was like God, or God himself, then all men were like God or could be God himself.'[3] He could accept Jesus as a martyr and teacher, and his death as a great example, but he could not comprehend the doctrine of the atonement.[4]

Despite these reservations, however, Gandhi revered Christ throughout his life and, as a good Hindu he drew on the Gita, the Koran and the Bible. No consideration of his political role can be understood without a full acknowledgement of this basic fact, for Gandhi always saw politics and religion as inter-woven.[5]

Above politics Gandhi set a higher ideal. In his studies of the *Bhagavad Gita* he defined his conception of a holy person:

> He is a devotee who is jealous of none, who is a fount of mercy, who is without egotism, who is selfless, who treats alike cold and heat, happiness and misery, who is ever forgiving, who is always contented, whose resolutions are firm, who has dedicated mind and soul to God, who causes no dread, who is not afraid of others . . .[6]

Gandhi's profundity was already evident during his time in South Africa, where he worked as a lawyer. He saw suffering as a key to *satyagraha*, the passive resistance he and his followers used so powerfully when faced with political obstacles.[7] In his small book *Hind Swaraj*, he argued that every day small quarrels in millions of families disappeared before the face of truth and love. And what was true of families and communities was true of nations, for there was no reason to believe that there was one law for families and another for nations.[8]

Gandhi tried to live out this conviction while he was in South Africa. During the Boer War he took the side of the British (and again in the First World War), and in Durban he learned how deep was the racial prejudice there. One of the most formative experiences of his life occurred on a twenty-four-hour train journey, when he read Ruskin's *Unto This Last* and learned that the good of the individual is contained in the good of all; a lawyer's labour is no more significant than that of a barber, and a life of labour is the life worth living.[9] At this time he was also greatly affected by Tolstoy's *The Kingdom of God is Within You* and corresponded with him. In Natal, Gandhi founded the Phoenix Settlement and he tended the Zulu wounded during the Zulu rebellion.

Once, in 1905, Gandhi became engaged in a controversy with the Muslim community, which must have sensitized him both to their presence and their demands. During a lecture in Johannesburg, he argued that Muslim converts in India came from the lower classes. Zeal, or passion, was a mighty force of Islam, and the remarks triggered off a protracted debate. In June 1905 Gandhi apologized to the Muslims, saying he did not want to prolong the uproar. Some months later he reiterated his apology in an attempt to end the dispute and sorrowfully appealed to Muslims to forgive him if he had committed an error.[10]

It was while in South Africa that Gandhi developed his approach to civil disobedience – this involved him in a jail sentence, the first of many. He and his followers formed a Passive Resistance Association which confronted the government on a number of issues affecting the Indian population. Their main focus was the Asiatic Registration Bill, which was designed to prevent Indians who had left the Transvaal during the Boer War from returning; also to stop future Indian immigration. Some concessions were achieved on immigration, and a head tax was abolished and arrears cancelled. However, the restrictions preventing Indians moving freely from one province to another were retained. The result was thus a compromise, but Gandhi saw it as a victory for his *Satyagraha* movement, as it was now called. Gandhi also negotiated with General Smuts (then the minister in charge of Indian Affairs) regarding a law under which only Christian marriage was legal. An agreement was reached that all Indian marriages solemnized by Hindu, Muslim or Parsi tradition would be recognized as valid.

Just before he and his wife sailed from South Africa in 1914 Gandhi sent a pair of sandals he had made in prison as a gift to General Smuts. They were returned by Smuts to Gandhi as a gesture of friendship on Gandhi's seventieth birthday in 1939. Speaking about the incident, Smuts is recorded as observing:

> I have worn the sandals for many a summer – even though I may feel I am not worthy to stand in the shoes of so great a man. It was my fate to be the antagonist of a man for whom even then I had the highest respect . . . He never forgot the human background of the situation, never lost his temper or succumbed to hate, and preserved his sense of humour even in the most trying situations . . .[11]

In August 1914 Gandhi went to London where he tried to organize a small Indian ambulance corps. Radical Indian friends wanted him to wrest political concessions from Britain but Gandhi was too loyal. The ambulance corps lasted only a short while and Gandhi became ill because of the climate. He decided, therefore, to leave London, arriving in Bombay in January 1915 to start his life's main work.

The debate about India's relation to Britain and Europe had already been active for some time. Tagore, the great Indian poet and Nobel Prize winner for Literature, wrote in July 1915 to C.F. Andrews, the friend of Gandhi who was to mediate a new image of English people to Indians:

> The gravest danger is when Europe deceives itself into thinking that she is helping the cause of humanity by helping herself, that men are essentially different, and what is good for her people is not good for others who are inferior. Thus Europe, gradually and imperceptibly, is losing faith in her own ideals and weakening her own moral supports.[12]

Despite this, Tagore, unlike others, welcomed the contact of India with the West, regarding it as providential.[13] His openness to other cultures was one side of a debate which went on for decades, as Nehru and Gandhi, Tagore and Jinnah (the Muslim leader), struggled for a new India.

The event which finally antagonized even Indians who were pro-British, and was to prove as symbolic an event as the Indian Mutiny, occurred on 13 April 1919 in Amaritsar. (It caused Tagore to renounce his knighthood.) As a protest against British policies, Gandhi had proclaimed a *hartal*, a cessation of work. In Amaritsar, a city of 150,000 in the Punjab, it had been successful in stopping the business there without any collision with the police or violence. Five days later Brigadier-General Dyer arrived to take command. On 12 April 1919 he issued a proclamation prohibiting processions and meetings. The next day there was a big meeting, and when the crowd refused to disperse Dyer told his officers to fire. The firing continued for some ten minutes.

The Hunter Report set up to enquire into the Amaritsar disaster (Gandhi was one of those who had testified to it) estimated that there were 329 dead, 1137 wounded or '1516 casualties with 1650 rounds fired'.[14] All Indians were appalled, as were some of the British; but, though Dyer was dismissed, on his return to Britain he was heralded as a hero.

Whatever the defects of the Raj and Gandhi's disillusionment, unlike other Indians, Gandhi refused to give way to hatred. Writing in his paper, *Young India*, he said he would rather have India use her arms to defend her honour than remain a helpless victim, but he considered that non-violence was superior to violence and that forgiveness was more manly than punishment. Forgiveness should be offered even 'when there was the power to punish'.[15] Moreover, hatred had to be transformed into pity.[16]

That December the Indian Congress declared its intention to attain self-government in a year. Gandhi urged national consecration to that goal. The means to this end was to be a campaign of 'non-co-operation', of denying and ignoring the authority of the British government. Congress also urged people to boycott cotton cloth flooding in from England and undermining the Indian textile trade. In advocating such action Gandhi urged his followers to ask forgiveness for every unkind thought or deed spoken or done. Hindus and Muslims should cease suspecting one another's motives. Hindus should call no one unclean or inferior and cease to regard the 'pariah' class as untouchable.[17]

Gandhi toured India incessantly, tireless in all weathers, addressing mammoth meetings of 100,000 without the help of microphones. Everywhere he went he encouraged strikes and civil disobedience. He also encouraged the crowds to take off their foreign clothing and put it on a heap, which he would then set alight. This was a challenge to Indians to sit up and be self-reliant and to shape their own future. 'It is high time the British people were made to realize that the fight that was commenced in 1920 is a fight to the finish,' he argued. ' ... I shall only hope and pray that God will give India sufficient humility and sufficient strength to remain non-violent to the end.'[18]

By December 1921, 20,000 Indians had been jailed for civil disobedience and sedition. During December and into January 1922, 10,000 more were thrown into prisons for political offences.

Not all Indian leaders agreed with Gandhi's self-help and civil disobedience programme. One of his sternest critics was Tagore; he took issue with Gandhi both over non-co-operation and the burning of Western clothing, but Gandhi was adamant, arguing that when he burned his foreign clothes he burned his shame. Despite the injustices evident in Britain's rule in India, Tagore refused to support what he saw as the spreading of a 'blind passion all over the country. It would be like using the fire from the altar of sacrifice for the purpose of incendiarism.'[19]

Tagore was surely right to be worried, for communal riots had occurred in Bombay in the wake of the cloth boycott. In February 1922 twenty-two policemen were burnt alive by an infuriated mob, leading Gandhi to suspend the movement in which one million were involved and to undertake a five-day fast of penance. He had, he told Nehru and other Congress leaders who were upset by this unilateral action by their president, already been troubled by the violence elsewhere as a result of civil disobedience policies.

At first the authorities had not taken civil disobedience seriously, but after the February riots they acted. In March 1922 Gandhi was arrested, yet he remained convinced that he and the Congress were rendering England and India a service by showing, through non-co-operation, a way out of the 'unnatural state' in which both nations were living.[20]

Gandhi spent twenty-two months in prison at this time and whilst there he read the *Gita*, reserving the right to amend it! In 1924 Gandhi had an operation for appendicitis and was released from prison.

During his absence hostilities had developed, especially between Hindu and Muslim communities. This was a subject to which Gandhi was always addressing himself, arguing that before Hindus and Muslims could think of freedom they had to be brave enough to love and trust one another and tolerate each other's religion.[21] 'Cleanse your hearts and have charity. Make your hearts as broad as the ocean. That is the teaching of the Koran and of the Gita . . .' 'Love never claims,' he considered, 'it ever gives. Love ever suffers, never resents, never revenges itself . . .'[22]

Always he was determined to show that his approach was for all peoples. 'To me God is Truth and Love . . . He is all things to all men . . . He is ever forgiving for He always gives us the chance to repent,' he maintained.[23] The oneness of God was a consistent thread throughout his political life, never more movingly stated than shortly before his arrest and imprisonment in 1922:

> India's greatest glory will consist not in regarding Englishmen as her implacable enemies fit only to be turned out of India at the first available opportunity – but in turning

them into friends and partners in a new commonwealth of nations in the place of an Empire based upon exploitation of the weaker or underdeveloped nations and races of the earth.[24]

Because Gandhi's political work had religious roots, there was a consistency about his appeals, as he worked for an India in which all communities could live together in harmony. Besides his concern for Indian–British and Hindu–Muslim relationships, he was much preoccupied with the 'untouchables', the *Harijan* as he called them, children of God.

During one of the many times he was in jail (in all he served 2,089 days in Indian prisons) Gandhi decided to fast, if necessary to death, as a protest against Hindu mistreatment of India's 60 million 'untouchables'. The day before the fast began twelve temples in Allahabad were made accessible to the *Harijans*. On the first day some of the most sacred temples did the same. Each day more opened their doors. Nehru's orthodox Hindu mother said she had accepted food from an 'untouchable'. At the Hindu Benares University the principal and others dined publicly with street-cleaners, cobblers and scavengers, as a pressure for reform, penance and self-purification swept over India. Others followed suit.[25] Gandhi himself negotiated with Hindu leaders and 'untouchables' and agreed to break his fast, knowing that he had achieved some improvements. In February 1935, once again in prison, he started a society to help the *Harijans* and began another fast. On its first day he was released from prison.

There was no pause in his work for Indian independence. One of the injustices that Gandhi perceived was the monopoly held by the government on production of salt. In a letter to the Viceroy (in March 1930) he wrote: 'I cannot intentionally hurt anything that lives, much less human beings, even though they may do the greatest wrong to me and mine. Whilst, therefore, I hold the British rule to be a curse, I do not intend harm to a single Englishman or to any legitimate interest he may have in India . . .'[26] He pleaded with the Viceroy to abolish the salt monopoly and gave notice that if there was no response he and his co-workers would act.

On 12 March, there being no response, Gandhi set off for

Dandi, south of Ahmedabad, with seventy-eight men and women. They walked along winding dirt roads, as they moved from village to village, covering two hundred miles in twenty-four days. At Dandi he intended to flout the salt laws, vowing he would not return to his ashram until they had been repealed.

> Gandhi's journey to Dandi was compared by his disciples and followers to Jesus' journey to Jerusalem; many Hindus who could read bought copies of the Bible and read it. Gandhi himself apparently thought that he might have to die in Dandi, as Jesus died in Jerusalem. He and his followers arrived there on April 5th and spent the night praying on the beach. In the morning, he walked into the sea to bathe and purify himself. Then he and his followers went through the process of making salt from sea water and so became criminals in the eyes of the law.[27]

For a month they camped nearby. At first the government did nothing, expecting the campaign to fizzle out. But the story went round the world, and in India itself others went on their own salt marches. There was little violence as Gandhi's followers emulated his practice of *satyagraha*. Civil disobedience spread to other forms of protest as the salt campaign became Gandhi's biggest action.

On 5 May, in the middle of the night, Gandhi was arrested, and action was taken against anyone of importance involved in the civil disobedience campaign. It has been estimated that 60,000 offenders were arrested.

Later that same month another march took place, this time to the government's Dharasana Salt Works, 150 miles north of Bombay: 'Suddenly at a word of command, scores of native policemen rushed upon the advancing marchers and rained blows on their heads with their steel-shod lathis. Not one of the marchers even raised an arm to fend off the blows. They went down like tenpins . . .'[28] The story was carried by newspapers in every continent. Tagore, writing in the *Manchester Guardian* (17 May 1930), said: 'For Europe this is, in actual fact, a great moral defeat that has happened.'[29]

Gandhi was released from prison by the Viceroy, Lord Irwin, on 26 January 1931, the date Congress had fixed as the day for Independence. This was taken by Gandhi as a gesture of

friendship and conciliation. On 5 March 1931, the Gandhi–
Irwin Pact was signed, after many interviews between the two
men.

In Britain steps were in hand to draw up a constitution for an
independent India. A report of the Simon Commission (which
had been boycotted by the Indian National Congress when it
visited India in 1928) formed the basis of negotiation at three
Round-table Conferences held in London. The first of these
comprised leaders of the British political parties and Indian
representatives, mainly rulers of the princely states but including
also leaders of the Muslim League. It reached agreement on a
federal system which involved a measure of self-government.
The Indian National Congress was not involved in these discussions.

In August 1931 Gandhi sailed from Bombay to take part in
the second Round-table Conference; this time the Congress
had been invited, and Gandhi was to be their sole representative.
In a broadcast to America the day after his arrival in London
he reiterated what he had said in 1927: 'The world is weary of
hate.'[30]

At the Conference Gandhi argued passionately for independence, but the British government, whilst committed to responsible federal government in India, was not yet ready to release
power, and divisions between Congress, the Muslim League
and the Indian princes came to the surface. Gandhi returned
home, disappointed and with a deepened awareness that he had
to contend with his own fellow-citizens as well as the British.

His visit to Britain had caused a great stir, as he met distinguished people and visited Oxford colleges and the Lancashire cotton mills, which had suffered greatly from the cotton
boycott campaigns. He explained the reasons for the boycott to
Lancashire workers.

> There is a telling photograph taken outside Greenfield Mill
> at Darwen, Lancashire, showing Gandhi, wrapped in white
> cotton and squeezed in amidst cotton factory workers, most
> of them women, one of them holding his hand, and all of

them cheering the Mahatma, and smiling. He made friends among those whom he hurt.[31]

An Act to bring in a new constitution for India was passed in 1935. Self-rule was to start with the transfer of provincial government powers to popularly elected bodies. Congress was divided over this, but eventually those who urged co-operation prevailed and Congress took part in the provincial elections held in 1937.

Early in the 1930s Gandhi had given up membership of Congress, but was drawn back into politics when Indians were drawn into fighting in the Second World War. He was urged again to lead civil disobedience campaigns. But he did not wish to stab Britain in the back and came up with a plan for a succession of individual acts of civil disobedience. The first was by Vinoba Bhave, who received three months in jail; the second by Nehru, who received four years. Over a period of twelve months some 23,000 Congress workers went to prison, Gandhi managing the campaign and this time staying out of jail.

He remained convinced of his non-violent approach to politics, even though Europe was slipping into a vicious war. Earlier he had written: 'Having flung aside the sword, there is nothing except the cup of love which I can offer to those who oppose me. It is by offering that cup that I can expect to draw them closer to me . . .'[32] Now, even though he was aware of the difficulties of his philosophy, he recommended it to others in predicaments vastly different from his. Indeed, some have queried if he ever really understood what was happening in Europe. He wrote in *Harijan* (the successor to *Young India*) of a Jewish friend, Herman Kallenbach, who was then living in Gandhi's ashram, that the man's anger was so great against German atrocities that he, like thousands of Jews, had no space for loving an enemy.[33]

His advice to some nations anticipating an imminent German invasion was this: while their country was being invaded by Germany they should, as non-violent resisters, 'offer themselves unarmed as fodder for the aggressor's cannon . . . The unexpected surrender to the will of an aggressor must ultimately melt him and his soldiers.'[34]

By now a world figure, Gandhi would at one time be writing to the Japanese saying how intensely he objected to their 'attack upon China' and would, if not frail, come 'to plead with you to desist from the wrong you are doing in China, the world, and therefore to yourself'.[35] At another time he would praise the French surrender in 1940 as brave statemanship, a term he had also used to describe the Munich agreement.[36] He even urged the British to lay down their arms.[37] 'He spoke,' writes Stanley Naron, 'from the Himalayan heights of Hindu romanticism, urging upon them the example of Harischandra'.[38] Yet, inconsistently, he wrote to Chiang Kai-shek that he would agree that the Allied powers, under treaty with India, would keep their forces in the country as a base against Japanese aggression.

As he grew older and more and more separated from Congress he grew less realistic. Indeed at no point was Gandhi only interested in the transfer of sovereignty; he wanted liberation from the inroads of modern society, a return to traditional Indian values. Hence, as he viewed the modern world, he responded with a critique of its whole behaviour. 'Devotion to Truth is the sole justification for our existence,' he maintained so often[39] that he must surely be seen as exemplifying certain Jain teaching, especially in *ahimsā*, the giving up of violence. It seems then that he had really become a *yogin*, one who employs asceticism as a path to truth.

But was this approach, certainly meaningful in the context of Indian tradition, the only valid Indian path? In Jain Yoga 'the intending yogin should practise absolute non-injury to all living beings (*ahimsā*), absolute and strict truthfulness (*satya*), absolute sexual restraint (*brahmacharya*) and the acceptance of nothing but that which is absolutely necessary (*aparigrapha*)'.[40] With this as his real objective it is hardly surprising that Nehru and Congress parted company from Gandhi. Nehru was interested in ending caste and religious prejudice and in modernizing and industrializing through a form of Indian socialism. But Gandhi's aim was to lift up the people of the villages where he felt the strength of India lay. This was one reason he spent some time each day spinning.

In the 1940s Gandhi's influence on Indian politics waned.

The ambivalent attitude of Congress to the war, the 'Quit India' movement (launched in Gandhi's name in 1942, but conducted mainly by people who had little faith in non-violence), the sharpening of communal violence, the growth of extremist forces on the Left and the Right, and the dramatic developments leading ultimately to both Independence and the partition of India, left him effectively isolated. In statements like, 'My love of the British is equal to that of my own people,'[41] he showed the same old fire and was genuinely upset over the wartime destruction in England which he called 'heartrending'. As ever, he felt Britain must quit India and purge herself thereby. He felt also that Britain, and America too, had no right to be fighting for freedom for themselves without also helping countries in Asia and Africa to gain their freedom.

After the end of the Second World War negotiations toward independence were resumed. A British delegation met with Congress leaders and consulted Gandhi, who had come to Delhi to meet them and was staying in the slums among the 'untouchables'. The Muslim League, however, were unwilling to co-operate. They were talking of partition; to Gandhi this was blasphemy.

Perhaps lacking sufficient historical perspective on the roots of the Hindu–Muslim conflict, Gandhi continued to believe that, if people from both religions had enough faith in 'everlasting friendship', all would be well.[42] He never wavered in this conviction but, except in their opposition to British rule, the 'nationalist' Muslims, led by Mahomed Ali Jinnah, had little in common with the essentially secular leadership of Congress. The Muslims' demand for a separate state was the final expression of their separatist attitude under British rule, but its roots surely lay in the earliest period of Islam, for had not the Prophet himself enjoined them to found Muslim states where Allah was to be revered above all other? How could such a view coexist with Hindu syncretism, let alone with conservative Hindu nationalism?

On 12 August 1946 Lord Wavell, the Viceroy, commissioned Nehru to form a government. Mr Jinnah was offered a choice of places in the government but refused. Gandhi suggested that Jinnah should form the first administration, making his own choice of personnel, but Gandhi was reminded that Jinnah could not command majority support.

The Muslim League announced it would abstain from the newly formed national Constituent Assembly and called for a 'Direct Action Day'. Rioting broke out in Calcutta, leaving 5,000 dead and 15,000 wounded. On 2 September 1946, when Jawaharlal Nehru became Prime Minister, Jinnah proclaimed a day of mourning. Gandhi was horrified at events, especially as British troops had to intervene to restore order.[43]

Widespread Muslim attacks on Hindus took place during October 1946 in rural areas of East Bengal. Gandhi went there immediately and suggested that one Hindu and one Muslim should together visit each affected village, guaranteeing (though aware they might themselves be killed) the safety of returning Hindu refugees.

During the following months Gandhi stayed in forty-nine villages. Arriving in one place he would go straight to the hut of a peasant, preferably a Muslim, and ask to be taken in with his companion. If refused, he would try the adjoining hut. He passed his seventy-seventh birthday at this time.

In Bihar, where more than 10,000 died, Gandhi was joined by the Pathan leader Badshah Khan, the one Muslim figure who followed Gandhi's lead. Often he recounted how Badshah Khan had transformed the dreaded Pathans of the Frontier to non-violence – the non-violence of the fearless and strong that Gandhi wanted Hindus to emulate.[44]

The division of India, by now almost inevitable, caused the deaths of around one million people. There were 15 million refugees, the largest movement of people in history. The threat of partition provoked a war in Kashmir, over which Gandhi supported Nehru. Opposed as ever to partition he visited refugee camps outside Delhi, urging self-help. To the Hindus in particular he addressed words about being wrong, arguing that they should never think they were blameless. The killings in Delhi ceased, no doubt due in part to his presence, but Gandhi's policy of non-violence and of Hindu–Muslim accord was in shreds.

By February 1947 Britain was ready to transfer power to India, united or not. Lord Louis Mountbatten was sent to Delhi as Viceroy to supervise the transfer of power. In June he announced a procedure for legislators and their leaders to vote for or against partition whereby those areas where the majority of the population was Muslim – West Punjab, Sind, the North-West Frontier and Baluchistan together with East Bengal – would become a separate state. After much negotiation Congress and the Muslim League voted for partition, and the new independent states of India and Pakistan came into being on 15 August 1947.

J. B. Kripalani, President of Congress, and a follower of Gandhi, addressing his colleagues after the decision for partition, said:

> Some members have accused us that we have taken this decision out of fear. I must admit the truth of this charge ... The fear is that if we go on ... retaliating and heaping indignities on each other, we shall progressively reduce ourselves to a state of cannibalism ... I have been with Gandhi for the last thirty years ... Why then am I not with him [now]? It is because I feel that he has as yet found no way of tackling the problems [of Hindu-Muslim violence] on a mass basis.[45]

Gandhi fasted twice 'unto death' for the restoration of religious tolerance to independent India. The first, in Calcutta, served, in Mountbatten's words, as 'a one-man boundary force' to stop Hindu and Muslim groups from repeating the massacre of the previous year. Gandhi broke each fast only after receiving pledges from Hindu, Muslim and Sikh leaders that they would seek to help their people live in peace.

The second fast lasted from 13 to 18 January 1948. On the final day, just after noon, over one hundred men from all the communities, led by the new Congress President, entered Gandhi's room and promised peace. Gandhi replied saying he was moved and insisted the promise applied to all India, not merely to Delhi. The fast was broken with recitals from scriptures. A Hindustani hymn was sung and also Gandhi's favourite Christian one, 'When I survey the wondrous Cross'. He took fruit and shared it with all present.

For some time Gandhi had been the centre of violence. A mob had stoned his residence, a bomb had been thrown on a train carrying him, and during the fast itself he had been confronted with the slogan 'Let Gandhi die.' After the second day of the fast a bomb explosion had failed. Gandhi's response was to say that if he fell victim to assassination he hoped he would have no feeling of anger against his killers.[46]

Gandhi was now to experience the last violent act against him. Nathurum Vinayak Godse was the founder of two tabloid newspapers crusading for Hindu rule. 'I sat brooding intensely on the atrocities perpetuated on Hinduism and its dark and deadly future if left to face Islam outside and Gandhi inside,' he explained later, at his trial, ' . . . I decided all of a sudden to take the extreme step.'

On 30 January 1948, while Gandhi was on his way to a prayer meeting, Godse went up to him, bowed, took out a pistol and shot him dead. He was one of a number of Hindu extremists who had taken part in the conspiracy. Gandhi's disciples and followers urged that his life be spared, but he and his accomplice were later hanged.

Nehru, despite his many political differences with Gandhi, was grief-stricken. 'Even in his death,' he wrote, 'there was a magnificence and complete artistry. It was from every point of view a fitting climax to the man and to the life he lived.'[47]

What contribution did Gandhi make to forgiveness and politics? Was it because he was dealing with the British that he was able to help bring freedom to India and handle history forgivingly? For he was manifestly unable to handle the Hindu–Muslim conflicts. 'He taught us to shed fear and hatred,' Nehru wrote, 'and of unity and equality and brotherhood and of raising those who had been suppressed . . .'[48] Yet he who taught all these things, and of the need for forgiveness, was shot by someone who felt Gandhi's ideas were out of the reach of ordinary people.

However mistaken Gandhi may have been over India's economic future, without doubt he did strike a chord in the Indian masses through his Hindu perceptions. But how far is Gandhi's way, especially his practice of non-violence, applicable outside India? That is a key question in trying to assess his contribution to forgiveness in politics. Martin Luther King applied Gandhian philosophy successfully in the civil rights campaigns in America. But although the principles of non-violence have to some extent permeated peace movements in the West, is it realistic to expect that his approach, rooted as it was in a specific religious tradition, can be taken up in a radically different cultural setting?

If we agree with Gandhi's assassin, who maintained that Gandhi's views were not applicable to the complexities of political life however admirable personally, we are surely on a road to destruction. There is no doubt that, toward the end of his life, Gandhi's idealism soared to unreasonable heights. But does this invalidate his fundamental insights about how to respond to enemies?

Gandhi's sense of the need for forgiveness ('To forgive is not to forget. The merit lies in loving in spite of the vivid knowledge that the one that must be loved is not a friend') and his appreciation of our fallibilities ('To err is human and it must be held to be equally human to forgive if we, though being fallible, would like rather to be forgiven than punished and reminded of our deeds')[49] are surely the core of his contribution.

Perhaps what Thomas Merton wrote, from the Abbey of Gethsemani in April 1964, may yet prove a saner assessment of Gandhi than many others: 'Gandhi's principles are, then, extremely pertinent today . . . There can be no peace on earth without the kind of inner change that brings man back to his "right mind".'[50]

8

BRITAIN AND IRELAND

IN EUGENE O'NEILL's play *A Long Day's Journey into Night* one of the characters is heard to say that the past is not only the past: it is the future as well. This well describes the kind of trap in which Ireland finds itself today. 'It is the terrible years of the Great Hunger which are remembered, and only just beginning to be forgiven,' Cecil Woodham-Smith observed,[1] writing about the time in the mid-nineteenth-century when the potato crop in Ireland, as elsewhere in Europe, failed and the responses of the British government were less than adequate.

The Great Hunger of 1846 and its legacy of bitterness – in both America, where many fled for work and food, and mainland Britain with a population of over one million Irish and more with Irish connections – is one of many factors which complicate the centuries of hostile interaction between the two islands and makes the work of forgiveness between Britain and Ireland, and within Ireland, extremely difficult. The story is compounded too by centuries of conflict in Europe between Roman Catholicism and Protestantism, and also by Britain's imperial role: Elizabeth I's colonization of Dublin and the two periods of Presbyterian–Scots intrusion in the seventeenth century, the latter under Cromwell being the most savage. In addition there were penal laws aimed at suppressing Catholics. Then, when both Protestant and Catholic Irish rose up against Britain's unjust rule in the 1798 Irish Rebellion, they were crushed with a determination made worse by Britain's fear of Napoleon, who the Irish hoped would help them win their freedom.

The opening of the twentieth century saw the culmination of Irish demands for independence. Already Gladstone had come to grief through his 'Home Rule' policy and had been outman-oeuvred by Lord Randolph Churchill, who supported the demands of the Ulster Protestants for the continuance of the Union of Britain and Ireland, which had been effected in 1801 (as a result of the 1798 rebellion) when the Dublin parliament for all Ireland had voted itself out of existence. 'Ulster will fight and Ulster will be right,' was the slogan of Lord Randolph Churchill but, as it happened, it was the southern Irish who fought.

In 1916 there was the Easter Rising in Dublin, which was ruthlessly crushed by the British. The Irish were so appalled – even those who had not supported the rebellion, including leaders of the Roman Catholic Church – that they determined to end the British connection. Some two years later, Irish representatives who had been elected to the British parliament in the election of December 1918 met in Dublin the next month to form their own parliament, the Dail Eireann, where they affirmed Ireland's independence.

Thus it was that in the 1918–1921 period Lloyd George, then the British Prime Minister, set out to negotiate a new settlement with Ireland. His task was difficult. He was by no means assured of his position in the House of Commons and the Ulster Unionists, as they came to be called, were against any 'Home Rule', and certainly against any independent Ireland, even though from the time of Wolfe Tone, a northern Presbyterian, there were leaders like those in the United Irishmen Movement who favoured independence.

Lloyd George's Treaty was ingenious, too ingenious the southerners felt. They could not agree amongst themselves, a disagreement which led to Pro- and Anti-Treaty Parties and a civil war in the south. Furthermore, the predominantly Presbyterian north wished to remain part of Britain and the south (where there was a minority of Protestants) wanted independence. There emerged, therefore, Eire in the south and Northern Ireland, comprising six of the nine counties of historic Ulster, with its own parliament at Stormont. Provision was also made for a Council of Ireland so the two parts could interact and make any necessary boundary adjustments, but this never met.

In his speech at the opening of the Stormont parliament King George V hoped that his coming to Ireland may prove to be the first step towards an end of strife amongst her people, whatever their race or creed. In that hope I appeal to all Irishmen to pause, to stretch out the hand of forbearance and conciliation, to forgive and forget, and to join in making for the land which they love a new era of peace, contentment, and good will.[2]

He hoped that in the south an occasion parallel to his Stormont address would be possible soon.

But the situation there was less simple (although in the north also there was a built-in problem, which re-emerged in the 1960s as a group within the Catholic population showed itself permanently disaffected from the state). One Sinn Feiner in the south told Thomas Jones, Lloyd George's cabinet secretary:

Freedom for all Ireland is all we care for. And yet a gen-erous act of trust would bring forgiveness and forgetting more swiftly from us than from anyone. The Dail Eireann would pledge itself wholeheartedly against any coercion of a minority if Great Britain would equally pledge itself and remove its forces.[3]

The activities of a specially recruited British troop, nicknamed the Black and Tans, were a specific indictment of British mili-tary activities and provoked the Sinn Fein, led by Éamon de Valera, into even greater determination to win freedom. 'As for myself and my colleagues,' de Valera wrote to Lloyd George in August 1921, 'it is our deep conviction that true friendship with England, which military coercion has frustrated for centuries, can be obtained most readily now through amicable but absolute separation.'[4]

De Valera remained convinced that a solution to the majority-minority problems of Ireland was possible. 'If your Government stands aside, we can effect a complete reconciliation,' he wrote. '. . . The sole cause of the "ancient feuds" which you deplore has been, as we know, and history proves, the attacks of English rulers upon Irish liberties . . .'[5]

In December 1921 a treaty with Britain providing for the creation of an Irish Free State, with a dominion status similar to that of Canada, came before the Dail. In the debate there, a strong appeal for its acceptance was made by Michael Collins.

It gave, he said, 'not the ultimate freedom that all nations desire and develop to, but the freedom to achieve it'. The Republicans fought it bitterly; de Valera rested his case on a proposal for 'External Association', but in effect stood out for a republic. The narrow vote approving the treaty, 64 to 57, was less about de Valera's views than an expression of how the recent Irish past had already become stereotyped so that it cast a shadow over the future.[6]

De Valera then resigned as President of the Dail and was defeated, 60 to 58, when he sought re-election. A provisional government was set up to take over from the British administration until the Act was passed and the Irish Free State came into being.

In January 1922 the Lord Lieutenant handed over Dublin Castle to Michael Collins, and the slow evacuation of British troops began. The new and untried Irish administration set to work to become a government and deal with the complexity of British legal arrangements bequeathed to them. But de Valera had formed the Republican Party (Fianna Fail) and, by the middle of March 1922, seemed bent on encouraging violence in the south and raising support among the dissident elements in the Irish Republican Army.

In Northern Ireland the new government there started complaining about the Boundary Commission which, they claimed, had been imposed on them by an arbitrary fiat of the British government. Winston Churchill, then Colonial Secretary, made great efforts and succeeded in bringing together James Craig, the Ulster leader, and Collins. For a brief moment there seemed a prospect of reconciliation, but by March 1922 intensified Irish Republican Army (IRA) outrages and equally violent Orange reprisals had created a situation where no peace was possible.

Despite this, after 1922 Ireland drifted slowly away from mainstream British political life and became the concern of the Colonial Office (for the south) and the Home Office (for the north) rather than the Cabinet as a whole. The seeds of civil war in the south had been sown and, as W.B. Yeats wrote, 'a terrible beauty'[7] was born, when 'the centre cannot hold.'[8]

The new government in Dublin had a difficult task to perform.

Violence was near the surface and IRA irregulars on the loose. The problems of bringing a new state to birth were immense, as de Valera and his party refused to co-operate. Perhaps the worst immediate outrage was the murder of Michael Collins in August 1922. When Lloyd George heard the news he sent a message to the press. 'His engaging personality won friendship even among those who first met him as foes and to all of us who met him the news of his death comes as a personal grief and sorrow . . . ,' he wrote.[9]

More bloodshed followed. The Irish Cabinet, in which Kevin O'Higgins was Home Secretary, had to take the tough decision to execute a number of irregulars. O'Higgins had been negotiating with Lord Carson, the Protestant leader by then in retirement, over the possibility of a dual monarchy system for Britain and Ireland, on the model of the Hapsburgh Empire which, if accepted, would have enabled the Protestants of the north, led by the aging Carson, to join with the south in some form. The idea, bizarre as it must seem in the event of subsequent history, was for the British King to be crowned King of Ireland in separate ceremonies in both Dublin and Belfast.[10]

Not long after, in 1927, Kevin O'Higgins was assassinated by two gunmen on his way to Mass.[11] The assassination shocked the nation. 'He lived,' according to the writer of a poem published in *The Irish Independent*, 'to echo Calvary's great cry, "Father, forgive".' The words had been spoken on O'Higgins' deathbed. He was not the only person to die in such a spirit, for in 1922 Rory O'Connor, one of the irregulars, had written to his sister Eily as he went to his death: 'I forgive all my enemies. I have never felt any feelings of revenge . . . Rory.'[12]

Such a forgiving spirit, however, was seldom in evidence as the two Irish states settled down to their separate business. In the early 1930s de Valera changed course, and his party, Fianna Fail, the bearer of the Irish national and republican traditions, became the dominant party in the Dail. Fine Gael, O'Higgins' party, was to rule only occasionally and always in coalition with others.

In the 1930s Irish history took another turn. Under the 1937 constitution, introduced by De Valera, the Roman Catholic Church was given a special status. An attempt was made to see Ireland as predominantly a Catholic and Gaelic nation, despite the fact that Ireland's history had been as polyglot as mainland Britain's. Moreover the whole of the island of Ireland was claimed as the national territory, a claim much resented by the new state of Northern Ireland.

As the south was becoming a Catholic state for a Catholic people (though the Protestants that remained survived, some taking senior positions in the state), the north looked increasingly like a Protestant state for a Protestant people, despite the fact that some one-third of the population of Northern Ireland were not Protestant. Indeed, in the case of cities like Londonderry the boundaries for local elections were so rigged as to give a permanent majority to the Protestant Unionists, even though Derry city itself had a permanent Catholic majority.

The language issue was ignored too, and there was also severe discrimination against Catholics in jobs and housing. Sporadic violence occurred as, of course, it had for several centuries. The tensions over land, cultural identity and wealth, evident from the time the Protestants had driven out the Catholics from the rich farmlands, simmered continually. The seeds were being sown for the turmoil of recent decades, as Protestants in Ulster struggled, as they always had done, to keep their identity under the British crown.

With the start of the Second World War the north was loyal to Britain, even providing outstanding generals like Auchinleck and Montgomery. The south remained neutral, a difference which further exacerbated the north-south divide.

Ireland's neutrality never wavered. But de Valera could be reached. The story is told of how, in 1944, his speeches softened towards Britain. When asked why, he replied that he had met a British serviceman whose family had once been great Irish landowners of a particularly bad kind. This officer had told him that, if he survived the war, he would return and make amends for his family's misuse of their estates. The story moved de Valera deeply. Alas, the officer was never to make amends as he was killed on active service.

From 1950 to 1968 the problems of Ireland seemed to be as distant as ever from the House of Commons, and the Irish in England and Scotland were in the main not disposed to raise their heads too high on issues which worried them. The departure of the Republic of Ireland, as it came to be called, from the British Commonwealth in 1949 confirmed the northern Unionists' convictions about the south. The Ireland Act that year made the necessary adjustments, with Irish citizens in the United Kingdom being given full citizenship if working or living there, a decision reciprocated by the Dail in the early 1980s for some 30,000 British citizens resident in the Republic.

From 1959 to 1973 de Valera, as President, was above active party politics, but his legacy in Fianna Fail was always there. Indeed it was not until January 1965 that Sean Lemass, successor to de Valera as leader of Fianna Fail, and Taoiseach (prime minister) from 1959 to 1966 – who had never been an enthusiastic supporter of de Valera's Catholic, Gaelic and rural utopia – surprised everyone with an historic visit to see the Northern Ireland Prime Minister, Terence O'Neill. He also initiated and later served on an all-party committee to review the de Valera constitution; it recommended that territorial claims on Northern Ireland be rephrased as an aspiration to Irish unity.

In the autumn of 1968 the present troubles in Northern Ireland began with violent reactions by some Protestants to the civil rights movement which had already emerged, led in part by Catholics who had benefited from British higher education. At first the British troops deployed the following year were regarded as protectors by the harassed Catholic population, especially in Derry city, but this picture changed as the civil rights movement grew and the British army acted with brutality, particularly on Bloody Sunday in Londonderry at the end of January 1972. The scene was set for the emergence of the Provisional IRA, with a corresponding group of extreme Protestant para-military organizations growing stronger as it gave support to the aims of the Rev. Ian Paisley, whose sectarian Presbyterianism cleverly played on paranoid fears, especially in working class and rural areas. This revealed a split in the ranks of Protestant Unionism, the official Unionists henceforth holding their ground only in the middle and upper class areas.

All politics in Northern Ireland have been forcused on the constitutional position, so the emergence of a Labour Party, as in mainland Britain, was unthinkable; even the Social Democratic and Labour Party (SDLP), led by Gerry Fitt, has its base and support almost entirely in Derry and West Belfast Catholic communities.

Hence, while it is incorrect to describe the cause of Northern Ireland's troubles as religious, because religion and politics are so intimately intermingled in both parts of Ireland, there is always a religious component, however secularized, to politics there. Though it might appear that the Protestant and Catholic working-class districts of Belfast have more in common, in their deprivation, with each other than with anyone else, this has not led to any expression of common political interests; it is the commitment of Protestant communities to maintaining the Union with Britain and the Catholic reaching out to the Republic of Ireland, that override all else.

So the two traditions exist side by side, unable to resolve the double-minority problem at the heart of Ireland's anguish: the Protestants a minority in the whole of Ireland, and the Catholics a minority in Northern Ireland, often regarded as potential, if not actual, traitors to the state. The 'solution' of 1921 has in effect compressed the whole long-standing Irish question into the six counties of Northern Ireland.

To compound the problem each side relies for its arguments and perceptions on myths intertwined with history, sometimes going back centuries. Each group can remember bloody massacres, not only of recent origin, and terrible deeds done; there is, too, a sharp awareness of the wrongs committed by Britain. Ironically, the Unionists themselves are deeply ambivalent toward Britain, however much they plead loyalty to the crown and to Westminster. For were not their forebears 'planted' in Ulster, mainly from Scotland? And though now indigenous, they were in the past as much passive recipients of British policies as the southern Catholics have been.

Once the Protestants' deep sense of conviction became linked with economic and cultural questions, let alone those of identity, or a threat to the state itself, all manner of conflicts were bound to develop. Moreover, how the British, with their long and often bad record in Ireland, could imagine their troops would be able to help in the complex interaction in Northern Ireland, or that their presence there would be other than an irritant to the south, bringing on occasion to the surface unworked anger from history, is and remains a mystery. 'You Irish remember too much,' said a member of the British cabinet to his secretary who was Irish. 'You British remember too little,' was the reply.

Remembering and forgetting is vital to forgiveness in politics in the context of Britain and Ireland – the British to remember, the Irish to forget. Yet few British seem to be aware of the need to make amends, like the English officer who reached de Valera's heart. Perhaps some public act of recognition could do that, as the cross-bench peer Lord Hylton advocated in his letter to Margaret Thatcher. 'I believe', he wrote, 'that the time has come for Britain to face up and ask forgiveness for the immense wrongs it has done to the people of Ireland.'[13]

Some redressing of wrongs has been attempted in Northern Ireland.[14] After the initial stormy days of the civil rights marches and the demands of the Catholics for a proper say in the institutions of state, as well as adequate fairness in jobs and housing, the Northern Ireland government did institute some reforms. But how could any prime minister of Northern Ireland accommodate legitimate Catholic demands without losing out to militant Unionists who were not willing to give 'an inch'. The Unionist cry of 'No surrender' is a powerful rallying phrase and has been used as such by many an Orange Lodge, the handmaid of Ulster politicians since their inception in 1789. But the phrase has served to convince Catholics that the way of the bullet is the only one which would force the British to withdraw from Northern Ireland. Then, goes the IRA myth, in some magical way one million Protestants in the north (who in the main are unwilling to be linked with Dublin) would happily be joined with all Irish people, hopefully in a thirty-two counties socialist republic. Such is the power of this myth that it has persuaded many to support the IRA actively and many more covertly, some of them in America.

As attempts at reform through Stormont failed and Northern Ireland drifted further into chaos and killings, Edward Heath, then the British Prime Minister, suspended the Stormont parliament in 1972. A new post, Secretary of State for Northern Ireland, was created, and a number of distinguished British Labour and Conservative ministers have held the job over the years. One of them, now Lord Whitelaw, put forward a bold and imaginative proposal for a power-sharing Executive of Catholics and Protestants who would jointly run Northern Ireland from Stormont. The plan was nearly stillborn but – saved by a request for forgiveness for anything amiss in what he had said by the Unionist leader, Brian Faulkner – it survived for some months until a workers' strike in Ulster and a change of government in London brought it down. It was significant, in that the Dublin government had agreed to the plan and thus acknowledged for the first time that unity could only come by consent.

Strangely, despite all the atrocities – the murder of Lord Mountbatten in the Irish Republic, the Darkley killings in a Pentecostal Church, shootings by the army in West Belfast and many other such incidents – Northern Ireland has been described by the Bishop of Salisbury as 'one of the most Christian places' he has ever visited.[15] For in the midst of the troubles numerous groups have sprung up to address themselves to the place once described as having 'a problem to every solution'.[16]

The most well-known has been the 'Peace People' who emerged after the death of three Catholic children killed in a terrorist incident in West Belfast in August 1976. The local community was outraged and feeling against the Provisional IRA ran high. At this point two local women, Mairead Corrigan and Betty Williams, both new to public affairs and the peace movement in Ireland, began to organize protest meetings across the Catholic areas of Belfast. They were joined by Protestant women who sympathized with their actions, and soon a wave of opinion surfaced to support their appeal for an end to violence.

Their campaign was given widespread press and television coverage. People in mainland Britain, in Europe and elsewhere, gave support. At the heart of much of this work was a remarkable Protestant leader, Saidie Patterson, who had grown up in the Protestant Shankill area of Belfast. After some scepticism about a proposed peace march in the Shankill, she eventually sought support for it by knocking on doors in her area, persuading one of the members of the local Orange Lodge, a former shop steward, to marshal the women of the neighbouring streets.

The march has been described graphically:

... To shouts of 'Welcome to the Shankill', the crowds

mingled – 50,000 strong, with equal numbers of spectators. Nothing like this had ever been seen on the Shankill before. Nuns, dressed in fashions unfamiliar to the Loyalist districts, stretched out hands to clasp and be clasped by Protestant women; priests and Protestant ministers walked as brothers; and strangers from either side of the 'peace-line' linked arms as they had not done since the troubles began.[17]

The price of this act of forgiveness was high, for a group organizing a follow-up march on the Falls Road was stoned by IRA supporters. Many marchers were attacked and injured, Saidie Patterson among them. Beaten by the mob, she was rescued by a group of Catholic women, but was in hospital for four months with an injured spine.

As groups like the Peace People rose and passed their peak, many began to query the effectiveness of community action. 'Is it worth it?' outside commentators were tempted to ask, when faced with so many groups. What effects can groups like the Corrymeela Community, or Lagan College (for Protestants and Catholics to be educated together), or communities like Columbanus, Columba House and Rostrevor have? Do the activities of the Ballymascanlon talks on Christian Unity, the Peace Education and Resources Centre of the Irish Council of Churches, the community development work in east Belfast and in Londonderry have any political impact?

The answer surely must be a qualified 'Yes', for each of these groups is making cross-community links. It is the possible success of these which is feared by both Protestant and Catholic extremists; so each atrocity is calculated to keep fear in the communities at fever pitch, thus blocking the discovery of creative solutions.

The work of Maura Kiely of the Cross Group is a good example of communal forgiveness. The aim of the group is to bring together women who have been bereaved through political killings. Among the group's members are two women who saw their husbands shot dead in front of them. One woman was seven months pregnant. Another member of the group is a woman whose husband died with sixteen others when the IRA blew up a truck at Warrenpoint and all the soldiers in it were killed. Maura Kiely herself lost her nineteen-year-old son when he was the victim of two gunmen who fired indiscriminately at worshippers leaving a Sunday evening Mass.

There are many people like Maura Kiely whose attitude is one of forgiveness. Florence Cobb is the widow of a murdered RUC inspector. She wrote a letter to the killer of her husband, forgiving him. He in turn showed it to a fellow prisoner, an ex-member of the Ulster Defence Association (UDA), who was also in prison. The letter so moved him that he invited Mrs Cobb to visit him in the Maze prison where he, too, was serving a life sentence for murder. She did; they fell in love and antici-pate marrying when he is released in 1997.

Gordon Wilson's act of forgiveness for the IRA, after his daughter died one Remembrance Sunday in a bomb outrage, went across the world through the media. Wilson received hun-dreds of letters and was specifically mentioned that Christmas in the Queen's broadcast to the Commonwealth.

Liam McCloskey is another person who has discovered the power of forgiveness, in his case linked with a profound experi-ence of repentance. In 1975 he joined the Irish National Liber-ation Army and was arrested in December 1976 charged with having arms, taking part in hijackings and armed robberies. A year later he was given a ten-year jail sentence. In prison he agreed to go on the blanket protest in the H3 block of the Maze prison, and there, at a friend's suggestion, he began reading the Bible. It made him think about his half-hearted attitude to prayer and Bible-reading. When the warders had been rough with some of the men on the protest, he decided to keep calm if maltreated. 'During my three and a half years on protest,' he has said, 'many times anger, hate and resentment welled up, but a line from the Our Father kept speaking to me: "Forgive us our trespasses as we forgive those who trespass against us . . ." '18

Liam McCloskey later broke with his old associates and became involved in peace and reconciliation work, especially as it is expressed in the charismatic movement. This movement has had a profound effect in both the Roman Catholic and Protestant Churches. It has had a specific impact on both UDA and IRA prisoners, leading some of them to become friends despite what they have done to each others' communities. One public reconciliation took place between two ex-paramilitaries who at one meeting crossed the room and clasped one another, tears running down their cheeks.

All these and many others, like a British soldier, Stephen Cummins, shot dead by the IRA, who left his parents a letter asking them to forgive those 'who trespass against me',[19] have not allowed instincts of vengeance to overpower them. Rather they point to a need for communal forgiveness to motivate the politics of human life. It is this sense which also motivates those politicians who see Northern Ireland as a British-Irish problem, like those from the parties in Dublin and the SDLP in Northern Ireland who produced the New Ireland Forum Report which suggested a new Ireland either as a federal or a unitary state; or a joint authority in Northern Ireland supported both by Britain and the Republic of Ireland.

Father Denis Faul, whose actions helped to bring about the end of the Hunger Strike in the Maze prison, in which Bobby Sands died, has also called for forgiving politics. He argued in December 1982, and again at Christmas 1985, for a release of prisoners based on forgiveness. 'The result would be a ground-swell against paramilitary activity among the large extended families of the Catholic community.'[20]

Another priest, Father Desmond Wilson, argued similarly in 1979:

> . . . forgiveness is not greatly concerned with the past, after all. It is very much concerned with the future and what we intend to do with it . . . When Jesus said, 'Father, forgive them,' he released his followers for ever from any obligation they might have felt to avenge him.[21]

Some people have become symbols of a forgiving spirit in situations where crimes have been committed for political purposes. They include British citizens like Jane Ewart-Biggs, whose husband was blown up in a car-bomb explosion in Dublin, and Joanna Berry, daughter of Sir Anthony Berry, the Conservative MP killed in the bomb attack in 1984 on a Brighton hotel where the Cabinet was attending the annual Conservative Party conference. In the Republic of Ireland, Una O'Higgins O'Malley, daughter of the murdered Kevin O'Higgins, has stood as a symbol for healing through her support in the early 1980s for two Walks of Remembrance in Dublin to places associated with the dead of the Irish Civil War. Her long-standing exploration of the need for new approaches in the Republic, as well as her contacts with Northern Ireland and Great Britain, have also won her great respect as she tries to articulate the complex inter-relationships between both parts of Ireland and England, Scotland and Wales.

When, as Prime Minister, Mrs Thatcher took her Foreign Secretary, Chancellor and Northern Ireland Secretary to Dublin for talks in 1980, it was surely a first public indication of a desire by the British government to be seen to be dealing with the Republic of Ireland in its own right. And when the Irish prime ministers, first Mr Haughey and then Dr Fitzgerald, both talked of the 'totality of relationships' between the two islands, this was a further step in a politics of forgiveness.

If, as some suspect, Northern Ireland is the scene for the working out of the unresolved hate between Britain and Ireland, then, as the Bishop of Salisbury has observed, 'the first thing to put right' is our relation with 'our neighbour'.[22] Factors which impinge on this – the role of the Roman Catholic Church, confirmed by the spectacular success of the Pope's visit to the Republic in 1979, and American pressures, reflecting the residual hatred arising from descendants of the famine victims of the nineteenth century – should not be allowed to stop this development. The recognition, too, in the New Ireland Forum Report of the legitimate traditions of *both* Unionism and Republicanism in the North is also a step in a constructive direction. However, the decision in a referendum, held in the Republic of Ireland in the mid-1980s, to put a clause forbidding abortion into the Irish constitution, and a subsequent one in similar vein against divorce, seems to caution against any easy solution to issues of civil liberties in the eyes of northern Unionists.

The 1985 Anglo-Irish Agreement, signed by Dr Fitzgerald and Mrs Thatcher, is also, despite the objections to it, part of this process, marking in fact the first change in relations between Britain and Ireland of a major nature since the 1921 Treaty, and of significance therefore to events in Northern Ireland. An earlier comment in a British newspaper is pertinent here:

It is time to start reorganizing the relations between Britain and Ireland so that they take account of the facts. The first important fact is that Britain and Ireland are not foreign countries. They are different. They are sovereign. But they are not foreign . . . The second important fact is that notwithstanding the representation of Northern Ireland in the House of Commons and not in the Dail, in spite of frontier posts and customs sheds, six-ninths of the province of Ulster cannot be held to belong entirely to Britain and not at all to the hinterland of Ireland. The partition of Ireland was an expedient that failed in its purpose. The severance of ties between Britain and Ireland was an act of perversity.[23]

The setting up in 1989 of a permanent group of members from the Dail and House of Commons (an important aspect of the Anglo-Irish Agreement) is one further step in reversing this 'act of perversity'. For surely the wish of the Protestant people of Northern Ireland to be part of the life of the British world, and the desire of the Catholic people to share in the life of all Ireland, are both correct instincts. As an editorial in *The Guardian* maintained:

It is surprising that two peoples, the English with a genius for constitution-making and the Irish with a genius for making metaphysics a part of everyday life, should have found the joint task so bewildering for it is a mixture of both. For example, Dublin envisages a federal, or confederal Ireland. An excellent notion, in our view, but why stop there? Why not a confederated British Isles? Or, if the term is disliked (though it is purely geographical) a confederation of North Atlantic Islands. It already exists in practice, why not in the constitutional theory which is what the argument is about . . .[24]

A letter in *The Observer* drew out a further paradox in the inter-relationships:

Already the citizens of the Republic have a consultative role in all the boroughs of Britain in which they happen to live: they have the vote. And very right and proper too.
The involvement of the Republic in the governance of

the North is legitimate and long overdue recognition of the same principle: that the infrastructure of Britain – its roads and buildings, its towns and cities – as well as its political movements and its social structures owe as much to the blood, brains and labour of the Irish people as they do to the English and the Scots. The reverse of this principle, though, is not true.[25]

Much, as has been indicated, has been done in Northern Ireland itself to redress wrong – but not enough. There are human rights still to be attained; but why not a Bill of Rights for *all* of Britain? What must not happen, in any new arrangement, is for a new wrong to be done to northern Unionists, for that would be to redistribute the suffering in Irish politics unfairly. But it would be foolish to think that political arrangements can ever avoid some inevitable suffering.

Maybe there are two essential aspects of forgiveness in politics that need to be explored before many new initiatives can be taken. The first is a desire for repentance, such as was symbolized in Derry City on Good Friday 1985 when three hundred people, led by clergy, proceeded through the city carrying a large wooden cross. At the ceremony a representative of the Protestant community read out a confession and asked forgiveness for using the name of God for political advantage, abusing political processes and perpetuating discrimination in jobs and housing; the confession also regretted the support given to men of violence and the lack of support from clergy and people for justice. Then a 'Confession of the Gaelic Irish', read by a local Catholic, included a confession of unresolved anger over centuries, leading to atrocities in Ireland and England; of claiming to follow Christ, but not forgiving enemies; of glorifying violence and seeking a united Ireland above the Kingdom of God. 'Lord, before you and one another we ask pardon for the pain caused to people in mixed marriages,' the Confession went on, and asked for ways to eliminate such pain. The Church's contribution to a rapid breakdown in values was also acknowledged, and then pardon was sought from 'our Christian brothers and sisters'. The final prayer, a 'British Confession of Sin', was read by an Englishman. This included repentance for British sins against Irish people 'of both traditions', especially those involving coercion, and for the actions of armies and governments which had killed the dispossessed Irish people, also regret for acts of Church and state curtailing religious freedom, and for neglect 'especially of Northern Ireland . . .'[26]

Why cannot 'every town, every city, indeed the whole nation, have such a Repentance Day?' asked the group who had initiated the service in Londonderry. To date this suggestion has led to similar events taking place only in London, Belfast and Dublin on Good Friday 1988. In London there was a silent procession from the steps of Westminster Cathedral to the nave of Westminster Abbey where, in a short service, similar confessions were read out.

But maybe the second aspect of forgiveness in politics, needed over and above services of repentance and reconciliation by Irish and British together, is attention to social justice. Can there be forgiveness before at least some of the injustices experienced by the poorer sections of the population in both Britain and Ireland have been dealt with?

If, however, the British and Irish can discover a new fraternity, which spills over into a concern for all members of society, then maybe they will find that 'the stone which the builders rejected' – Northern Ireland – 'has become the cornerstone'.[27] Perhaps only then can forgiveness change the past and the future of both Britain and Ireland.

9

THE NORTH AMERICAN EXPERIENCE

'IN 1976 I WAS REMINDED of the good that can flow from a friendship that is mended,' Queen Elizabeth II said in her Christmas broadcast that year.

> Two hundred years ago the representatives of the thirteen British colonies in North America signed the Declaration of Independence in Philadelphia. This year we went to America to join in their Bicentennial Celebrations. Who would have thought two hundred years ago that a descendant of King George III could have taken part in these Celebrations . . . Wherever we went the welcome was the same, all the way to Boston where the first shots in the war between Britain and American were fired . . .[1]

Events in the United States of America during those two hundred years have often lacked that spirit of reconciliation; as Billy Graham has noted, 'the Americans feel guilty over the American Indian and the way the Black man has been treated'.[2] Indeed, what happened to the Indians in the Americas has parallels in the treatment of the aborigines of Australia and the Maoris of New Zealand, where a similar guilt is felt by the descendants of those who took over native land. 'I leave behind in the Indies', wrote Fray Bartolome de Las Casas, 'Jesus Christ our God, whipped, afflicted and crucified, not once, but a million times over.'[3]

The supreme irony of American history is surely revealed in the final paragraphs of a narrative by Dee Brown of how the West was 'won'. Here he described how soldiers went over the Wounded Knee battlefield, gathering up the Indians still alive after their battle with the American cavalry and loading them into wagons. As a blizzard was approaching the dying Indians were left where they had fallen. The wounded Sioux reached the destination of Pine Ridge after dark and were left in the open wagons in biting cold as an army officer searched for shelter. Eventually the episcopal mission was opened, its benches removed and hay scattered across the rough floor.

It was the fourth day after Christmas in the Year of Our Lord 1890. When the first torn and bleeding bodies were carried into the candlelit church, those who were conscious could see Christmas greenery hanging from the open rafters. Across the chancel front above the pulpit was strung a crudely lettered banner: PEACE ON EARTH, GOOD WILL TO MEN.[4]

From that day to this the United States has been unable to acknowledge its need for forgiveness for what has been done, or to make sufficient reparation to the native Indian peoples. There are probably more than one million people in America who identify themselves as Indian, but in a population of over 250 million they seem insignificant. Most of them belong to the 266 tribes recognized by the Bureau of Indian Affairs. Under the terms of the nineteenth-century treaties by which they ceded much of their territory, they normally receive special federal services and trusteeship for what remains of their lands and assets. The Bureau also recognizes some 216 Eskimo, Aleut and Indian communities in Alaska.

How have the Indians fared under such arrangements? According to the 1970 census the average *per capita* income for Indians was $1,573, lower even than the figures for blacks or chicanos and half that for whites. For rural Indians and those on reservations the figure was even lower.

Moreover, land possessed by Indians has not been sacrosanct. In the reservation created for Paiutes in 1859 around Pyramid Lake, near the Nevada-California border, whites squatted on Indian ancestral land. In 1924 the US government decided to legalize this theft by making the squatters pay a small 'sale-price' to the tribe. After a long legal battle, five white families who did not pay up were ordered to move, but there was no one to serve the eviction orders because the US marshals were all appointed by the trespassers' main advocate. The Paiutes fenced the disputed land back into their reservation. 'In retaliation for this action neighbouring farmers cut the Indians' irrigation channels and Paiute cattle began to die for lack of winter hay.'[5]

There has been an Indian Claims Commission (1946–1978) by which the United States government has sought to eliminate Indian grievances over their treatment, 'an admitting of guilt on the part of the government and asking for forgiveness', in the view of Professor Francis Paul Prucha, 'and this resulted in compensation of over 800,000,000 dollars, but did not end Indian complaints'.[6]

In 1968, the incoming President, Richard Nixon, asked an expert on Indian matters to advise him on the administration of policy. Many reforms were advocated, but the Indians themselves were less than enthusiastic, probably because of the paradox at the heart of the constitutional arrangements between the Indian communities and the United States government.

> Indian tribes are composed of United States citizens, who nevertheless have a governmental power that antedates the United States and is in a sense separate from and independent of the sovereignty of the general government. The catch, of course, is that it exists only at the will of Congress, and is subject to complete annulment if Congress should so act.[7]

Though the Bureau of Indian Affairs is unsatisfactory, many Indians argue it is better than anything which might take its place. Attempts at reforming the Bureau have been made often, from the time of the Meriam Report of 1928 (the first assessment of what has happened since the end of the Indian wars), but even relocation policies have been unproductive.

By the end of the 1950s concerted opposition had emerged from among Indian leaders. The Second World War, and US involvement in the Korean war, brought not only 25,000 native servicemen but also many thousands of Indian war workers into contact with white society; this gave restless Indians less fear of their fellow Americans.

By 1960 they had been able to bring a halt to the gradual extinction of tribes which economic and other pressures were causing. Stimulated by the civil rights and Black Power movements the Chicago American Indian Conference of 1961 issued a 'Declaration of Indian Purpose' which ended:

> What we ask of America is not charity, not paternalism, even when benevolent. We ask that the nature of our situation be recognized and made the basis of policy and action. In short, the Indians ask for assistance, technical and financial, for the time needed, however long that may be, to regain in the America of the space age some measure of the adjustment they enjoyed as the original possessors of their native land.[8]

The Indian Youth Council, founded in 1961 by ten college-educated Indians, went into action. Its campaign included 'fish-ins' and demonstrations, to draw public attention to Indian problems and to compel the government to act in defence of rights guaranteed in its own treaties. When the Bureau of Indian Affairs delayed, the Indians sent in armed men to stop or resist interference by state governments. There were a number of confrontations, but the campaign succeeded in both highlighting issues and forcing the government to file charges against states on behalf of the Indians.[9]

President Nixon's administration *did* implement changes. After a five-month Senate battle the Blue Lake (of Taos Pueblo), taken without consultation in 1906, was restored to the people of Taos. A few tribes, such as the Zuni, took over responsibility for almost all their federal programmes. The congressional sub-committee on Indian affairs became more sympathetic to Indian needs, and the Indian Education Act, framed after much consultation, gave unprecedented opportunity for native communities to run their own schools. In addition, an Alaskan native was put in charge of the Indian Education Office and made an Assistant Commissioner with direct access to the White House.

During the 1970s Indian protests continued to grow. At the end of 1972 the 'Trail of Broken Treaties', organized by the American Indian Movement and several other groups, converged on Washington to present a list of grievances and a twenty-point programme to stress treaty rights and make possible a 'honest relationship' between natives and government.

When the demonstrators arrived there was no decent accommodation for them. As it became clear they would be cold-shouldered, they occupied the Bureau for Indian Affairs building, leaving only after six days of considerable tension. There was no bloodshed or prosecution but a promise to answer their twenty points was rescinded when it appeared they had taken documents while occupying the offices.

A few months later, in February 1973, the village of Wounded Knee, the scene of the 1890 massacres, was occupied and attention drawn to Indian problems yet again. The occupation lasted seventy-one days, and there was world-wide publicity as two Indians were killed. Finally a truce was negotiated.

In 1975 Congress set up a further Commission (the first since the 1928 Meriam Report), which reported two years later, making two hundred recommendations. That same year President Carter appointed the first Assistant Secretary of State for Indian Affairs, a Blackfoot Indian who had considerable Indian support.

However, disenchantment has continued and many Indian groups have sought redress through the legal system. Settlements include one with the Penobscots and the Bassamaquoddies, who are to receive 300,000 acres of underdeveloped land and $27.5 million in extinguishments of their rights to 12.5 million acres. More recently, $162 million in land, services and money, in return for giving up its claims to valuable real-estate, have been agreed with the small Puyallup tribe, who live on the Puget Sound in Washington State, one of the most expensive settlements of American Indian land claims.[10] However, one of the larger western tribes, the Oglala Sioux, have refused to accept over $100 million offered to them for the sacred Black Hills in South Dakota, saying they are not for sale. At the heart of the situation is a constitutional problem: 'If the federal government retains responsibility (now increasingly called "trust responsibility") for Indian programmes, it must maintain some control of them. But federal control negates full tribal self-determination.'[11]

All these inter-relations imply some degree of repentance and forgiveness. But they lack the kind of courage shown by Trudeau's administration in Canada, which admitted mistakes and invited criticism. It then set up a forum for the discussion of major problems and issues, especially land claims and revisions to the Indian Act. (In November 1975 came the first major claims settlement with the Quebec government, involving land and money. A similar settlement was worked out for the Yukon.)

The black minority in the United States, the descendants of the slave trade, have faced much suffering and vast problems, especially in the southern states. At all times religion and politics, hope and change, have been intermingled in their struggles. However, 'whereas the whites asked Jesus for forgiveness, the blacks primarily asked for recognition'.[12]

In wedding themselves to Christianity, for that is what most slaves did, American blacks both trapped and liberated themselves at the same time. If in their songs they could express – under guise of yearning for a new world in the next life – a hope for a new order here on earth,[13] it was awaited with too much calm.

> The black variant of Christianity laid the foundations of proto-national consciousness and at the same time stretched a universalist offer of forgiveness and ultimate reconciliation to white America ... The synthesis that became black Christianity offered a profound spiritual strength to the people at bay; but it also imparted a political weakness, which dictated, however necessarily and realistically, acceptance of the hegemony of the oppressor.[14]

It took one black American to galvanize this slumbering yearning. When in the 1950s the black civil rights movement selected Martin Luther King to lead it, its leaders chose wisely. For, while black America has had greater writers (James Baldwin, with his scorching writing in *The Fire Next Time*, *Nobody Knows My Name* and *Go Tell It On The Mountain*[15]) and more vocal militants (the Black Muslim group led by Malcolm X), it was King, with his wide reading, gift for oratory and commitment to the way of Gandhi, who emerged as the prophet of the hour.

In one of his books King recorded his debt to Gandhi, setting it in the context of moves toward violence made after the seeming failure of the Montgomery bus boycott of 1956 and other non-violent protests. He argued that earlier twentieth-century revolutions had been based on hope and hate, hope for freedom and justice, hate for the old order, and it was these which had made the revolutions violent. Gandhi sought to build a revolution on hope, love and non-violence. The civil rights movement in America followed the same course as Gandhi.[16]

Gandhi was always in the forefront of King's thinking, despite other influences. Yet King felt there was a delicate balance to be maintained between struggle for justice and loving one's enemies. At a meeting to consider bus segregation in Montgomery – especially what happened to Rosa Parkes, when she protested at being given a seat at the back of the bus – King declared that they were there that evening to say to those who mistreated them they were tired of segregation and humiliation. But, unlike the Ku Klux Klan, there would be no cross burnings or brutal murder. Citing Jesus's words to love one's enemies he quoted Booker T. Washington, 'Let no man pull you so low as to make you hate him.' His hope was that one day, if they protested with both dignity and Christian love, history books would record that there once lived black people who had the courage to stand up for their rights and give society a new meaning.[17]

In January 1958 King was speaking at a mass meeting when he heard his house had been bombed. Back at home he found a crowd of blacks around it and white police trying to hold them in check. From his porch he looked on the crowd, held up his hand and stilled the people. 'My wife and baby are all right,' King said. 'I want you to go home and put down your weapons. We cannot solve this problem through retaliatory violence . . . We must love our white brothers, no matter what they do to us . . .'[18]

In March 1957 King and his wife Coretta visited Ghana for its independence celebrations. There he felt that the world's one-and-a-half billion blacks, plundered and oppressed by Europe, were on the move, 'in revolt against social and political domination'.[19] In May, back in America, in a speech at the Lincoln Memorial he argued that if blacks were given the vote they would bring good deeds to birth and fill the legislative halls with people of good will. They would send to Congress people devoted to justice and would provide state governors who felt 'the glow of the divine'.[20]

In September 1958 King and others were brought to court for trivial offences which were dismissed, but still he refused to be bitter. Later that month he was stabbed and near death; many whites wrote to express solidarity with him.

The following year King flew to New Delhi and dined with Nehru, who described to him his country's efforts to deal with the problems of low-caste Indian 'untouchables'. Nehru told him that now, if an untouchable and a high-caste Indian competed for college admission, the school had to take the 'untouchable', arguing that this was the Indian way of atoning for centuries of injustice that high-caste Indians had inflicted on 'untouchables'. 'To equal that,' King is reported as saying, 'President Eisenhower would have to take a negro child by the hand and lead her into Central High School in Little Rock.'[21]

By April 1963 King was in jail again through his civil disobedience campaign. From there he wrote his 'Letter from Birmingham Jail' in which he stressed the interdependence of all communities. 'Injustice anywhere is a threat to justice everywhere,' he argued.[22] By August he and the civil rights movement were at the heart of America's consciousness, as the largest ever, integrated protest march reached the steps of Lincoln Memorial in Washington and King made one of his most famous speeches:

> Five score years ago a great American, in whose symbolic shadow we stand, signed the Emancipation Proclamation. This momentous decree came as a great beacon light of hope to millions of Negro slaves who had been seared in the flames of withering injustice . . . But one hundred years later, we must face the tragic fact that the Negro is still not free . . . So we have come here today to dramatize an appalling condition . . .[23]

Continuing, he said that, despite the difficulties of the present time, he still had a dream that all would be able to live as equals:

> I have a dream that one day on the red hills of Georgia the sons of former slaves and the sons of former slaveholders will be able to sit down together at the table of brother-

hood. I have a dream that one day even the State of Mississippi, a desert state sweltering with the heat of injustice and oppression, will be transformed into an oasis of freedom and justice . . .[24]

The speech went on with the hope of an integrated Alabama, as people below joined hands and swayed to and fro, shouting out, 'Dream some more.' Here were biblical echoes with straight politics, all couched in a powerful rhythmic style as he called down freedom for Pennsylvania, Georgia, Tennessee and Mississippi.

Essentially, even in this speech, King was a typical American. Indeed black and white Americans have more in common with one another than they have with Africans or Europeans. 'It is only by understanding each other that the mixed American race can earn its unique inheritance.'[25]

King certainly understood that, revealing the calibre of his thought in another book, *Strength to Love*. It was published in June 1963, when Governor Wallace was trying to prevent the court-ordered integration in the University of Alabama. King wrote:

A third reason why we should love our enemies is that love is the only force capable of transforming an enemy into a friend. We never get rid of an enemy by meeting hate with hate; we get rid of an enemy by getting rid of enmity. By its very nature, hate destroys and tears down; by its very nature, love creates and builds up. Love transforms with redemptive power.

He then described how President Lincoln made his arch-enemy, Stanton, the Secretary of War, arguing that he was the best person for the job.[26]

On 6 August 1963 King was again in Washington, as President Johnson, having signed the Civil Rights Bill, faced the media in front of the statute of Lincoln and spoke of the day as a 'triumph for freedom as huge as any army has won on any battlefield'. Later that day Johnson met the leaders of the Conference on Civil Rights, including King, who had lobbied for the bill on Capitol Hill.[27]

The legislation was strong: it outlawed all illiteracy tests and similar voting restrictions, allowed the Attorney General to supervise Federal elections in seven southern states by appointing examiners to register those kept off the rolls, and instructed him 'forthwith' to challenge the constitutionality of the limited polls taken in elections in the four states where they were still law. Political commentators attributed the voting reform to King's campaigning; without that pressure it might have taken years to extract such legislation from Congress.

Selma, the old 'black-belt' town where the campaign had started, felt the impact quickly. Within a few years the city's racial caste system was finished, the obstacles to negro voting gone, the city council and the police force were both racially mixed, and the schools and public accommodation all desegregated, though racial prejudice did continue to afflict the white community.

'We must develop and maintain the capacity for forgiveness,' King had once said. 'He who is devoid of the power to forgive is devoid of the power to love. There is some good in the worst of us and some evil in the best of us. When we discover this, we are less prone to hate our enemies.' Moreover, 'forgiveness is not an occasional act; it is a permanent attitude'.[28]

It was this astonishing power to forgive which eventually led King into disagreement with other leaders. In June 1966 King's aides had been horrified by Stokeley Carmichael's extolling of 'black power', and King shared their disquiet. Though blacks like Paul Robeson and Adam Clayton Powell had used the term before, it now caused a sensation as media writers seized on it.

King spoke about those who were urging blacks to be violent like their oppressors. He was, he maintained, tired of violence, especially in the Vietnam war, and would not use it, whoever urged him to do so.[29] He said the same to Carmichael and others in a five-hour talk in a small Catholic parish house. Carmichael disagreed, arguing that power alone was respected and blacks must obtain it at any cost; he thought King was not political enough.[30] To a Berkeley crowd in October Carmichael said that King was a man full of mercy and love but lacked the power to deal with Lyndon Johnson.[31]

Young Black Power supporters argued with King in his home.

Quoting Fritz Fanon and his *Wretched of the Earth*,[32] they argued that violence for oppressed people was psychologically healthy and tactically sound. King retorted with the evident fact that blacks were outnumbered ten to one in the USA; what chance would they have? To combat Black Power civil rights leaders signed a statement in October 1966, repudiating violence and demagoguery and welcoming the participation of whites.

The civil rights movement faced set-backs. Congress rejected open housing legislation sponsored by the Administration, and the media grew critical. 'After more than a decade of the Civil Rights Movement,' one magazine stated, 'the black American in Harlem, Haynesville, Baltimore and Bogalusa is worse off today than he was ten years ago ... The movement's leaders know it and it is the cause of their despair.' In his last book King argued back: Negro electoral registration was up 300 per cent in Virginia, 600 per cent in Alabama. It would take time, after centuries of oppression, for blacks to become as resourceful as the whites.[33]

King's vision began to widen, and he became the most prominent of a group of Vietnam war protesters. He called the Vietnam war 'one of history's most cruel and senseless conflicts'.[34]

His concern now extended to poor people of any race, not only in the United States but in the whole world. He urged Mexican Indians, Puerto Ricans and Appalachian whites to become creative dissenters who would lead America to a higher level of awareness.

King also conceived a Poor People's March on Washington. As he explained in broadcasts that autumn 1967 the crisis in America was 'inseparable from an international emergency which involves the poor, the dispossessed, and the exploited of the whole world'.[35] He saw the campaign as edging the United States towards a Christian commonwealth where individual and corporate activities and concerns were fused in a unique way, an old American dream. On 3 April 1968 he made a speech in Memphis. It seemed he had a premonition of what was to come, speaking about being allowed to go up the mountain and look over. 'And I've seen the Promised land,' he reported. Yet he felt he might not get there with the people. 'But I want you to know tonight, that we as a people will get to the Promised Land ... Mine eyes have seen the glory of the coming of the

Lord . . .'[36] The next day he was shot on his hotel balcony and rushed to hospital, where he died.

Stokeley Carmichael considered it was white America which had killed King and thus declared war on blacks. He urged blacks to get their guns. Riots flared up in 110 cities and 39 people were killed, mostly blacks. More than 75,000 troops and National Guardsmen patrolled the streets. Hundreds of fires blazed in Washington DC and ten people died. It was, as with Gandhi, a final ironic twist to a life of consecration.

Did Martin Luther King succeed? He was, as his father told his friend Rabbi Friedlander while they stood at King's grave, 'my Isaac', and such sacrifice often bears fruit. Since then, the King family has been a kind of icon of forgiveness in America's violent history. When 'Daddy' King died, a London newspaper, reporting his death, drew attention to the murder of his wife and of his first son. It said he had refused to bow to tragedy, speaking always to his people of what it meant to love. The elder Martin Luther King, the report concluded, said on several occasions that he had forgiven the murderers both of Martin Luther King, Junior, and of his wife.[37]

In the 1970s and 1980s, as more blacks reached positions of power in local and national government, King's way seemed vindicated. Yet could his aims have been achieved without the fear which Stokeley Carmichael and his friends generated? It is difficult to judge. What *is* clear is that by the 1980s there were six black mayors in major American cities, and a substantial increase of blacks in the police force and in senior civil service posts. Moreover, when Jesse Jackson, a follower of King as a young man, set up the Rainbow Coalition and stood for the Presidency he demonstrated that history had moved a long way from where King and his friends were in the 1950s.

Jimmy Carter, when he stood for the Presidency, acknowledged a debt to King. 'I stand before you a candidate for President, a man whose life has been lifted as yours has been by the dream of Martin Luther King,' he declared. Some said he would fail, as he was from the south, but he stood by the dream despite the ever-present injustices. 'Martin Luther

King's dream and your dream,' he maintained, was his dream, too, for it 'is our national dream'.[38]

Once in office Carter acted in ways to implement King's hopes. Indeed, the mere fact of a southern President and a southern black, Andrew Young, formerly Mayor of Atlanta and now the US representative at the United Nations, spoke of a new deal for America. In addition Carter refused to be high and mighty. 'Killer nanny in White House', screeched a newspaper headline over a story of how a woman, serving life for killing a man, had become nursemaid to Carter's nine-year old daughter. The Carters, the woman said, 'know what forgiving is all about'.[39]

President Carter showed clemency also in more public acts. For example, on 21 January 1977 he issued a proclamation of pardon for violations of the Selective Service Act, thus bringing to an end an anxious period in the life of hundreds of Vietnam war resisters, many of whom had fled to other countries rather than serve in a war they felt was wrong.[40]

Besides these political acts there have also been small, personal actions. Few have been as daring as John Howard Griffin, who changed the colour of his skin and then told the story of how Americans treated him as a black man, and of the contrasting world in which black and white live.[41] But the story of Dixie Whitted shows similar courage. On the evening of 9 April 1968, the day of Martin Luther King's funeral, four young blacks jumped aboard a bus in San Francisco. There was a single shot and the young men, hands full of money, left the bus. Its white driver, Martin Whitted, was dead. This shooting did not lead to riots; in a tense situation Mrs Whitted said her husband had been killed in a robbery and not because of colour. She had been helped by the example of Coretta Scott King's bearing at her husband's funeral, and she proposed a memorial fund in her husband's name for both blacks and whites.[42]

Were the actions of Martin Luther King and President Jimmy Carter but small let-ups in the relentless round of hard politics? As Martin Luther King Day was observed on 20 January 1986, one journalist wrote, 'King's day has come but not his dream. He is the first American national hero to be honoured by a holiday so soon after his death. (George Washington had to wait eighty years.)'[43]

By 1986 there were 6,000 blacks in posts at city and country level – out of a total 490,000 posts. At the University of Alabama, where George Wallace held on to segregation so long, black students had become unexceptional; throughout the country 1.1 million college students were now black. Yet there was still a great disparity between blacks and whites at work, and positive discrimination policies were being challenged in the Supreme Court. As one black broadcaster argued: 'White society has psychologically made up its mind that it has paid black America off for slavery.'[44]

There are other views:

> King left us with the provocative question of how to put together revolution and non-violence. How do we create a loving, tough, persistent, righteous, justice-seeking revolution? King was struggling with that ... [But] we must never assume that because we believe in love and non-violence we cannot believe in revolution.[45]

Can America really rise to such a challenge, for it is caught in the complexity of its diverse styles? When President Ford gave ex-President Nixon a pardon for his involvement in the Watergate Affair, was this not more a convenient way of healing a wound in the Republican Party than a demonstration of the kind of forgiveness for which Martin Luther King and his friends lived and died? Moreover, can the wounds of Vietnam, with some 58,000 American servicemen dead or missing (and many others having since then committed suicide) ever be healed? If the USA could not even give medical and psychological help to those returned soldiers who were made to feel they had disgraced their country, what use now is the memorial in Washington to the war dead, or the requiem held for them? Maybe a recent visit by some Vietnam war veterans to help Russian soldiers returned from Afghanistan will be a source of healing for both Russian and American soldiers, and a most unexpected result of *glasnost*.

Thus we see a nation trying to deal with memories of its

recent history. But history has a perverse way of returning, as the individuals going up to the war memorial in Washington and looking for specific names on it indicate. Somehow the issues of forgiveness, reparation, memory and healing are all interlocked.

These are the same themes which currently preoccupy Japanese Americans. 'When, during World War II . . . we ripped 100,000 Japanese-Americans out of their California farms and shops and confined them to Mid-western camps, we were indulging the paranoid side of our realistic fears of Japan . . . ,' the playwright Arthur Miller once observed. That order, which affected 77,000 Americans of Japanese ancestry and 43,000 Japanese nationals, was rescinded by President Ford thirty-four years after its promulgation. But can history be thus reversed? Surely not so easily, for back in 1942 President Roosevelt *did* yield to Californian pressure against the Japanese.

'An honest reckoning must include a recognition of our national mistakes as well as our national achievements,' stated President Ford. This is a start, but although the Commission on Wartime Relocation and Internment of Civilians (1983) has pointed out ingredients for a national apology – a joint resolution of Congress, signed by the President, recognizing the injustice done, and a presidential pardon for those convicted of violating the statutes imposing a curfew – these have yet to be taken up.

In all these tangles maybe it is the Indian and black communities who can help white and Japanese America? For what is needed is a liturgical healing of corporate memories, something with which Martin Luther King and his friends were wrestling. Perhaps it is asking too much, for memory scorches, but without some such public exorcism, can America ever become free of the burdens of its past? Maybe the blacks, with their deep awareness of the need for mourning rituals, and the Indians with their sense of reverence for creation itself, can help white America find a new path and purpose.

10

LATIN AMERICAN RESPONSES

R AUL TASIGUANO and his brother, along with others
from their Indian community in Llano Grande, Ecuador,
were attempting non-violent action as a means to bring changes
to benefit their oppressed group. It was 1969, and their first
project was to obtain adequate bus services. Walking home one
night Raul was clubbed unconscious and a waiting bus twice
driven over his body. 'He was killed,' wrote his friend, Estella
Horning, 'because his vitality and spiritual strength were a threat
to the power, the purse and the self-image of persons who
couldn't bear the thought that an "Indio" considered himself
as good as they.' Estella Horning described how *she* was torn:
'I live with pain and sorrow, anger and guilt. I accept pain and
anger, yes, even the guilt, until there is formed a better world.'[1]

That story of the death of an idealist is symbolical of much
of Latin America's violent history this century. Back in 1899
there was a frontier dispute between Argentina and Chile, and
by Easter 1900 the armies of the two countries were ready to
strike. That Easter Day a passionate appeal for peace was
preached by Monsignor Benevente in Buenos Aires. The sermon's contents reached Chile and a bishop there took up the
message. The swell of popular opinion led the two governments
to submit the frontier dispute to arbitration – in fact to King
Edward VII of Britain. This led to a new treaty and a symbolic
reconciliation in the form of a great bronze statue of Christ,
which was carried 13,000 feet up the Andes mountains to the
frontier. It was unveiled in 1904 and stands on that frontier to
this day.

There were many other, more serious, disputes during and

after the founding of the nation states of Latin America. Since then, there has often been oppression as democratic rule has been overthrown by dictators with the help of the military. From Argentina to Mexico, Ecuador to Brazil, the people of Latin America have known severe poverty and regimes which often have been inherently unstable. Brooding over the countries has been the United States of America, which has always felt able to intervene in its own interests: stage-managing Panama's separation from Columbia in 1903; intervening militarily, until this policy was stopped by Roosevelt in the 1930s; helping, through the CIA, to remove a left-wing regime, as in Guatemala in 1954; or engineering opposition to Allende in Chile in 1973.[2]

Because of the Portuguese (in Brazil) and Spanish colonial influence, Latin America has been predominantly a Roman Catholic continent. Protestants, until recently confined mainly to the middle classes or ethnic minorities like the British in Chile and Argentina, have had less impact. The advent of an indigenous Pentecostal movement in Latin America, however, has led to a growth of grass-roots Protestant communities. In addition there are influences, as in Brazil, from African religious traditions, which reach right into Venezuela.

Recently Latin American Christians have changed their outlook in response to the poverty. There has, of course, always been a strand in Christianity which has sided with the oppressed, but now a declared 'option for the poor' – by theologians and church leaders like Helder Camara in Recife, and the murdered Archbishop Romero in El Salvador – has given a high profile to liberation theology. No longer can the Church be seen as necessarily on the side of the establishment. This has led to conflicts with those in power in Church and state. In Nicaragua, for example, a number of priests, most notably the poet Ernesto Cardenal, joined the government, despite official disapproval in Rome, which has also tried to silence radical theologians, like Leonardo Boff, for their views.

What is the core of this 'revolution' striking Latin America? The Brazilian educator Paulo Freire has described it as an attempt to allow the powerless to use what power they have to change their situation. Born in Recife, Freire knows poverty at first-hand and what he has called the poor's 'culture of silence'. This understanding has led Freire, eventually banished from

Brazil as too dangerous, to speak of a 'pedagogy of the oppressed', whereby people, by studying their own situation and the forces which impede them, are able to participate in their own liberation. As he has observed:

> No pedagogy which is truly liberating can remain distant from the oppressed by treating them as unfortunates and by presenting for their emulation models from among the oppressors. The oppressed must be their own example in the struggle for their redemption.[3]

Latin America raises starkly the problem of how to deal with wrongs committed by governments having at their disposal all the forces of law and order which a modern technological state can command. What was true for Argentina under the Generals, culminating in the Falklands War, is equally true for places like Guatemala, or for Peru where, according to Amnesty International, over one thousand men, women and children have 'disappeared' after being seized by troops or police since a remote area of the country was placed under military rule in 1983. Hundreds of others have been killed in custody, often after torture.[4]

Repression and wave after wave of arrests was the pattern in Chile under the rule of General Pinochet after the violent overthrow of the democratically elected Marxist government of Señor Allende. From September 1973 to March 1978 there was a state of emergency, and a less severe rule was introduced. But in the early 1980s popular protests demanding a return to democratic government in Chile, which gathered momentum, led to further repression and an Anti-Terrorist Law proclaimed in May 1984.

Faced with such contrasts and stark alternatives many Christians have joined the revolution and, relying on the Christian tradition which argues that it is lawful to take up arms against unjust rulers, have supported the guerrilla movements across Latin America, as they seek to overthrow, by force if necessary, governments which refuse to reform themselves. What then becomes of forgiveness and politics in these contexts? Surely, it is argued, forgiveness is a tool in the hands of the oppressors for ruling in the same way as before. No real change is required of them.

Patently this will not do for Latin America. As Gustavo Gutierrez, the Peruvian priest who is one of the pioneers of liberation
theology, has written,

> There is no peace without justice. This is a hard,
> uncomfortable truth for those who prefer not to see these
> conflictual situations, or who, if they see them prefer palli-
> atives to remedies . . . In the political context of Latin
> America, this means we have to recognize the fact of class
> struggle and accept the fact that we have class enemies to
> combat. There is no way not to have enemies. What is
> important is not to exclude them from our love.[5]

Loving them surely presupposes forgiving them but how can
you love people who preserve an unjust *status quo* to keep a
small group of wealthy people in power and ignore the cries of
the poor?

A look at events in Nicaragua will pin-point many of these
issues and perhaps help in the exploration of forgiveness in the
Latin American context. On 20 July 1979 the caretaker President (General Somoza had left the previous Monday) fled from
Managua as the Sandinista National Liberation Front (FSLN)
installed its five-member junta in Leon.

Even the United States accepted that there could be no
compromise government in Nicaragua and that the Sandinista
Revolution had succeeded in driving from office a fifty-year
dictatorship. At the takeover in Leon, four of the five junta
members were 'met by 30,000 who sang, paraded with flags and
posters, and stood quietly for a ceremonial service in honour of
three fallen Sandinistas . . . The service was conducted by the
Sandinista poet-priest Ernesto Cardenal, who said the guerrillas
had fallen fighting "a sainted revolution".'[6]

Though there were still pockets of resistance a revolution had
been won. It took several unusual turns: for example, one of
the first acts of the new government was to abolish the death
penalty. 'Nicaragua's spirit of forgiveness' was described by
Charles Elliott when, as Director of Christian Aid, he visited
the country in 1983:

Again and again we met people, from simple *campesinos* to ministers of state, who emphasized to us the readiness of the people of Nicaragua to forgive and be reconciled with those who currently harass and kill them ... Some of the stories are now well known. Tomás Borge, for example, is now the Minister of the Interior. In 1979 he was in prison, tortured. His wife was raped and then murdered. After the revolution, he visited the main prison in Nicaragua where many of Somoza's Guards were being held.

He recognized two of them. 'Do you know me?' he asked them. With downcast eyes they refused to answer. 'I am Borge,' Tomás said, 'whom you tortured – and whose wife your colleagues killed ... Now you are going to discover the full weight of this Revolution ... I forgive you ... Go on. Out through the door. You are free.'

Borge, Elliott continued, was strongly criticized for his release of over 5,000 national guardsmen, most of whom fled into Honduras and soon joined the American-backed Contras to fight against his government. Justifying his action Borge has said: 'We will never create a more human society if we use hatred, if we answer abuse with vengeance.'[7]

That spirit has been exemplified by others in Nicaragua besides Borge. Carmen, for example, the mother of a four-year old girl killed by the Contras, had on her door the official notice proclaiming an amnesty for the very people who mortar-bombed her home. Two mothers, who both lost sons in the fighting in Jalapa, spent time with the families of men who had joined the Contras, to convince them of the genuineness of the amnesty and the welcome the returning *muchachos* would receive. At a parish mass Father Ramon asked people what turning the other cheek meant in Jalapa today. Pain, they replied, not without a struggle.[8]

A BBC television series on Nicaragua showed a reporter on a national paper there visiting a guardsman who had murdered his nephew. Now the guardsman felt nothing but contempt for what men like him had done. Both guardsman and reporter were interviewed. 'I trust the Revolution,' said the guardsman, 'and I know they might release me early.' 'There is', said the reporter, 'no comparison between the present and the past. I cannot but be proud when I think how we have treated the others [the opposition]. You have to learn how to forgive. I've learnt that from this revolution. You've no idea how difficult that was . . ."[9]

Despite the pressing demands of national reconstruction and development for such a poor country, efforts have been made to transform the brutal prison system inherited from Somoza. The aim has been to enable prisoners to be productive and to encourage a sense of social responsibility. In 1981 over 3,000 ex-national guardsmen and others convicted of crime under Somoza worked on the cotton harvest with minimal supervision. This successful experiment led to the setting up of the first open prison, housing fifty ex-national guardsmen in a farm on the outskirts of Managua. There were no walls and no armed guards, just two wardens. Since the farm opened in 1982 seventy-six inmates have been released and only five have escaped. According to a report, 'An Irish psychologist who is investigating the success of Nicaragua's open prison system in rehabilitating ex-prisoners into the community, has found less than 15 per cent recidivism.'[10] Most prisoners, however, were still in ordinary jails but eligible for a place in an open or semi-open prison if considered suitable.

This unusual Nicaraguan approach is seen also in an account by Henri Nouwen, writer and priest. In 1984 he went with a party of 150 North Americans on a 'Witness for Peace' visit to Nicaragua. In Jalapa, close to the Honduran border, there had been many attacks on the town by the counter-revolutionaries, and only the previous month many in Jalapa had suffered from the fighting.

Nouwen has recalled how, during a prayer vigil, the group were joined by five Nicaraguan women:

> They stood very close to one another and quietly spoke to a group of about twenty North Americans . . . One of the women raised her voice and said, 'A few months ago the counter-revolutionaries kidnapped my seventeen-year-old son and took him to Honduras. I have never heard from

him anymore, and I lie awake during the night wondering if I will ever see him again.'

Then another woman spoke: 'I had two boys and they both have been killed during the last war. When I grieve and mourn, I grieve and mourn not only because they have been killed but also because they who killed them dismembered their bodies and threw the parts over the fields so that I could not even give them a decent burial.'

Then the third woman spoke: 'I had just been married and my husband was working in the fields. Suddenly the Contras appeared – they burned the harvest, killed my husband and took his body away. I have never found his body.'

There was a long and painful silence. Out of that silence a voice was heard. One of the Nicaraguan women said, 'Do you know, we found US-made weapons in our fields? Do you realize your Government paid for the violence that is taking place here? . . .'

For a long time no one said a word. What could be said. But then a question came from us that sounded like a prayer. Someone quietly asked, 'Do you think you can forgive us? Do you think it is possible for you to speak a word of forgiveness?' I saw how one of the women turned to the others and softly said, 'We should forgive them.' She then turned to us, looking us in the eye, and said clearly: 'Yes, we forgive you.' But it seemed we could not fully hear it.

Someone else said, 'Do you really forgive us for all the sorrow and pain we have brought to your village and your people?' And the woman said, 'Yes, we forgive you.' Another voice spoke: 'Do you truly forgive us for killing your husbands and children?' And the woman said, 'Yes, we forgive you.' And there was another voice, 'Do you also forgive us for all the fear and agony we have brought to your home?' And the woman said, 'Yes, we forgive you.' And as if we were still not hearing it fully, another begging question was heard, 'But do you forgive us too the many times we have invaded your country in the past and for the fact that we have made you subject to our decisions and rules for most of this century?' And again the woman said, 'Yes, we forgive you.'

As this prayer was going on Nouwen realized he was being lifted into a litany of forgiveness. It was as if he could see for a moment

> that the broken heart of the dying Christ, stretched out on the cross of the Americas, was being healed. . . . The five women of Jalapa are the women standing under the cross. They speak for us that divine prayer: 'Father, forgive them, they do not know what they are doing' (Luke 23:24). They are the voices of the dying Christ speaking of new life being born in suffering . . .[11]

The group, with Henri Nouwen, returned to the United States to help its citizens to see the effects of their government's involvement in Nicaragua. Many on that visit in July 1983 were radically changed by it. Robert Bonthius, for example, a Presbyterian pastor from Maine, described the experience of being part of a crowded, festive scene in Managua on the 4th of July. Conscious of the day and its significance for citizens of the USA, Nicaraguans asked the group to sing their national anthem. 'I hadn't sung it with any enthusiasm for a long time,' Bonthius explained:

> I have been so aware of the contradiction between America's constitutional ideals and what we are doing in places like Nicaragua. We have not been true to the best of our national heritage and gifts. The experience of being in Nicaragua helped me to appreciate the American heritage in a way I haven't for thirty years.[12]

The story of the revolution in Nicaragua cannot be left there, for mistakes have been made, especially the government's treatment of the Indians. All over the continent the relation of the local, and original, inhabitants to the inheritors of the *conquistadores*, has been uneasy, despite inter-marriage and the syncretist religion which has often emerged. In Nicaragua the government tried to move the Indians to new areas of the country, less near the borders, and also to introduce reforms without due consideration of the Indians' cultural inheritance. These attempts misfired; the Indians fought and eventually were allowed to return to their ancestral homelands.

Another problem has been over human rights. Since 1979 Amnesty International has issued a Human Rights Record of events in Nicaragua, in which a pattern emerges of frequent, though generally short-term, imprisonment of prisoners of conscience, incommunicado detention before trial, violations of the right to fair trial in political cases and poor prison conditions. Military personnel have been convicted and punished for abuses of prisoners, including murder and rape, but some reported cases of killings and 'disappearances' have not been officially resolved. There have been also examples of torture and execution of captives by anti-government military forces.[13] The suspension of a wide range of civil rights during the state of emergency declared by President Daniel Ortega indicates the measure of opposition it faced, as America's involvement escalated. A further twist to the story was reported in June 1986: 'Just when the Sandinistas were about to accept US peace proposals President Reagan changed his mind and went all out to win direct aid for the Contras – a move condemned by the World Court.'[14] More recently the change of government in Nicaragua, following the Sandinistas' defeat in an election, indicates the willingness of its politicians to move away from previous patterns into multi-party politics.

Behind all the struggles in Latin America lies liberation theology with its specific approach to caring. One of its exponents, José Miguez Bonino, explains this as he draws attention to the importance of the part which the

> . . . radical motivation of love and the motif of 'laying down one's life' for the brothers and sisters has played and continues to play in liberation language in Latin America. It is central in the thought of even the more radical leaders. Perhaps it is a testimony to the Christian presence within such movements; perhaps it is the age-old Christian tradition asserting itself – in a diffused way – even among non-Christians. In any case, this love-language stands in sharp contrast to the hate-language of repression with its

constant mythologizing of the struggle and 'demonizing' of
the enemy. In the mind and conscience of Latin Americans
committed to liberation, we are engaged in a project of
love, not of hatred.[15]

Another writer has expanded on this as he considers the
problem of class struggle and whether Christians can be
engaged in it, believing as they do in reconciliation. 'By com-
manding us to abandon neutrality, the gospel forces us to create
enemies and to combat them . . . The Christian must love every-
body, but not all in the same way; we love the oppressed,
defending and liberating him; the oppressor, accusing and com-
bating him.'[16] As Cardinal Arns of Sao Paulo, Brazil (where 70
per cent of homes have no sewerage and half no water), has
said, 'We have to go as the Christ did in his life.'[17]

Vamos Caminando and his colleagues try to teach local groups
in Peru in a similar spirit. In his catechetics he tells the story
of Emilio, who sells sombreros for thirty instead of twenty-five
dollars. When confronted about this, he admits his selfishness
and is thrown out of the co-operative in which he works, the
co-operative itself dissolving shortly afterwards.[18]

Essentially this story, echoed all over Latin America, raises
the issue of whether Emilio's severe punishment was justified.
Can a group be purified by throwing out its members who
commit errors? God, the text goes on (citing Luke 15:1-7;
Matthew 18:21f. and Matthew 18:35), does not act in that
way. The catechism continues by narrating what subsequently
happened to the group. They were thinking about the biblical
texts and decided they must stop being vengeful and forgive.
So they make plans to speak with Emilio, ask his pardon for
what they have done and celebrate their reconciliation. 'In this
way the group can start up once again. Forgiveness is a step
from death to life,' the catechism points out, and asks the
question, 'How can a rural community express its collective
forgiveness?' with a reference to Matthew 5:31 about loving
your enemies.

In the next section the catechist describes how the pardon
given to Emilio enables him to put in order certain domestic
problems he has had with his wife, who had been having an
affair with his cousin. Thus there is seen an intimate connection

between corporate and personal forgiveness, which is then linked with the sacrament of reconciliation and with the celebratory side of Jesus, who frees us from sin and urges us to free each other.[19]

It can be seen from this that liberation theology has a strong emphasis on the deeds of Christ. It tries

> to overcome the most radical dualism in theology; that of the believing subject and history, of theory and practice . . . that to understand Jesus is to follow Jesus; that to understand sin is to take sin upon oneself; that to understand the world's wretchedness is to liberate the world from its wretchedness; that to understand God is to journey to God along the paths of justice.[20]

At the heart of this is the Eucharist, the focus for discipleship. This 'imitation of Christ' was demonstrated most dramatically on 24 March 1980, when Archbishop Romero was at Mass. 'This body broken and blood shed for human beings encourages us to give our body and blood up to suffering and pain, as Christ did,' he said, 'not for self, but to bring justice and peace to our people. Let us be intimately united in faith and hope at this moment.'[21] The next moment Archbishop Romero was shot dead.

In Latin America civil strife has been the norm, truces at best a glimmer of hope.[22] The violence and feuding between the conservatives and liberals in Colombia have gone on for decades; military intervention in 1953 led to a slaughter which may have claimed 250,000 or more lives. The conflict there was dramatically highlighted when the priest Camilo Torres joined the revolutionary cause.

In 1984 President Betancur, a devout Christian, sought to bring peace by forging ceasefire pacts with the warring groups. But would the military really stop harassing and fighting? Would the revolutionary groups really abide by the agreement that would pave the way for a return to civilian life under a general amnesty? A headline 'Bang goes the consensus in Bogota' told the bitter truth while the report that followed described how the peace process came to a violent end; guerrillas took over the law courts and this was followed by a dramatic siege.[23] There are, it seems, almost inevitable results when it comes to dealing with revolutionaries for whom forgiveness and politics can never mix.

Despite Latin America's violent history over many decades, a thread of forgiveness can be discerned. In Chile in 1891, for example, civil war broke out between parliamentarians and loyalists to the President. Yet within five years of a parliamentarian victory a prominent Chilean, who had been a loyalist, was made governor of a province. Attempts at amnesties are also part of this process, albeit partial – however low a level of forgiveness they may represent and whatever the political reasons for such amnesties – for the vicious cycle of violence and counter-violence must somehow be broken. And the lesson from Nicaragua seems to be that political forgiveness can encourage new growth which would otherwise be impossible.

Can Churches as institutions have any role in helping to shape history? They failed in the Falklands-Malvinas conflict for, though both British and Argentinian Churches made statements and had access to politicians, they were unable to stop developments leading to outbreak of war. A Mass celebrated in Rome by British and Argentinian Roman Catholics was a powerful testimony to a desire to be together and to recognize a common humanity, but did it have any tangible effect on the course of events? Seemingly as little as the Pope's appeal during his visit to England, which coincided with escalation of the war.

The same strictures may apply to numerous statements of the Latin American Churches, especially those made by the Roman Catholic hierarchies. The declaration 'Responsibility and the Common Good' by the Uruguayan bishops in May 1984, stating that the use of national resources for the primary ends of people and for human and social development should have priority over other commitments, together with a plea for reconciliation through 'a change in the attitude that trusts in the systematic elimination of the adversary as the means of achieving power,' indicates the stance of the bishops. Yet they are only too aware that changes cannot be achieved without a new consciousness and a new spirit.[24]

The Colombian bishops' plea in May 1984, that 'the blood of our brothers be spilt no more and that we may construct a real civilization of love,' appeared to do to little to help resolve the bitter conflicts described earlier. But would the situation have been even worse without their statement?

Similarly ineffective in influencing government policies was the appeal by the Chilean bishops in April 1984, urging all sides to eschew inflammatory language and actions, and the military to 'renounce all unnecessary repressive violence' and to remember 'we are all Chileans and brothers by race, culture and faith,' but it does indicate the anguish of the episcopate and the struggles of Chile under military rule. 'Nobody should feel authorized to beat up, wound or kill those they consider to be their enemies . . . ,' it continues. There follows a moving testimony to the forgiving power of the women of Chilé, resembling perhaps that of the Nicaraguan women:

> To the women, who have shown their decisive and healthy influence on our civic life, we ask them to exercise all their powers of tenderness and compassion at home, in their work and meeting places and in public life, in the services of peace – peace with dignity, peace with justice, peace with love – and against violence, hatred, lies, and all irresponsible adventures.

Finally they implore everyone to 'remember God created us, loves us, forgives us, and will judge us'.[25]

To read the statements of the Argentinian bishops over the past twenty years is to get some impression of the depth of anguish of that country. In their document, *The Church and the National Community*, they are always pleading for an appropriate and mature response to national affairs, based on a consensus. To converge towards unity the spirit and practice of reconciliation is needed, based on truth and justice, they argue. ' . . . we Argentines need to go beyond even justice with solidarity and love. We urgently need to reach that superior form of love: forgiveness.'[26]

Another document from the Argentinian bishops, *The Road to Reconciliation*, was set in the context of the Pope's visit during the Falklands/Malvinas war. Again calling on Argentinians to seek reconciliation with each other, the bishops argued that it was not merely a matter of reconciling divergent viewpoints 'but of curing an enmity which is taking over the souls of many Argentinians.'[27]

What effect do such statements have? If read out to local groups at Mass they presumably help to mould and shape attitudes in a neighbourhood in one direction rather than another. But although the Roman Catholic Church commands allegiance from the overwhelming majority of the population in Latin America, there is an intimate interaction between Christ and culture, here compounded of Indian, Marxist and Roman Catholic ingredients, and the perception of what is stated by the bishops might easily be seen through distorted lenses. Yet it remains true that the Churches, as political institutions – for that they are – must have some impact on groups, large and small, as they seek to guide the political leaders, many of whom are Catholic, as well as the local communities.

Amidst all the theological exhortations, however, there is an uneasy feeling on the part of some observers that the attempt by the more cautious church leaders and the Vatican itself to ignore class conflict is not sufficiently rooted in biblical realities. Hence the struggle since the important Puebla talks in 1979 between the theologians of liberation and the more cautious Latin-American church leaders supported by the Vatican. Out of these came a demand for a 'preferential option for the poor' as a dimension of Christian faith itself.

This is the theological foundation of the many grassroots communities of Latin America, with their celebratory Masses and their committed priests and laity. What seems to be at issue is the legitimacy of using certain Marxist terminology to interpret Latin American reality, and linking it with the thrust in the Old and New Testaments for liberation.

On the one hand are those, with Reinhold Niebuhr perhaps, who see the ever-present ambiguities of history and consider:

> Nothing that is worth doing can be achieved in our lifetime; therefore we must be saved by hope. Nothing which is true or beautiful or good makes complete sense in any immediate context of history; therefore we must be saved by faith. Nothing we do, however virtuous, can be accomplished alone; therefore we must be saved by love. No virtuous act

is quite as virtuous from the standpoint of our friend or foe as it is from our standpoint; therefore we must be saved by the final form of love which is forgiveness.[28]

On the other hand are those, like Gustavo Gutierrez, who perhaps must be allowed a last, if not final, word on the vexed relation of forgiveness to politics in Latin America:

> ... the true pulse of history can be taken only by listening to the heart of the lowly, so often anonymous, Latin Americans ... Here is where we can seize both the old and the new – both in what lingers on in the panicky spasms of the oppressor, and what is fresh and irreversible: the forward movement of the oppressed in Latin America.[29]

Yet does forgiveness come after liberation, or during it, or is it offered freely, unconditionally, generously? That is the crux revealed by a consideration of Latin American paradoxes. Does the powerlessness of Jesus mean that the powerless stay that way for ever? This is how a Chilean refugee in London sees it:

> Forgiveness is a must if we are to break once and for all the spiral of violence fed by fear, anger, punishment and vengeance. However, forgiveness must come after victory over oppression, which is costing two million lives per year in Latin America alone. Otherwise, a unilateral forgiveness act could well have the result of entrenching evil even further ... As I see it, what is important, even vital, is that Latin Americans involved in the Liberation Struggle should undertake this crusade without hatred even if force and violence becomes unavoidable ...[30]

11

AFRICAN IDENTITIES

'TODAY THE WHOLE CONTINENT of Africa, that sleepy giant, is stretching its limbs as it awakes to its own new and thrilling dawn. From Algeria to the Cape every part of it is astir,'[1] wrote Trevor Huddleston in 1959. As in Latin America the cry of the nationalists has been for liberation, from the legacy of slavery and from colonialism. Surprisingly the search for a post-colonial identity, the preoccupation of so many thinkers and leaders, has been conducted with a minimum of bitterness. The Martinique poet, Aimé Césaire, speaks for many blacks in his prayer: ' . . . my heart, preserve me from all hatred, do not make me that man of hate for whom I have but hate; you know that it is not through hate of other races that I make myself a digger . . .'[2]

After the terrible scourge of the Atlantic slave trade on West Africa came to an end, some local slave-trading continued to flourish in Mauritania, Mali, Niger, and Chad, along the drought-stricken southern fringe of the Sahara. However, the primary experience in most of non-Islamic Africa was its continuing encounter with Western colonialism – Belgian, French, German, English, Spanish and Portuguese.

Maybe Albert Schweitzer, fascinated by Africa from the moment he stood in awe in front of a sculpture in Colmar of a black man, lived out another aspect of this encounter – the desire to make atonement. 'Why do I forgive anyone?' Schweitzer asked. 'Ordinary ethics say, because I feel sympathy with them.' There is, though, a deeper ethic in his view, called 'reverence for life'. It was this which he commended to others and applied to himself in all his encounters.[3]

A felt need to atone for oppression committed by earlier generations of Europeans is probably among the motivations that have sent white teachers, medical and other workers to Africa. A need to repent and atone may be experienced even by a child, as one father recalls:

> Many years ago I saw the effectiveness of such repentance when my wife and I were invited to address the inhabitants of a village in Ghana. To our surprise our twelve-year old son, who at that time was somewhat reticent, asked if he might speak. He described a visit to a castle at Cape Coast, once a centre of the slave trade, and his shock at finding, directly above the dungeons where the slaves were kept, a chapel where, as he put it 'my people, the white people, could pretend to worship their God'. He went on to apologize for the past and to commit himself so to live that such things could never happen again. The headman then told how the last time white men came to the village, he and his friends had fled into the bush, and he promised to write down in a book what our son had said. Many years later our son was one of those described by the BBC and *The Guardian* as 'intermediaries' at the Lancaster House talks who helped the leaders of Zimbabwe to reach a settlement.[4]

Single acts of repentance, however, do little to heal the historic wounds of Africa. Some people, like Bishop Lesslie Newbigin, have visited Elmira Castle, where slaves were kept before despatch across the sea, and want a more corporate response. 'I am always amazed that these crimes can be so easily forgotten. Ever since that visit I have wished that some representative Englishman – an Archbishop or Prime Minister – might come to Ghana and go down into that dungeon, kneel down on the floor and offer a prayer of contrition. I still hope it may happen . . .'[5]

To free themselves from colonial domination African countries have paid a heavy price. In some cases there has been an armed struggle, whether against the French in Algeria, or the British in Kenya, or the Portuguese in Angola and Mozambique.

The politics of Ethiopia indicates the second stage in the struggles of African countries, for often, after the ruling groups have left, a great mass of problems confronts the new leaders. Their governments have faced massive increases in population and times of drought and famine, as well as trying to meet the rising expectations of their people for more education and a higher standard of living. They have been beset by so many problems that the disaffection which has ensued has, in many countries, paved the way for rule by soldiers, as now one, now another politician is shot, put under house arrest or flees into exile. Few African countries have been as politically stable as Tanzania under Nyerere. Even the seemingly prosperous Ghana and Nigeria have experienced immense economic problems and corruption.

Civil war has racked the Sudan, with its difficult majority-minority tensions. The people in the north are mainly Muslim and Arab, while those in the south are of several different black ethnic groups and include many Christians. Despite the mediation of the World Council of Churches which led to a temporary resolution of the Sudanese conflict in 1972 and the granting of regional independence to the South, fighting broke out again in the 1980s and still continues. An editorial in the magazine *Africa* pointed out that the Sudanese civil war is one of the factors 'which keeps the historical and psychological gap between Arabs and Africans' alive.[6]

Uganda, which started its independence with an unhappy conflict between the Kingdom of Buganda and the rest of the country, has also fared badly, with several changes of government as leaders have been overthrown. Idi Amin's rule during the 1970s, besides being tyrannical, also raised fears that the Muslims were seeking to take over a country where, unlike the Sudan, they were in a minority. The murder of Archbishop Janani Luwum came as a great shock. He died in mysterious circumstances in February 1977, martyred for his stand against the atrocities of the Amin government. Few could reach the heights of Bishop Festo Kivengere, who has written:

> I had to ask forgiveness from the Lord and for grace to love President Amin more, because these events had shaken my loving relationship with all these people. He gave assurance of forgiveness on Good Friday, when I was one of the congregation that sat for three hours in All Souls' Church in London, meditating on the redeeming love of Jesus Christ.[7]

More recently, under the government of President Museveni, some of the wounds of the past have at last begun to heal.

Perhaps the Nigerian civil war provides the clearest example of the tensions existing in a newly independent state, whose boundaries were drawn by colonial powers to serve their own interests and which now often enclose many and varied ethnic groups. And the aftermath of that war shows a particularly African way of attempting to resolve conflict.

The conflict in Nigeria arose out of its majority/minority problems: a Muslim majority, especially in the north, and a large Ibo population, with a Christian background, in the east. An attempt to deal with this had been made in the constitution established when Nigeria became independent in 1960 by setting up three main regions in a federal system. But, because of their greater numbers, the northerners dominated the new federal government. This was resented by the Ibo, who made up a large part of the army. A military coup in January 1966 led to the murder of the Federal Prime Minister, a northerner, and brought the army chief, Major-General Ironsi, to power. This was followed by widespread attacks on Ibo people living in the north. In May 1966 Ironsi proclaimed a unitary state, but in July he was killed in a counter-coup by northern army officers, and the federation restored under a military council headed by Lieut.-Colonel Yakubu Gowon.

During the next few months several attempts were made to work out new constitutional provisions, but no agreement could be reached. The most significant of these was held in January 1967 at Aburi near Accra, at the invitation of the Ghanaian head of state, General Ankrah. Gowon's concern was for a new command structure for the Nigerian army; Colonel Ojukwu (the Eastern Region leader) wanted federal arrangements that would allow every region full control over its internal affairs and a veto over policy decisions taken by the central government in Lagos. Their final communiqué renounced the use of force to settle differences, but since the Supreme Military Council reaffirmed its belief in maintaining 'the existing institutions subject to the necessary safeguards', nothing was solved. Four more peace talks were held, under the auspices of the Organization for

African Unity and the Commonwealth Secretariat, yet none could stop the war.[8]

A further attempt toward a structure that would be fairer towards Nigeria's ethnic and religious groups was made when General Gowon announced, in May 1967, the creation of twelve states: the Northern Region was divided into six; the Western and Eastern Regions into three each. But despite this, Ojukwu was urged by the Eastern Region's Consultative Assembly to declare 'at any early practicable date Eastern Nigeria as a free, sovereign and independent state by the name and title of the Republic of Biafra'.[10] This he did on 30 May. Gowon responded by declaring a state of emergency and reactivating a blockade against the Eastern Region. Civil war broke out and continued until January 1970.

Over one million died during the war, many from starvation. But a prediction that the end of the war would be marked by many deaths was proved wrong. There were no mass trials of 'war criminals', and very little recrimination among the people. Indeed post-war rehabilitation and reconstruction in the war-affected areas, and the reintegration of the Ibos into Nigerian society proceeded comparatively well.

Much of the credit for this must go to General Gowon, whatever the defects he was to show later on. 'We honour the fallen of both sides of the tragic fratricidal conflict,' he declared. 'Let it be our resolution that all those dead shall have died not in vain. Let the greater nation we shall build be their pride.'[11] Colonel Effiong, who had taken over from General Ojukwu the leadership of Biafra and declared the end of secession, also urged people to 'avoid sectional interests and selfishness', and asked all Biafrans to 'forget the past and join hands with their fellow Nigerians to reconstruct Nigeria. I trust that Ibos can rise up to the challenge of the occasion . . . They should not feel disgraced. They should not feel bitter. The important thing is to learn the lessons of the war.'[12]

Not all Nigerians, however, could rise to this challenge. Ntie-yong U. Akpan, Chief Secretary to the Government and Head of the Eastern Nigerian Civil Service from 1966–1970, preached a sermon which, he recorded afterwards, called for Christian charity, 'love, forgiveness. Immediately after the service of worship, a hostile and disapproving group of women surrounded me and remonstrated . . . They considered it inhuman that one should even suggest that the Hausas should be forgiven and loved after what they had done.'[13] There were too, as Chinua Achebe has told, hard-liners in 'Gowon's cabinet who wanted their pound of flesh, the most powerful among them being Chief Obafemi Awolowo, Federal Commissioner for Finance . . .'[14]

Bearing in mind that many of the Nigerian leaders were Christians, what part did the Churches play in the conflict? One leading speaker urged repentance from Church and nation: 'Such repentance is not weakness; it is sometimes the fruit of courage of the highest order.'[15] At the service to commemorate the murdered head of the government and of the armed forces the preacher said: 'You and I then, must go on living in brotherhood, a human brotherhood that has its roots in God's power and love. We must forgive as we hope to be forgiven.'[16]

A consultation of laity at Ibadan called 'all Christians to social repentance. The whole nation needs to repent, but we call on Christians to lead the nation in this way . . . Unless we repent, we cannot forgive one another,' the consultation considered. 'Unless we show deep penitence, God cannot forgive us. And we need to be forgiven for we have sinned much.'[17]

Such statements surely had a steadying effect. General Gowon certainly was aware of his Christian responsibility but after the scars began to heal he had a different task: to create a new constitution. But he seemed to lack the qualities needed for this and other post-civil-war tasks, even changing the date for the return to civil government. Thus in July 1975 there was a further military coup and Gowon was overthrown.

General Obasanjo, who became Head of State, built on the basis for stability laid by General Gowon, and carried through programmes which enabled a reunited Nigeria to be returned to a democratically elected civilian government in October 1979. Under him the new constitution was confirmed (the previous twelve states were subdivided into nineteen), voter registration and the formation of political parties encouraged. Elections to the national and state assemblies were held, as well as the election of state governors and the first Executive President.

Despite these immense labours, involving much forgiveness and many-faceted political action, Nigeria did not fully resolve its tensions. On New Year's Eve 1983 President Shagari's four years of civilian rule was brought to an end and another military ruler, Major General Buhari, took over, alleging that the politicians had been 'corrupt, insensitive and inept'.[18] Then he, too, was overthrown in another military coup.

In Nigeria there had been a relatively peaceful transition from British colonial rule to independence. But in some other British colonies the road to independence was complicated by the presence of white settlers who had already assumed much political power, as in Kenya and Zimbabwe (formerly Rhodesia); there the nationalist struggles were primarily to gain 'majority rule' as an essential preliminary to independence.

To trace the development of Kenya, from the Mau Mau movement of the 1950s to its independence in 1963, is to see the power a charismatic personality may have in politics – in this case, Jomo Kenyatta.

After a long period in London, studying, writing and working for liberation for his country, Kenyatta returned to Kenya in 1946. He worked to improve education among his people, the Kikuyu, and, as president of the Kenya African Union, to build a nationalist movement that would secure freedom from domination by white settlers.

The Mau Mau rebellion, which broke out in 1952, had its roots in traditional Kikuyu secret societies, but increasing anger over the allocation of land to white settlers and other injustices turned it into a political movement. In October that year the Governor, Sir Evelyn Baring, declared a state of emergency, and Kenyatta, along with other African political leaders, was arrested on suspicion of connections with Mau Mau. Kenyatta regarded the Mau Mau uprising as due 'to outstanding grievances of the Kikuyu people and also other Africans . . .' but had already denounced its actions. 'Last Sunday', wrote a member of the Legislative Council, 'Jomo Kenyatta himself publicly condemned Mau Mau at a meeting of 30,000 Kikuyu, all of whom held up their hands at his request to signify that they approved his denunciation of Mau Mau.'[19]

Despite this denunciation, Kenyatta was brought to trial in January 1953, convicted of managing Mau Mau and sentenced to seven years imprisonment, which he spent in Lokitaung in the far north-west of Kenya. After serving the sentence he was restricted for a further two years in a remote village before finally being released in August 1961. Although he had been cut off from his people for nine years, Kenyatta was still regarded as the undisputed leader of the Kenyan nationalist movement. He had become 'Mzee' ('Old Man'), a title of respect.

Much of the information which had been used to convict Kenyatta had been garnered from needy informers who said what the government wanted to hear. But Kenyatta bore no grudge toward those who had imprisoned him, despite the wasted years. He could 'borrow from the New Testament philosophy: forgive them for they know not what they do,' he had written, adding, 'I have never been a violent man. My whole life has been anti-violence, and will continue to be when I am free.'[20]

On his release Kenyatta was determined to unify his people, Africans and others who saw Kenya as their home. On a British television programme he stated that 'an African government will retain the services of British advisers, technicians, and will readily accept aid without strings . . .'[21] To the press in Nairobi he stated categorically that an African government would not deprive people of their property, or rights of ownership.

In August 1962 he argued for unity through his party, the Kenyan African National Union (KANU). He stated that there would be no discrimination, but the laws must be obeyed.[22] To a mass meeting that September he was severe on those former Mau Mau fighters reported to be returning to the forests to create a civil war. 'Let us have independence in peace . . . ,'[23] he said.

Obviously, the psychological harm which Mau Mau had caused and the repression by the British rulers continued to worry Kenyatta. In an article written in April 1963 he returned to the theme of bitterness. 'I myself suffered for long,' he said, 'but I promise you I am not bitter. I ask those of you who still have hatred in your hearts to cast it aside. We cannot build a happy and progressive nation as long as man harbours ill-feelings about the past.'[24]

This was a magnificent triumph against adversity, for in eleven years he had experienced arrest, a spurious trial and verdict, and imprisonment followed by the isolation of banishment before his eventual homecoming. There followed assumption of leadership of the KANU party and then an election victory prior to Kenya becoming independent. In his speech at the independence celebrations on 12 December 1963, he was more than generous to the British:

> I think, my brothers, that our friendship with the Queen and the government of the United Kingdom will now be of greater value. Before, this was not our choice; it was being forced on us. But now, we have broken all chains, this friendship can be real and of great importance.[25]

He paid a moving tribute to the last Governor-General, Malcolm MacDonald.

'Harambee' (Let us pull together) was the keyword Kenyatta gave to the new Kenyan nation. The adoption of that motto, Malcolm MacDonald observed, 'reflected one of Kenyatta's fine qualities – his capacity to view the past as something that is finished – the lessons of which should never be forgotten, but which otherwise should be dismissed to its proper place in history, whilst everyone turns their attention to the new, challenging problems of the present and the future.'[26]

'One thing I want to make clear is this,' Kenyatta had said, addressing the white farmers in the rich farmlands of the Kenya Highlands in mid-1963.

> It is, we must also learn to forgive one another. There is no perfect society anywhere. Whether we are white, brown, or black, we are not angels. We are human beings, and as such are bound to make mistakes. But there is a great gift we can exercise, that is to forgive one another. If you have done harm to me, it is for me to forgive you. If I have done harm to you, it is for you to forgive me. All of us, white, brown and black, can work together to make this country great.[27]

Through Kenyatta's wisdom at the time of independence, and for some years afterwards, Kenya's path was more peaceful and straightforward than in, for example, Nigeria or Zimbabwe. As one commentator observed:

> Kenyatta's call to forgive and forget the past turned out to

be no empty phrase, it was the keynote of his government. Youth wingers and old nationalists who spoke of revenge were sharply rebuked; Mau Mau fighters who had grown accustomed to the ways of the forest and refused government resettlement schemes were quietly rounded up. White men and women who only a few months before had thought of Kenyatta with fear and revulsion now took Kenya citizenship.[28]

Kenyatta bore no grudges. When Sir Evelyn Baring, the former Governor who had been responsible for imprisoning him, visited Kenya as leader of the Commonwealth Development Corporation, Kenyatta welcomed him into his own home. Kenyatta believed in a one-party state and in November 1964 KADU, the opposition party, agreed to disband. Kenyatta showed no recrimination toward the KADU leaders; they were welcomed into KANU and given government posts.

Despite the undoubted success of Kenyatta's early years after independence certain nagging questions remain to be answered. Had he taken over the old colonial style with his personalized form of politics? What really lay behind the mysterious assassination in 1969 of Tom Mboya, the most promising younger Kenyan politician and possible successor to Kenyatta? Though doubtless Oginga Odinga did get out of hand as he sought to create a new party, and had to be rebuked after the riots of 1969, was the Kenyan model focused too much on one charismatic leader?

Having said this, it has to be admitted that Kenya has been remarkably stable since independence. Kenyatta, who with his roots deep in the soil of Kenya had seen drought and flood, hail and tempest, both in nature and in human affairs, brought to his land a new birth, based on forgiving and forgetting. 'One must learn to suffer and endure,' he once wrote, 'to replant and rebuild, to move on again. And as with farms, so with politics, the practitioner must never lose faith.'[29]

The road from white settler-controlled colony of Rhodesia to independent Zimbabwe in 1980 was long and tortuous. In 1979 Robert Mugabe, leader of the Zimbabwean African National

Union (ZANU) said in a ZANU Day speech: 'The sixteen years of our life as ZANU have been years of bitter experience gained through a bitter struggle.'[30]

Those sixteen years had seen also the Unilateral Declaration of Independence proclaimed in 1965 by Ian Smith as leader of the settler-dominated legislature, followed by the increasing isolation of Rhodesia as economic sanctions, imposed by Britain and many other countries, became more effective, and mounting guerrilla action by the nationalist movement put pressure on the administration.

In 1980 talks were held at Lancaster House, London, to seek a constitutional basis for an independent Zimbabwe. At the talks two 'enemies' – Rhodesian Prime Minister, Ian Smith, and General Tongogara, leader of the nationalist guerrilla army – came face to face. Their links, however, went back to the latter's childhood, when Tongogara had worked on the Smiths' farm in Selukwe. He sent greetings to Ian Smith's mother, who used to give him sweets as a boy. Some weeks later, when the Lancaster House talks were on the point of collapse, Tongogara remembered that time, and it made him realize that a negotiated peace was possible. 'I didn't want to destroy Smith or the old lady,' he commented; 'I did want to destroy the system he had built.'[31]

Agreement at the talks was reached partly because Samora Machel of Mozambique, who had provided a base for Zimbabwean nationalist guerrillas, pressed Robert Mugabe to accept the British Foreign Secretary's package.

As the time for transition to majority rule drew near, there was anxiety that General Walls, the Rhodesian military commander, angered by a breach of the ceasefire or other guerrilla action, might break away from the Lancaster House agreement and set up a government with Abel Muzorewa, a moderate African leader, thus leaving the British authorities impotent and the peace plan in ruins. Calm action by the Governor, Lord Soames, averted a potential coup. Soames knew that ZANU Patriotic Front troops had intimidated people more than other groups but he also knew that a partial ban on Mugabe's party would be unlikely to alter the result of the polls. He therefore took no action when pressed by Walls, Muzorewa and Nkomo (Mugabe's war-time ally), and some senior British officials. 'Soames' decision was the most important ever made by the British in Rhodesia,' commented a research fellow at St Anthony's College, Oxford.[32] Soames' role was critical and constructive, earning him the affection of the people of Zimbabwe to such an extent that Robert Mugabe attended his funeral some years later.

On 26 August 1980, Robert Mugabe gave an address to the United Nations as his country began its new life with a clean slate – the Zimbabwe Act of 1979 having granted an amnesty in United Kingdom law for political offences connected with UDI, and a similar amnesty in Rhodesian law, subsequently extended by the Governor to a general pardon, covering all political offences up to the elections. In his address he said their history had taught the Africans that the settler community would never voluntarily surrender power. 'War became to us therefore an instrument for creating peace.' He went on to praise Britain. 'We recognize the significance and courage of her final act and join hands with her in reconciliation and friendship as we face the future . . .' He hoped that in a policy of national reconciliation which his government was pursuing new energies could be released to create a non-racial society for all.[33]

'Let us forgive and forget, let us join hands in a new unity,' he said in a speech on Zimbabwean television after the election.[34] The following week he made General Walls supreme commander of the armed forces. (Walls was sacked and exiled a year later for plotting against the government.) Two whites were included in the first cabinet, and Joshua Nkomo was given the Interior Ministry. Nkomo, restless because his party, ZAPU, was subservient to ZANU, subsequently withdrew.

A remarkable degree of reconciliation was achieved as leaders of the Rhodesian army and the guerrillas were brought together in a new force. Ian Smith's son, touring the country with Arthur Kanodereka, a guerrilla leader subsequently killed, and Garfield Todd, former Prime Minister of Southern Rhodesia, exemplified those whites who wanted to make a multi-racial society work. Indeed, it was Smith's son who had encouraged his father to meet Robert Mugabe shortly before the Lancaster House negotiations, at a time when it must have been difficult for Ian Smith to do so.[35]

Slowly, however, and due no doubt to pressures from within

and without Zimbabwe, other feelings emerged. There were troubles in Matabeleland, the homeland of most ZAPU supporters, and mounting international criticism as the activities of the Fifth Brigade (the state's special military unit) became known. Mugabe defended the Fifth Brigade during the early months of 1983 as many African civilians suspected of aiding dissidents were being killed. 'If people give dissidents food, they are starting a war against the government . . . ,' he maintained. 'Don't cry if your relatives are killed in the process. It's the price of supporting dissidents.'[36]

Mr Mugabe is reported as saying, after Ian Smith's party won fifteen of the twenty seats in parliament reserved for whites under the constitution: 'The voting has shown that they have not repented in any way. They still cling to the past and support the very man . . . who created a series of horrors against the people of Zimbabwe . . .'[37] However, as one critic has observed, in assessing Robert Mugabe you have to understand the pressures on him: it is not what he *says* but what he does that counts. Indeed more recently there has been an amnesty for political prisoners and the split between the parties of Mugabe and Nkomo has been healed, assisted partly by heads of the churches. In December 1987 the two political parties signed an agreement to unite.[38]

In Mozambique the issue of collusion with the former colonial regime was of acute concern to President Samora Machel as he considered the 100,000 of his compatriots who had collaborated with the Portuguese regime, and who after independence would live side by side with other Mozambicans. He decided to bring one thousand of them to meet with him and senior members of Frelimo (the freedom movement which forced the Portuguese to leave in 1975).

They were sat in appropriate groupings: PIDE (secret police); former soldiers in the Portuguese Army; members of various political groupings. In other revolutions, said Machel, they would have gone before a firing squad; instead they would lose their civil rights, and pictures with their biographies would be put up at their places of work. The problem for Frelimo supporters was to forgive those who they saw as having betrayed the country. Machel maintained that the difference between collaborators and resisters had to be overcome. Rather than letting bygones be bygones, as some suggested, the past must be dealt with in order for the future to be different.

The proceedings of the five days were filmed, and subsequently made into a documentary by Dutch television called 'Treatment for Traitors'. Those interviewed included the son of a clergyman who had infiltrated student gatherings, paid to do this by PIDE; one of the founders of the Association of Mozambican Negroes, who had fled in January 1963, only to be protected by the Portuguese; and soldiers involved in the Wiriamu Massacre, two of whom told the story of the destruction of a whole village.

Machel drew out the horror of what each person had done. During his questioning one man specifically pleaded for forgiveness. 'Do you want to hear any more?' Machel asked the Frelimo supporters present. 'How much time would it take to liquidate them? Half a minute. With weapons or with bare hands?' But that, he said, was not the way, though the crimes could not be forgotten. In the hall the different groups had been sitting by signs indicating their role under the Portuguese. 'Let us unite and stand together for a strong and wealthy country,' Machel summed up. 'Socialism shall triumph. Put away these signs – there are no PIDE or traitors any more.'[39]

How indicative is this dramatic story of the true situation? For some allege that one-party states like Mozambique ruthlessly crush opposition (indeed, a war in some areas of the country has been waged for some years between government and rebel forces backed by South Africa). What pressures made those questioned say what they did, as the media relentlessly used its influence to build up the revolution? Compared with what has often happened after revolutions elsewhere, there surely *is* an original African element in this approach to those deemed to have been traitors. In the Mozambican situation forgiveness was no optional extra, for 100,000 people were involved, constituting what Machel called 'our national problem'.

Underlying all these examples is a question asked by Bishop

David Jenkins in another context: how can you advocate love and brotherhood *after* the revolution when the means by which it has been obtained has been the opposite of that? It is an issue with which President Kenneth Kaunda of Zambia has wrestled often. 'I ended up', Kaunda has written, 'supporting armed struggle in Zimbabwe because I could no longer believe that *anything* is preferable to the use of force.' He came to believe that it was a question of weighing one form of evil against another and asking 'for God's forgiveness as we undertook what had to be done'.[40]

Like others in the African independence struggle Kenneth Kaunda knew the long, drawn-out pain of it. In detention, weakened from malnutrition and frustrated by prolonged restriction, he was yet able to write, in 1959, 'I shall always pray that no bitterness shall come into the picture and we freedom fighters be forever colour-blind.' Throughout fourteen years of nationalist struggle he ceaselessly reminded his own supporters that 'black oppression is just as wrong as white oppression'.[41] Though by nature a conciliator, he found, after he had become President of independent Zambia, that he had sometimes to use force – for example, to quell the rebellion inspired by the prophetess Alice Lenshina. Yet in various speeches he has been at pains to talk about forgiveness. In his speech to the United Nations in 1964, for example, he said that Zambia had forgiven the past and would try to forget the years of humiliation.[42] In another speech, to the Organization for African Unity, he drew attention to the spirit of forgiveness which he saw in African leaders. 'You find it in the humblest village,' he said.

> Apologists or critics in other camps will say this is because we are underdeveloped. I don't accept that argument. What I do accept is that there is a challenge, and this is how to accept the good from both the East and the West and blend them with that which is good in our own, without losing that good in us. Amongst these is the preparedness to forgive . . .[43]

In one of his books he looks at the matter of forgiveness and politics in greater depth, admitting that the cross of Christ as 'political strategy' still eluded him.[44] Later on he argued that forgiveness is not a single act but a continual willingness 'to live

in a new day without looking back and ransacking the memory
for occasions of bitterness and resentment'. The nub is justice,
with which forgiveness must dovetail. 'To claim forgiveness
whilst perpetuating injustice is to live a fiction; to fight for justice
without also being prepared to offer forgiveness is to render
your struggle null and void.' To give way to hatred is to follow
a path of destruction. 'I have seen the bodies of innocent refugees in Zambia,' he writes, 'blown to bits by Rhodesian bombers
and my soul has been so tormented by my raging mind and
angry heart that had I not been able to forgive my enemies
because Christ has forgiven me, I should have become deranged
with fury.' But the difficulty of forgiving has been demonstrated
to him by some of the whites in Zambia, formerly his bitter
enemies, who have admitted subsequently they were mistaken.
This pleases Kenneth Kaunda, of course, but 'they *will* keep
harking back to those days . . . I try to say to them that they just
do not understand what forgiveness means.'[45]

Kenneth Kaunda is an unusual philosopher-politician; only
Julius Nyerere of Tanzania can be compared with him in sub-
Saharan Africa. For Kaunda sees many facets of the problem
of independence, urging Africans in their new-found freedoms
to realize we all need to be forgiven and that politics itself is
always made up of imperfect judges, policemen and rulers.

That perhaps is one lesson painfully being learned by the
new Africa – in the countries touched upon here and in the
many others, like Zaire, or French-speaking Africa, or Angola
debilitated by a 'fratricidal war'[46] – as the problems of the world
economic order and self-government have led to new crimes,
not all of which can be blamed on the legacy of the colonial
past which has been overthrown.

12

SOUTH AFRICAN POSSIBILITIES

THE CONFLICT IN South Africa is complex and has many causes. One of these, the intense and often exclusive nationalism of the Afrikaner people, has its roots in unhealed wounds inflicted by the British in the Boer War. Though the conflict of Boer and Briton started much earlier, the confrontation between English imperialism at its worst and the nascent Boer republics occurred just as the first African nationalist movement was coming into being. Forged in that crucible, the white Afrikaner tribe emerged from the experience both damaged and defensive.

During the Boer War as many blacks died on both sides as did English and Afrikaner and 'more adult Boers perished in the camps than fell in the field of battle, with over four times as many children'.[1] Even Kipling, in his poem 'The Settler', wrote about the stupidity of the war; he ended his poem with the hope that 'we may repair the wrong that was done'.[2] But his hope was only partially met, for though General Smuts, later to become a world statesman, was one of the signatories of the Treaty of Vereeniging (signed on 31 May 1902), underneath the seeming reconciliation was the smouldering resentment of Afrikaner nationalism. As William Plomer was later to write in his poem on the Boer War:

> Out of that bungled, unwise war
> An alp of unforgiveness grew.[3]

The peace treaty concluded outwardly the conflict between Boer and Briton and paved the way for setting up, in 1910, of the Union of South Africa. Generous financial help had fol-

lowed the end of the war, but many Afrikaners continued hostile
to the British, even though there was some intermarriage. But
Afrikaners could be reached at a deep level, as was shown by
Emily Hobhouse, an English Quaker who had opposed the war
and worked to relieve the sufferings of Afrikaner families in the
camps which had been set up to house them. Indeed, such was
her popularity that after her death her mortal remains were
interred in 1926 at the foot of the national memorial in Bloem-
fontein. 'We stood alone in the world, friendless among the
people,' Smuts declared then,

> the smallest nation ranged against the mightiest empire on
> earth. Then one small hand, the hand of a woman, was
> stretched out to us. At that darkest hour, when our race
> almost appeared doomed to extinction, she appeared as an
> angel, as a heaven-sent messenger. Strangest of all, she
> was an Englishwoman.[4]

What neither the British nor the Boers considered, other than
as a marginal presence, was the black majority. The whites saw
no constitutional role for them or for those of mixed-race and
the Indians – though in the Cape Province the latter communities had a limited franchise. Significantly, in the biography of
General Smuts by his son, published in 1952 shortly after
Smuts' death, there was hardly any mention of the black African
population. Indeed, by present-day standards Smuts can be seen
to have done little to prevent the continued growth of racialism
in South Africa. 'Unless the white race closes its ranks,' Smuts
said at his first big political meeting in Kimberley in 1895,
'its position will soon become untenable in the face of the
overwhelming majority of prolific barbarism', adding, 'the theory
of democracy as currently understood and practised in Europe
and America is inapplicable to the coloured races of South
Africa.'[5]

However, as white political groups were forming and Afrikaner nationalists quietly strengthened their political basis, some
black leaders tried to gain a hearing. Notable among these was
Sol Plaatje (1876–1932), the first secretary of the nascent African National Congress (ANC). Author of the first novel in
English written by a black South African, *Mhudi*, he sought in
it, through Barolong society, to present black South Africa as

having a culture and civilization of its own. His perspective on the Boers was sharp: 'In *Mhudi* they are viewed not as the embodiment of the advance of civilization, but as a strange and far from heroic group of travellers' obliged to turn to Africans for succour and assistance, one critic observed.[6]

Plaatje was more than a writer. He was a political campaigner of some power. He travelled to Europe to plead the cause of black South Africa, seeking help from the Great Powers. His campaign took him to Britain, where he met the prime minister, Lloyd George, and to the USA where he met black leaders like Marcus Garvey and W.E. du Bois. But though Lloyd George was willing to write a personal letter about the distressing situation of the black community he would not intervene directly, because the 1910 Act of Union allowed South Africa to run its own affairs. The price of Boer and British co-operation was manifestly the exclusion of black people in any political settlement. There was indeed in Afrikaner eyes only one place for them, as the Voortrekker Monument near Pretoria indicates – outside the *laager* in a servant role.

The political arrangements of 1910 had sowed seeds of destruction and set South Africa on its way of conflict. Yet for decades the blacks seemed able to accept their inferior status in a forgiving way. So long as the United Party was in power, English influence brought some flexibility, yet when Dr Malan's Afrikaner-dominated Nationalist Party overthrew Smuts' United Party in 1948 many of the apartheid laws then implemented had been on the statute book since the 1930s.

During the Second World War many black, as well as white, South Africans had taken part in the war, despite Afrikaner opposition to South Africa's involvement in it. As one commentator observed:

> In common with nationalists in other parts of Africa and Asia, black South African politicians tended to interpret the Atlantic Charter's endorsement of national self-determination rather more literally than its authors in the Allied camp intended. In 1943 a committee produced a document called 'African claims in South Africa'. Calling in its preamble for the application of the Atlantic Charter to all parts of the British Empire it went on to outline a bill of rights.[7]

(African claims had been rejected outright by Smuts when presented to him in 1941.)

In the context of this intransigence there developed in the 1950s a full-scale onslaught on the black population under Dr Malan's government. Now society was to be organized on the basis of *apartheid*, where each race had a place, but in separation from others. Those who dared to oppose this dream of the radical right were imprisoned, banned or killed.

Black South Africans have been peculiarly generous, with at times almost pacifist leanings. Like black slave communities in America, who took religion seriously – taking on board the ethics of the Sermon on the Mount and seeing an analogy between the Hebrew nation in bondage and their own situation[8] – something similar happened among the black South Africans who had become Christian. Perhaps the supreme example of this peaceful approach is to be seen in the life of South Africa's first Nobel Peace Prize winner, Chief Albert Luthuli, whose autobiography was appropriately called *Let My People Go*.[9] His response to the mounting pressures of *apartheid* during the 1950s was to encourage the passive resistance campaigns of the ANC. Luthuli's witness has to be understood in the context not only of a mass of people deeply influenced by Christian conviction, but also by the growing international concern about South Africa.

J.H.P. Serfontein, a young law clerk passionately interested in politics, who had just broken out of the Verwoerdian era of 'a narrow, restrictive Afrikaner ideology', as he has described it, met Luthuli at the time of the 1958 Treason Trial in Pretoria, where thirty black leaders, including Luthuli, were facing charges of high treason.

There he discovered a totally different South Africa, where blacks saw their struggle in the context of what they had learned of Afrikaner nationalism when it opposed British imperialism. 'In these discussions Luthuli spelled out his vision of the future – a non-racial South Africa with equal opportunities for all racial groups, on the basis of a common franchise for all.' One meeting above all left an impression on Serfontein both of Luthuli's stature and his forgiving politics.

Some three hundred people – academics, professionals, students and diplomats, including National Party supporters – had come to Pretoria to hear Luthuli speak. Many had never heard a black speaker, let alone seen Luthuli before that night. It was his first-ever speech to a predominantly Afrikaans-speaking audience. As he prepared to speak thirty young Afrikaner nationalists rushed into the hall and their leader jumped on to the platform. The chairman and others on the platform were thrown off. Albert Luthuli, unruffled, was knocked off his chair and jumped on before police arrived and order was restored. With blood trickling from his head Luthuli started his address.

> Almost apologetically explaining black demands and his vision of a non-racial South Africa and sticking close to his text written in a school exercise book, he emphasized the Christian principle of justice and neighbourly love with whites not to be driven into the sea. For the first time Afrikaans Pretoria saw a man totally different from the ogre usually presented in the Government press. His recipe was non-violence and peaceful negotiation.

What impressed Serfontein most was that in a forty-minute speech Luthuli never referred to the assault he had just experienced. 'Luthuli symbolized', he concluded, 'the patience, the tolerance, the amazing forgiveness, the essential moderation that characterizes black South Africa'.[10]

Alan Paton also described these characteristics in his novel of the 1940s, *Cry the Beloved Country*, and asked what if, when the whites have turned to loving, the others have turned to hating?[11] More recently there have been appalling acts of brutality – committed by members of all groups – as Africans have come to realize that 'There is no native problem, but a European problem of weakness, greed and robbery.'[12]

South Africa's problems are, of course, immense. But again and again individuals have emerged to announce there is another way through to social stability other than by repression, and some of them have been Afrikaner.

One of the most influential Afrikaner dissidents is Beyers Naudé. His father was one of the six Boer delegates who refused to give the unconditional surrender demanded by Britain at the end of the Boer War. And it was in his father's house, in 1918, that fourteen people met to plan the launching of the *Broederbond*, the secret society which behind the scenes has played a pivotal role in planning South Africa. Beyers Naudé himself attended the classes of *apartheid*'s chief architect, Hendrik Verwoerd, in the 1930s, and in 1938 he took part in the symbolic evocation of the Great Trek. Ordained a *dominee*, he later held high office in the Dutch Reformed Church. He was himself a member of the *Broederbond* and associated closely with the leaders of Afrikaner nationalism. At one time a supporter of *apartheid*, he came to repent deeply of this.

It was in September 1963 that he told the Dutch Reformed Church of his decision to leave. He explained that he could not agree with its dissociation from other South African Churches over the joint Cottesloe Declaration against *apartheid* which demanded the revocation of the Mixed Marriages Act and other restrictive legislation. This declaration had been drawn up by the Churches after long debate following the Sharpeville shootings in 1960 when police opened fire on a peaceful protest against the pass laws, killing many.

In the 1960s Naudé founded the Christian Institute which, until it was disbanded in 1977, and its officials including Naudé banned, acted as a focus for radical dissent in the churches and beyond. In June 1983, this distinguished Afrikaner, unable to deliver the Dom Helder Camara lecture at the Free University of Amsterdam in person, spoke through a friend. The South African situation, he observed, was seen by whites as 'the total onslaught of evil communist powers against a white Christian society which strives for the maintenance of law and order'. The blacks, on the other hand, saw it as 'a struggle for national liberation'. Yet most blacks and coloureds wanted a South Africa for all, with a democratic government, as in the Western world.

> In this attitude two highly important ideas of the blacks are reflected, firstly, their demand for the full and total acceptance of a non-racial society where everyone, regardless of race of colour, has equal rights and an equal place; and, secondly, their readiness to forgive, as becomes clear from this conscious or unconscious attitude towards the

whites, who caused them so much suffering and injustice, in as long as they are prepared to abolish the *apartheid* strategy altogether.[13]

Naudé went on to explain that many blacks are aware of the complex pressures playing on them and that they reject tinkering with the structures instead of real reform. They reject, too, the allegation that the liberation movements favour violence as the solution to the country's problems. The ANC had been founded in 1912 and pursued its goal peacefully until after 1960 when it was banned. This led their leaders to react to the violent acts of the regime with limited counter-violence. Repeatedly, he argued, black leaders had called for a national convention where all races could seek a non-violent solution to South Africa's problems. Thus, Naudé concluded, there is a build-up of inevitable conflict between relentless white selfishness and indomitable black conviction. Unless new factors emerge, he foresaw either a long, bitter guerrilla war, or a war with urban terrorism as its hallmark.

How is it possible to change systems and structures of injustice and oppression with little violence? he asked, adding, 'It calls for us to live in accordance with the highest ethical values of love, brotherhood, tolerance and forgiveness.' He saw need also for international help.[14]

Two other figures of comparable stature to Naudé have emerged in South Africa. One was Steve Biko, killed by the police in the 1970s. Biko, the founder of 'black consciousness' in South Africa, understood that blacks had to recover their dignity and sense of blackness. It was this conviction which lay behind the South African Students' Association (SASO), and all that Biko lived for. 'In order to achieve real action you must yourself be a living part of Africa and her thought; you must be an element of that popular energy which is entirely called forth for the freeing, the progress and the happiness of Africa,' he said.[15]

What is the task? he asked. It is to reclaim the blacks' inheritance: 'Our kindness has been misused and our hospitality turned against us. Whereas whites were mere guests to us on their arrival in this country, they have now pushed us to a 13 per

cent corner of the land and are acting as bad hosts in the rest
of the country. This we must put right.'[16] Black South Africans
should not see themselves tribally as Zulus, Xhosas, Vendas, or
even Indians (tribalism had been the bane of Africa), Biko
maintained, speaking cogently for an understanding that 'we are
oppressed because we are black'.[17]

But 'black is beautiful,' he proclaimed at his trial. 'We believe
ultimately in the righteousness of our strength,' he asserted
before Judge Boshoff in May 1976. The trial, taking place six
weeks before the spontaneous uprising in June 1976, when
hundreds of school children in Soweto were shot and maimed
by the police, made Biko the toast of Soweto's shebeens.[18] Still
committed to peaceful change, Biko argued in the courtroom
for a process of bargaining. 'We are not interested in the armed
struggle' he said. Eventually, he felt, it was inevitable that the
whites would agree to change. 'Our methods ... give hope ...
That is what black solidarity is all about.'[19]

Was there an exaggerated idealism in Biko's approach? He
argued, as did the ANC Freedom Charter, for a non-racial
society, with no guarantees for minority rights because this
would imply recognition of a racial basis for communal life. Yet
across the world, even countries with universal voting rights
continue to experience majority-minority conflicts. How, too,
would blacks themselves react to Biko's vision? When asked
how blacks could live without giving vent to their rage after
what they had been through, he merely stated that people had
to be educated to live in a non-racial society.

Why was Steve Biko killed? Surely it was because he fought
for a new humanness for blacks and for a new open society in
South Africa. Biko, his friend Aelred Stubbs maintains, was

consistently free from any spirit of hatred, bitterness or
resentment. When questioned about this he laughed and
said these would take too much time and energy and must
be eschewed. It may be said at the very heart of an authentic
Christian witness is the spirit of forgiveness. To suggest
that words of forgiveness were at any time during his passion on Steve's lips would be, in my view, unjustifiable, but
that does not make him an unforgiving person ... There
is no reason to suppose that Steve did not meet expressions

of repentance with demonstrations of forgiveness. The whole aim of the 'selfless revolutionary', . . . 'the liberation not only of the oppressed but also of the oppressor', presupposes not only that the oppressor can be brought to the state of repentance, but also that at that moment he is embraced, and so liberated by the forgiveness extended to him by the oppressed.[20]

Steve Biko, like the biblical Stephen, died a martyr of hope. Thousands attended his funeral, though some fled from the onslaught of the police with batons, sjamboks, and guns, reinforced with vicious police dogs.[21] As a friend wrote, his life had served to brighten 'the spirits of mortals on bitter winter days'.

The second figure of comparable stature to Naudé is Archbishop Desmond Tutu, another recipient of the Nobel Peace Prize. Whereas Biko's main influence was inside South Africa, Tutu has received, with the help of the international media, world-wide attention. Like Biko, he has followed a road of non-violence and has always warned of the inevitable escalation of violence if legitimate demands are not met. 'Non-violence', he has said, 'assumes a certain minimum moral standard among those it is directed against. Gandhi succeeded in India, and Martin Luther King in the United States because they could appeal to people who were appalled at what was happening.'[22] Tutu has continued to hold that non-violent protest could bring change in South Africa, if given decisive intervention from the international community, but has said elsewhere, 'If I were white I would need a lot of grace to want to change.'[23]

Tutu's stand is rooted in theology. In his enthronement sermon as Bishop of Johannesburg he talked of the need to be thankful for so many things in life – for God's presence, for Christ, 'for the forgiveness of our sins not once but many times over', for nature, music, food, love and friendship. He saw the task of Christians in prayer to carry 'the cries that come from the wretched of the earth to the mercy seat of God . . .' Also they were to be a 'forgiving fellowship of the forgiven'.[24]

Tutu knows that healing in South Africa will be costly and he sees that true reconciliation with God comes through our participation in the cross of Christ. He also sees the need to act forgivingly. While General Secretary of the South African Council of Churches, he sought to reach out to the Dutch Reformed Church, who were not members of the Council, though he received little response. He has written:

> It is, I believe, a miracle of God's grace that Blacks can still say they are committed to a ministry of justice and reconciliation and that they want to avert the bloodbath which seems more and more inevitable as we see little bending on the crucial issues of power-sharing. We are told that the Afrikaners have found it very difficult to forgive, certainly to forget what the British did to them in the concentration camps. I want to say that Blacks are going to find it difficult, very difficult to forgive, certainly difficult to forget what Whites have done and are doing to us in this matter of population removals.[25]

Nevertheless, Desmond Tutu can speak movingly of Afrikaner love, as when he speaks of the Dutch Reformed minister, Frikkie Conradie, who, with his wife and family, worked under a black minister, serving the black community in Alexandra Town.[26]

The question of how to act when people refuse to repent, is one which perplexes all South African reconcilers like Tutu. What chance was there for group forgiveness when the two main wings of the South African movement for freedom, the ANC and the Pan-African Congress (PAC) were forced underground, after being banned in 1960? Originally non-violent, as we have seen, the ANC came to the conclusion that this would not work in the South African context and so turned to violence against selected targets.

The crux of the struggle is, of course, the rights of over twenty-seven million blacks in South Africa. In addition there are three million of mixed-race, nearly one million Indians and other minorities, and some five million whites from diverse backgrounds. How are they to live and share together, and under what political arrangement? The ANC wants a non-racial, one person/one vote government, but others say that will not guarantee the rights of minorities. Hence the source of the

conflict as South African whites, with one of the highest standards of living in the world, refuse to share the land and other
resources equitably. Indeed, under legislation going back many
decades, blacks were allocated only 13 per cent of the land and
urban blacks forced to live on the edge of the cities. With no
votes, except in 'homelands' which many of them have never
seen, they are determined to take no more oppression. The
government imprisoned their leaders, like Nelson Mandela and
Robert Sobukwe (the former leader of PAC), set up a vast
network of informers, yet it found it could no longer intimidate
the black majority by its sophisticated weaponry.

Not only did pressures from outside South Africa intensify,
especially the banning of fresh loans and investments, but inside
South Africa itself the clamour for change grew. This focused,
after Nelson Mandela's meeting with President Botha, in 1989,
on the expectation that he would eventually be released.

Mandela's message – no doubt conveyed in private talks he
held with the government leaders while still in prison – was
consistent with all his other statements. Through his daughter
Zinzi he spoke to a meeting at the Jabulani Amphitheatre. He
was, he said, surprised at the conditions the government wanted
to impose on him in return for his release, as he was not a
violent man. From 1952, when he and others wrote to Dr Malan
asking for a round-table conference, they had sought a peaceful
resolution of South Africa's problems. They had asked this of
other leaders, too. He had urged Mr Botha to renounce violence
himself, to lift the ban from the ANC, free those in prison
and dismantle *apartheid*. He said that he was in prison as a
representative of the people, and for the people, and for the
ANC. Freedom for him was, therefore, inextricably interwoven
with freedom for the people.[27]

Despite Mandela's release in February 1990 and the changes
that have taken place in South Africa since then, one question
is as pertinent as ever: Can there be group forgiveness to free
the people of South Africa from their pasts so as to create
together a better future? The crimes of the past are immense –
from the dismantling of Sophiatown in the mid-1950s, through
the emergence of the Bantu Education Act and the banning of

so many opposition groups, down to the declaration of the United Democratic Front as an 'affected organization,' meaning it could not receive funds from abroad.

The indifference of white South Africa, save for its dissidents and some liberals, has been massive. The dissidents from Afrikaner backgrounds have often fared the worst: for example, Abraham Fischer from a distinguished Afrikaner family, who became a communist and pleaded the cause of black nationalism. When he died his ashes were retained in prison for fear his grave would be made a place of pilgrimage.

This seeming imperviousness to suffering has been summed up well by Oswald Mtshali in his account of a time when a prison van broke down between Johannesburg and Pretoria. The policeman went off to seek help, leaving the prisoners locked inside and dying of suffocation from the heat as traffic passed by, unaware and unconcerned. His poem 'Ride upon the Death Chariot'[28] symbolizes the deaths of thousands in South Africa, anonymous except to those who loved them. It is the scandal of these deaths which has led some Dutch Reformed Church theologians to say now that *apartheid* is a heresy. It led, too, the Western Province of the South African Council of Churches to produce material for a memorial service for those who had suffered, which ended with a prayer for the end of unjust rule:

This day O God of mercy
We bring before you all those
Who suffer in prison,
Who are oppressed,
Who mourn those who die in freedom struggles;
In places like Soweto, Cross Roads, Uitenhage, Sharpeville,
    and many places known to us.
Deliver us from the chains of apartheid, bring us all to the
    true liberty of the Sons and Daughters of God.
Confound the ruthless and grant us the power of your
    kingdom.[29]

Is there any hope for forgiveness in the face of all this suffering? It is the question we heard earlier rising on the lips of Jews as they remember the Holocaust. As ever, the answer lies in the human heart. If Charles Kadhikwa, in prison without trial, in solitary confinement for five months in Namibia (one of eighty-five detainees) could write as follows, surely there *is* hope?

> Forgiveness means to me a new start in a hopeless situation so that the faults and things of the past no longer control the actions of the present. Forgiveness is a breakthrough from the darkness of hate into the light of love.

The context of this statement is amazing, for it came after torture by the police who had said, 'From now on you are going to suffer until you are dead. We shall torture you until there is nothing left of you at all.' Then had followed the usual process of handcuffing, of putting a sack over the prisoner's head, then transportation to an unknown destination. Kadhikwa's worst experience was being hung in the air and assaulted because he had refused to make a statement saying he was involved in military activities.

In prison something happened to him. He read the New Testament several times and prayed, asking why he had undergone such suffering? He was able to see that in the life of Jesus there had been a similar suffering and that, just as Jesus forgave, so should he. He was struck by the phrase in the Lord's Prayer about forgiveness and came to understand that his hatred was cutting him off from God. Slowly Charles Kadhikwa came to appreciate that the '*Our* Father' meant 'ours, although we are from different countries, backgrounds, cultures, colours ... Forgiveness goes first through your fellow human being, whether Christian or not ... When I started to forgive them I was still tortured, but I could feel the release inside me ...'[30]

A similar spirit was seen in a Muslim interviewed in a BBC television programme 'Last Supper in Hortsley Street', about a mixed-race family in Cape Town who were the last to be evicted from District 6. The father said, as he and his wife and children viewed their home disconsolately, 'I do not know what they do and yet I *do* know what they do,' adding, 'May God forgive them. Two thousand years ago Jesus said, "Father, forgive them, they do not know what they are doing." '[31]

The 'Eminent Persons Group' sent by Commonwealth leaders to visit South Africa saw this same spirit in Nelson Mandela. 'We found him unmarked by any trace of bitterness despite his long imprisonment. His overriding concern was for the welfare of all races in South Africa in a just society; he longed to be allowed to contribute to the process of reconciliation . . . ,' they reported.[32] Indeed, the Commonwealth representatives considered the quality of black leadership to be outstanding. 'Their achievement in bringing about popular and trade union mobilization in the face of huge odds commands respect. Their idealism, their genuine sense of non-racialism, and their readiness not only to forget but to forgive, compel admiration.'[33]

Thus South Africa is confronted by only two ways forward, one dominated by those who say, 'How can I forgive those who have killed so many before me for the sake of capital?'[34] or whatever may be the cause for killing, and the other by those who can sympathize with Dennis Brutus as he writes:

> To understand the unmanning powers of fear
> and its corrosive action
> makes it easier to forgive.[35]

With the emergence of F.W. de Klerk as President it seems that South Africa is about to explore the route hinted at by Dennis Brutus. First, de Klerk's unbanning of many organizations, including the Communist Party, and the release of Nelson Mandela from prison have given hope. Secondly, his announcement of the repeal of certain acts has convinced most people in the country that he is serious. As one editorial observed:

> President F.W. de Klerk has demonstrated beyond doubt that he is sincere in wanting to lead South Africa towards a multi-racial society. His announcement that three of the main pillars of apartheid, the Land Act, the Group Areas Act and the Population Registration Act, are to be abolished is the latest and most dramatic step that he has taken in that direction.[36]

This is the tangible sign of a change of heart in the Nationalist Party (though there are many on its right wing deeply opposed to these policies); there have been other, less precise, straws in the wind of change. When the Foreign Secretary, Pik Botha, said that 'to allocate rights and privileges on the basis of physical characteristics was really tantamount to sin . . . of sinning against God because He created all of us',[37] it seemed that the Dutch Reformed Church's declaration of *apartheid* as a heresy had taken root. He was echoing the remarkable *mea culpa* declared earlier by the Deputy Foreign Affairs Minister, with full cabinet approval, at a conference in Oslo in May 1990: 'Apartheid was a dreadful mistake that blighted our land and its people.' It was a root cause of much of the violence, he added.[38]

There is, of course, an economic aspect to the changes (business does not think *apartheid* is economically sensible), but the shafts of repentance must not be underestimated. Indeed, as if to underline Pik Botha's statement, his deputy said in parliament that the government had 'failed to listen to the laughing and crying of our people. That must never happen again. I am sorry for having been so hard of hearing for so long, so indifferent.'[39]

To help this process forward the government encouraged the Churches of South Africa to convene a national conference. Church leaders met at Rustenberg in the Transvaal in November 1990. Here the issues of peace, reconciliation, repentance, forgiveness and justice and reparation were explored. 'We come here,' said Desmond Tutu in his opening talk,

> not to engage in recrimination, not to engage in accusation and counter-accusation . . . We come to stand under the judgement, all of us, of the cross of Christ . . . We must ourselves be reconciled. The victims of injustice and oppression must be ever ready to forgive. That is a gospel imperative. But those who have wronged must be ready to say, 'We have hurt you by this injustice . . . We are sorry. Forgive us.' And the wronged must forgive.[40]

Speaker after speaker then took up different aspects of the theme. Pastor Ray McCauley, for example, read out a confession on behalf of the charismatic churches for their lack of opposition to *apartheid*, often by their silences, and asked for forgiveness. Beyers Naudé spoke of the need for penitence and restitution to achieve reconciliation.[41] Father Smangaliso Mkhatshwa addressed himself to the justice issue, especially over land distribution.

But the address that set the gathering alight was one by Professor W.D. Jonker from Stellenbosch University. 'I confess before you and before the Lord,' he said, 'not only my own sin and guilt, and my personal responsibility for the political, social, economical and structural wrongs that have been done to many of you, but *vicariously* I dare also to do that in the name of the NGK of which I am a member, and for the Afrikaans people as a whole. I have the liberty to do just that, because the NGK at its latest synod declared apartheid a sin and confessed its own guilt of negligence in not warning against it and distancing itself from it long ago.'[42]

The response to this declaration of repentance on behalf of white Dutch Reformed Christians was immediate and warm. Archbishop Tutu said that when confession is made 'then those of us who have been wronged must say, "We forgive you". Together we may move to the reconstruction of our land.'[43]

The implications of this gathering are immense, for it means that once again the Dutch Reformed Churches in South Africa can become a part of the South African Council of Churches and of the World Council of Churches. Since 75 per cent of South Africans are involved in churches, great possibilities for good can come from this gathering of leaders if worked out at the local level.

If the Rustenberg Declaration issued at the end of the conference, with its call for confession, repentance, forgiveness, and restitution for the sins of racism and unequal opportunities, and its summons to make a new start – a Bill of Rights, a democratic process for all, and a concern for more equality in housing, work, education, health and welfare – is attended to, then South Africa's long agony may be coming towards an end.

One major theme running through the Rustenberg gathering was violence: from the state (via the military and the police) and violence between blacks. The most tragic aspect of the situation, both before and since the release of Nelson Mandela, has been the constant outbreaks of fighting between sections of ANC and of Inkatha, the Zulu movement led by Chief Buthelezi – a conflict that has claimed several thousand lives, especially in Natal and in Soweto. The hostility seems to have arisen out of differing perceptions of political reality. Buthelezi, who has perhaps handled the Afrikaners with some measure of forgiveness, has allowed himself to be perceived as a government-sponsored leader, through accepting the status of a homeland for the Zulus under the *apartheid* system – though not accepting 'independence' – and through his non-participation in the mass democratic movement. However, Buthelezi made frequent calls for the release of Mandela from prison.

Since Mandela's release there have been several attempts to bring the two leaders together, and this was finally achieved in January 1991, when representatives of Inkatha and the ANC met. It was the first meeting between Mandela and Buthelezi for twenty-eight years. With both leaders urging the two sides to 'make peace' a new start has been made. The establishment of a joint commission to monitor alleged incidents and a joint tour of Natal Province all bring some hope to a situation that has been rapidly getting out of control. The acceptance by both Inkatha and the ANC of the right of the other to political existence is another step forward, however complicated it makes the process of negotiating with the government. Also encouraging is the meeting in Zimbabwe between the leader of the PAC and Mandela, initiated by President Mugabe.

Thus, despite a calamitous history in South Africa this century, a start is being made on forgiveness in politics at a national level, drawing on a thread which has been present all along, in individuals and groups. Perhaps South Africa is the only country of which this can be said in such a profound way. As one journalist has observed:

> The effect of an official National Party confession . . . would have a powerful impact on the black population, especially once Mr de Klerk has made good on all his promises to scrap apartheid. A readiness to accept a plea for forgiveness, and make that a solid basis for reconciliation, is one of the more striking characteristics of black culture in South Africa.[44]

If one's enemy can become one's friend, as has happened powerfully between Nelson Mandela and F.W. de Klerk, then it is indeed the morning after *apartheid*.

THEOLOGICAL REFLECTIONS
by Donald W. Shriver, Jr

WESTERN THEOLOGIANS reading this book are likely to be discomforted by the notion that forgiveness – or any other term signifying a claim central to religious scripture and religious history – is a 'fact' comparable to the facts of science. Current Western theology seeks to discern the special realm where 'the idea of the Holy', or the like, is safe from reduction to scientific description. For this theological method, faith in God and all its entailments involve the believer in negotiation with a unique set of realities, in principle little related to other things which humans call real. There has been some safety for theology in this ploy, but the safety has been purchased at the cost of divorcing faith and theology from the ordinary human world.

How very far from all this is the world of the Rumanian writer Petru Dumitriu, quoted by Frost near the end of chapter 2: 'Whence did I acquire the power to love and forgive except from the world, from life itself, which has bestowed it on me, ready for my own use when I was ready to use it?'

How difficult it is for any of us theologians and theological ethicists to comment on these chapters when most of us are ill-equipped by our education to accept *this* thought-world as the one in which theology can legitimately be at home. The American novelist Flannery O'Connor, a Roman Catholic, summarized this difficulty – and two hundred years of Western debate between theology and science – when she observed to a college audience twenty-five years ago: 'In twentieth-century fiction it increasingly happens that a meaningless absurd world impinges upon the sacred consciousness of author or character; author and character seldom go out to explore and penetrate a world in which the sacred is reflected.'[1] She could have substituted 'theology' for 'fiction'.

Christians and their theologians have a stake in the intellectual sea change called for here. Like peoples of some (not all) other religious faiths, our faith implicates us in relations between what we perceive as *real* and what we perceive as *important* in the human world. That is one thing we mean when we call the context of our faith 'historical'. Like our neighbours around the earth, we are concerned with the place of our human hopes in the matrix of reality as a whole. If some of the great concepts of our tradition – truth, justice, mercy, love, the sacred, the divine – have no place in the ordinary rounds of human life, we may be unconsciously preparing to abandon first these concepts and then the faith-tradition itself.

Classically, that tradition has called its adherents to behold, to follow, and to be transformed by the presence of God in human affairs. We cannot believe in a holy presence once in our history which has no continuity with our present. Even the most ardent Christian acclaimer of the centrality of the cross and the resurrection of Jesus as the true saving events of world history believes that the Spirit of God connects Jesus to us in the present moment. So of what does this connection consist? What is it like? Where is it visible for those with eyes to see? Is it present only in the deep sacred consciousness of individuals, or it is as truly present in some of the facts of some of the histories in which we presently live? If Jesus Christ really is a revelation of the Creator who made the universe, must we not expect to glimpse conformities between our knowledge of that universe and our knowledge of the One we perceive in that revelation? These are questions old to theological discourse in the Christian tradition. It is time we addressed them again, and this book is an aid to the addressing.

It aids us, not only because it assumes and tests the proposal that forgiveness is a fact in human politics; but also because it invites us to revisit the human world of the Bible and ask again if it is the same world in which we still live. The fashion in scientific, historical, and even theological sciences is to stress the differences between the world according to the Bible and many subsequent human worlds. From my reading of it, the

Bible is remarkably concerned with as human and as real a world as any that humans ever lived in. For all of its fictional and mythological features and for all of its dramatic unmodern-sounding evidences of the active presence of God in the world, the most striking thing about the Bible is that its characters are as humanly real as many of my neighbours. And they are a lot more real than many of those who march, in comedy or tragedy, across my television screen.

In saying this, I am opening a door to the possibility that God is as present to ordinary human life today as ever God was present to Moses and the disciples of Jesus. This is a vulnerable proposal on my part, for my perceptive apparatus is apparently clogged with filters that explain away the meaning of certain facts before theological discernment gets invited to perform on my personal intellectual stage. But I, like other present-day theologians, may be in great need of *metanoia*[2] on all these points. If I am properly to repent, as the Bible and the narratives in this book invite me to do, I will have to be vulnerable to some new ways of looking at old facts and some new discerning of facts overlooked. In being thus vulnerable, I may have to open up the ghetto of theology's niche to commerce with the prolixity of human concerns we call the 'public world'. In that world, in the centre of the village, as Bonhoeffer liked to say,[3] God is present – as truly present, Christians believe, as in the life, death, and resurrection of that most real of human beings, Jesus of Nazareth. We cannot believe in 'Jesus Christ, the same yesterday, today, and forever',[4] without believing that the powers, the teachings, the purposes, the centrality, and the saving grace of his life pertain to us still, *incarnately* and *eschatologically*, if I may use those great terms: incarnately, because God means to be present in human life and not just episodically to it; eschatologically, because the real world is on its way to a redemption 'above all that we ask or think'.[5] Let other theologians put the matter differently and more cautiously; but let us all open ourselves anew to the possibility that 'the one with whom we have to do' is at least as close to us concretely as is our neighbour next door. The author of such stories as the Good Samaritan and the healer of such people as blind beggars would seem to want us to think this way.

Regularly in the history of Christian thought the reform of

that thought has taken the thinkers back to the Bible for some elementary rehearsals of what God asks the faithful to think about. Hence my return, in the following pages, to some perspectives on forgiveness and politics discernible in the two testaments of the Christian Bible. At the end, I shall reflect on some issues which Christians, like Brian Frost and me, should continue to ponder, if we are to perceive accurately the relation of forgiveness to human politics.

EMMANUEL: GOD AS PARTNER IN OUR HISTORY

Like many other ancients, the early Hebrews encountered God in their midst, but usually as a surprise. As Creator, God was powerfully present everywhere; but as Companion and Protector of mere human beings, God was surprising. This double experience rings right through the opening verses of Psalm 8:

> When I look at thy heavens, the work of thy fingers,
> the moon and the stars which thou hast established;
> what is man that thou art mindful of him,
> and the son of man that thou dost care for him?[6]

'Majestic' is the 'name of God', cries the psalmist, 'in all the earth.' Not even the discoveries of modern astronomy concerning the size of the universe would have been likely to have intimidated the Hebrew mind on this point. The difficult point, then and now, was to believe in the special care of the Creator for creatures like the psalmist. From many a latter-day perspective, *homo sapiens* is an absurd example of species-egotism. The religion of the early Hebrews seldom failed to express astonishment at the possibility that humans are particularly important in the divine scheme of things, an astonishment fed and re-fed by Israel's belief that as a nation it had been 'created' in Egypt, in rememberable time and in circumstances of deliverance from great political evil. Remarkable in this theology of nationhood was the theme, asserted now and again by the Hebrew prophets, that the God of Israel had purposes for this people beyond their own immediate human purposes. Confusing the two was one expression of idolatry; observing the difference meant seeing Israel as the servant of a divine care for all of humanity.

In the social history of the Hebrews – as seen especially in Isaiah, chapters 40–66, the Book of Ruth, and the Book of Jonah – there thus lay the beginning of a universal perspective on the human drama and a universal ethic. In Israel, God is teaching the world something. In other nations, God is teaching Israel something, too. In them all, God is on the way towards the creation of a humanity that is human indeed by God's own measurement: humans delivered from captivities like those of Israel – from a society torn apart by idolatry, exploitation, violence, and self-aggrandizement to a society held together by reverence for the Creator, neighbourly mutual care, respect for life, and care for the community's survival.

All of these themes in the prophets and laws of Israel were at once matters of religion, ethics, and politics. The great debate over the institution of kingship in the post-Exodus period, for example, swirled around the memory, kept fresh by the prophets, that a divinized king had kept Israel in slavery in Egypt; and around the perception, clear to any honest political observer, that the religious absolutization of anything human leads to great corruption of the human. Idolatry has practical consequences, especially in politics. Right religion stays separate enough from the political realm to remind its leaders that they are sinful, fallible humans. But to do this, religion must remain in close touch with politics. The political realm must make room for the witness of religion here, there, and anywhere by the faithful; for God cannot be institutionalized. This is only one illustration of how religious faith influenced the political ethic and political culture of ancient Israel; but the illustration obviously relates to a key principle in modern Western democratic thought – the 'secular' character of government. (Culturally Westerners are almost in danger of losing the meaning of the word secular. Who can understand what secular means in the absence of the sacred?)

To speak this way is also to illustrate the inseparable connections of religion, ethics and social institutions in ancient Israel. What is religious faith if not the substance of the purpose and point of human existence itself? And who can grasp the meaning and the purpose of the God of Abraham apart from one's neighbours? And how do neighbours 'dwell together in unity'[7] without the communal structures and exchanges of politics? Ethics in Israel had to do with what bound people together into a community. It had little to do with that subjective individualism whereby every human conscience is expected to be its own guide. (On the contrary, in the book of Judges the description of social chaos is, 'everyone did what was right in their own sight'.) Individual judgement, like individual good, is not expected to be at radical odds with the judgement and good of one's neighbours. Nor is social law merely restrictive: individuals and communities have reciprocal obligations, which fulfil each other; and even the most imperative of divine commands have benevolence in their preface ('I . . . brought you out of the land of Egypt') and blessing in their consequences ('that it may be well with you').[8]

In Israel God was not only the author of the community's existence and the benevolent law that kept the community existing but was the intervenor on behalf of punishing those who violate the community and its law. The great theological problem of the prophets is here: why is the 'chosen people' so perverse in relation to their own good as defined in their own historical memory and law? The mind of the prophets turned towards a practical remedy for this mystery of Israel's iniquity: what would God do about it? The presumption of the question was that God had intents and purposes which no amount of human iniquity could permanently foil – not high-handed sin, not defeat in war, not exile. The community of humans, beginning with Israel, can be smashed by the sins of humans; but God can and will repair that community. And a leading name for the repair is the forgiveness of sins.

This general context is background for a puzzle that should intrigue any careful reader of the Hebrew Bible: deeply embedded in its religious grounding and strikingly absent from its social ethics is the concept of forgiveness. The nature of this puzzle, all in vivid connection with the religious spirit and political setting of much of the ethics of Israel, can be discerned in such documents as Psalm 51, a prayer of repentance attributed to King David 'after he had gone in to Bathsheba', i.e. committed adultery with her and had her husband killed to cover up the resulting pregnancy. This was ordinary idolatrous autocracy in the history of monarchy, then and now. But such kingly behaviour Israel ostensibly fled when it left Egypt. Carelessness about the welfare of the most ordinary citizens was not to be ordinary in Israel, where the flocks of the rich are not to increase at the expense of the lambs of the poor.[9] This total knot of royal sin gets public rebuke 'when Nathan the prophet came to' David, whose own consent to the justice of the rebuke remained embedded in the nation's memory of him as a king human enough to sin greatly and spiritual enough to repent deeply. The unknown author of Psalm 51 describes what he thought would be the interior personal appropriation of that repentance, which, remarkably enough, is addressed exclusively to God. 'Against thee, thee only, have I sinned, and done that which is evil in thy sight.' And from God alone he requests a restoration of his spiritual health: 'Create in me a clean heart, O God, and put a new and right spirit within me. Cast me not away from thy presence, and take not thy Holy Spirit from me.'[10] In a word, forgive me. God is the fundamental guardian of human good as the giver of life and law. God is the one fundamentally offended at insults to that good and the breaking of that law. So also is God the only one who can forgive.

All of this implies a 'high' doctrine of evil in the Hebrew Bible. Evil done a fellow creature is done to God, for whom the community of humans is an object of intense, jealous compassion. This implies a high doctrine of the forgiveness of sin – only God is capable of it. And it explains why forgiveness between humans is so rare a social expectation in ancient Israel. 'Vengeance is mine, says the Lord,'[11] and forgiveness is mine, too, not only as a jealous prerogative but as the unique power rightly to judge human sin and simultaneously to remove its guilt, its damage to the human self, its damage to the human community, and – above all – its damage to the divine–human relationship. Who but God can do all of this? The question is its own answer, the major answer of the Hebrew Bible.

THE NEW TESTAMENT ADVANCE

Biblical scholars observe that, at least in his rules for the behaviour of his followers, Jesus was not radically discontinuous with the teachings of the Hebrew scripture and the rabbis of his time. In the first century CE followers of the Jewish way and the Christian way did not owe adherence to a very different set of social-ethical principles.

There seem to be two major exceptions to this observation. The one is well known: through the theology and leadership of Paul, in particular, the early Christian church opened its membership and its mission to all humans whatsoever. In this sense the new Christian faith was more humanistic than the older Jewish faith; but it would be fairer to say that Christians exploited the universalistic themes of the Hebrew prophetic tradition more consistently than did many of their Jewish neighbours. This was a shift full of potential for future political good and evil. A non-tribalistic understanding of the human, more convincing than Stoicism, now confronted Graeco-Roman culture.[12] The old Greek habit of dividing the world between Greeks and 'barbarians' suffered a fundamental religious blow. But this new universal humanism also became available as a new resource to fortify state autocracy. By the end of the fourth century, the new religion of Christianity was in the saddle of power in a state whose emperor had declared this faith as the only legitimate one for citizens of the declining Roman Empire.

The other innovation in early Christianity stems rather directly, the New Testament suggests, from the teachings of Jesus: *forgiveness becomes the centre of the Christian social ethic.* Still in place for Jesus is the conviction that God judges and forgives human sin; but now the disciples of Jesus are to understand forgiveness as a transaction mandated between human beings, not reserved to the divine–human encounter. 'Forgive us our debts as we forgive our debtors,' he teaches his disciples to pray. There is no equivalent to this petition in the Hebrew Bible and none, to my knowledge, in the contemporary teaching of the rabbis. It is the only petition in the 'prayer which the Lord taught us' which he saw fit to underscore in the explanatory note of Matthew 6:14–15. There he makes forgiveness by God interdependent with (if not dependent upon) human forgiveness – a teaching that has caused Christians of Pauline persuasion untold difficulty. We can just barely understand that we are to be empowered to forgive our neighbours by the matchless forgiveness of God; but will the Great Forgiver, who saves us 'by grace through faith', wait to forgive us until we have forgiven? That is the implication of Jesus' teachings in this prayer, and little in either the Matthean or the Lukan version of the prayer suggests otherwise.[13]

More than once in the ministry of Jesus he himself offered forgiveness to others for their sins; and the resulting outrage from religious officials must have been genuine on their part. 'Who can forgive sins but God alone?'[14] A faithful Jew of the time had to understand that forgiveness is one transaction for which God alone can be responsible. But Jesus does not claim the power to forgive as merely proof of his unique divine powers. He meant to share that power with all whom he invited to 'follow me'. In turn, they are expected to share it. It is possible now for any human to recover from the sins of the past, to enter into a renewed community with both the Creator and fellow creatures. But once on that path, once in that community, the law of forgiveness reigns supreme. Forgiveness is the guarantee that the people of God will survive their own sins, their alienation from God and one another. Forgiveness is a decisive deliverance from one's own inclinations to evil. But not to forgive is, in turn, to yield to the most dangerous of temptations, the most blatant defiance of the vast kindness of God.[15] 'Vertical' and 'horizontal' forgiveness, for Christians, are now inescapably connected.

Jesus expected the connection to be expressed in the ordinary communal life of his followers, but from early times many must have understood forgiveness as a stance and action which their faith in him also required them to take *publicly* towards their own persecutors. Otherwise they would not have attributed a forgiveness-intercession to Jesus himself in the midst of his public execution, nor would the Book of Acts have recorded the martyr Stephen's imitation of that prayer in his own dying moments.[16]

Norms for Christian behaviour in public today are not the same, however, as norms that Christians have a right to expect the public and its officers to observe; and herein is one of the great issues of Christian theology and ethics from New Testament times on. This book is evidence of the continuing importance of the debate between those who expect much and those who expect little transfer from Christian to public ethics in the politics of the human world. As H. Richard Niebuhr so astutely typologized the debate in his book, *Christ and Culture*,[17] only one group of Christians – the dualists – have been willing to abandon the secular public world to the darkness of alleged ethical ignorance and incapacity. Others, in varying degrees, have affirmed a connection and even an identity between some strands of Hebrew–Christian norms and norms discoverable in this or that human culture. The most frequent connection between the two sources has been the norm of *justice*. Even today theological ethicists find themselves able to converse with politicians, political philosophers, and fellow citizens around their mutual allegiance to the political virtue of justice. I explore the issue further below: if Christians and others are to make good on the claim that forgiveness, too, is a political virtue, they will have to address questions about the interrelation of forgiveness and justice.

Leading theologians from Thomas Aquinas to Luther to Reinhold Niebuhr, however, have resisted the belief that these two can be much connected in the *political* sphere, by Christians or anyone else. Forgiveness in this tradition has been dubbed a rarefied, high level of Christian ethics, scarcely attainable in the Church and not attainable at all in the State. (Whether the Church as a human organization is more or less likely as a sphere of conformity to religious norms is another question. This, too, divides those who write of Christian ethics.) We can perhaps 'do justice', but it is less likely that we can 'love mercy' in the public sphere with its coercions, its violence, its law, its wars and its collective power struggles.

One can ask, in the context of Micah 6:8, if it is intellectually or spiritually legitimate for Christians to settle for justice as an achievable public ethic while relegating forgiveness to some special sphere, e.g. personal relationships. Who is to say that, once launched on the path of walking 'humbly with God', who made and loves this world, the faithful are to subordinate justice to mercy or mercy to justice? Why the hierarchy, in God, in the teachings of Jesus, in Christian ethics, or in human society? The avoidance of political idolatry depends on 'walking humbly with God'; who is to say that political cohesion does not depend equally upon justice and mercy?

To ask these questions is to be well on one's way towards raising a large range of issues which the biblical tradition, theological discussion down through the centuries, and the common experience of us all prevent us from ignoring. Below I have raised and pursued briefly four of these issues, some of them alluded to here. Implicitly and explicitly, many of them have already been addressed in the foregoing pages of this book; and all of them have been abundantly illustrated therein. A long exploration awaits the Christian or any other community which wishes to inquire into the possible indispensability of human forgiveness in human politics. The foregoing sketch of some biblical and theological roots of such inquiry suggest some of the reasons why this book should have been written. Below are the four major issues which, especially in light of the histories recorded here, seem to me to deserve long, diligent, systematic attention in the future. Christians must join others in asking and answering the questions posed here; for ours is an ethic that has to inquire about a public good which is good and public enough to include us all.

1. FORGIVENESS AND POWER

All human organizations, including religious ones, have their politics, because in them some groups and some individuals have power in relation to other groups and individuals. Empirical requirements for the accumulation and exercise of power occupy much attention among political scientists and more attention yet among practising politicians. Achieving power is the ordinary goal of politically ambitious humans.

The right to pardon wrongdoers, or to remit penalties deemed due them for their wrongs, has been claimed for the top officials in some political systems, most notably the Roman Empire, which expected its generals to 'spare the vanquished' and gave its emperors the right to commute a death sentence.[18] Most state governors in the United States have this power; but political systems tend to be stingy with it, for the political problem of lawbreaking can only be resolved with a reaffirmation of the authority and power of the law itself.[19] Whenever high officials relent in their meting out of penalties for wrongdoing, they always reassert that wrong was done. We have many illustrations of this phenomenon in this book. The Hebrew–Christian tradition long ago understood forgiveness in this light: it is a way of affirming norms in the very process of seeking to lift from wrongdoers the full penalty due them for their breaking of the norms. Perhaps the chief popular misunderstanding of forgiveness is here: to forgive evil is not to forget it or to abolish all penalty for the evildoers. Nor is it to ignore their repentance, acts of restitution, or other responses to the damage they have done. Forgiveness has to be consistent with just judgement on one side and just repentance on the other.

The formal right to forgive penalties rightly due offenders, however, is a power fraught with much ambiguity precisely for those political leaders concerned foremost with the preservation and increase of their own power and influence. The latter depends very much on how their publics perceive them in their actions *vis à vis* enemies of public law and justice. In my country, by pardoning Richard Nixon soon after his resignation from office for his part in the Watergate scandal, President Gerald Ford may have forfeited the margin of voter preference which he needed to be elected in 1976. On the other hand, by pardoning young men who had refused to participate in the Vietnam war, President Jimmy Carter probably gained more power than he lost, because larger numbers of Americans felt the need to heal the fissures in the body politic that were the public legacy of that war. In doing so, Carter surely lost support among those who felt, with some justice, that they had paid the cost of obedience to the draft law while others got away with disobedience.

Pardons can add some major increments of power to the pardoner: the power of gratitude is one, but more concretely and politically another is the power of restored human relationships and all that flows from them. Put over-simply, forgiveness can make friends of enemies; and that can be a politically powerful fact, as in the case of the post-World War II treaties between the Allies, West Germany and Japan. Frost's descriptions of these treaties make clear that the element of forgiveness in them had powerful political justification in collective interests;

but the element may nonetheless be real enough. In this context, one can rightly criticize the Versailles Treaty of 1919 as the short-sighted failure of the French and the British to serve their own future interest in living with a dangerous, temporarily pacified enemy. Here the apparent justice of reparation took precedence over national self-interest in avoiding another war. At Versailles, a certain injection of forgiveness would have proven politically prudent.

All this may seem remote from the theology propounded above, but not if one takes seriously the political power of forgiveness. The power to forgive remains one of the awesome powers of human being as well as divine being. As portrayed in the writings of Hannah Arendt, quoted below, the power to forgive, like the power to enter into new social covenants, is an essential power for social change. As we have seen illustrated many times in this book, getting rid of the overpowering under-tow of revenge, resentment, and assorted other hostility can tie a society up into its own past. The power to say, 'Enough! We condemn the evil but resume relation with the evildoers!', is a human action which belongs to the array of powers of those who exercise and increase their power for the building and maintenance of societies. Again, Christians and others who perceive the wisdom of the Bible do not hesitate to make anal-ogies here from God's power to human power: for does not God have to reconcile the 'conflicting truths' of hatred for sin and love for sinners? Any power that effects that reconciliation is a very significant power. The analogy to society-building and society-maintenance among humans is strong. What more difficult political task is there than to build social relationships between humans who have a history of offences against each other? For Hebrew and Christian theology the ultimate pos-sessor of this power is God. No one in the Hebrew Bible stood more in awe of this divine power than Hosea, who 'overhears' the inner struggle of the one who called Israel from Egypt, mourning in mixed anger and grief over the subsequent perfidy of this people. It is the mixture of justice that condemns evil and love that wills a continued relation with evildoers:

> How can I give you up, O Ephraim!
> How can I hand you over, O Israel! . . .

> I will not execute my fierce anger,
> I will not again destroy Ephraim;
> For I am God and not man,
> the Holy One in your midst,
> and I will not come to destroy.[20]

The power to combine justice and love in an act of forgiveness *is* an awesome power, supremely in the God of Abraham and the God of Jesus. But, as we have seen, if for Jesus, too, the divine power to forgive was unique, it was not exclusive. Humans now must share that power towards each other. To refuse to forgive is to refuse repair of a broken relationship. To forgive is to save that relationship. In the 'divine comedy' that plays out its course down to the end of the historical tragedies of humanity, forgiveness is the way of divine victory. It is also the way of at-one-ment – not, we read, between God and Christians only but between God and the world.[21]

2. COLLECTIVE REPENTANCE

Western moral theology has often treated repentance exclusively in the context of individual behaviour. Often in the histories recorded in these chapters, however, we have illustrations of calls by political leaders to confession, memory, and new behaviour on the part of their own or other collectives (see, for example, the speech of Richard von Weizsäcker to the West German Bundestag in May 1985, summarized in chapter 3). There is something biblically resonant about such calls, in spite of the discomfort of individual-minded ethical theories on which most Westerners were educated. Not that the wrestle to distinguish individual from collective responsibility for wrong is foreign to the Bible: Ezekiel foresees a time in the nation's life when no longer will 'the children's teeth be set on edge' because their ancestors have 'eaten sour grapes'.[22] But often in human history burdens of responsibility for politically enacted evil fall on ordinary people remote from the centres of political power. In the aftermath of the Second World War it was impossible with precision to distinguish 'good' Germans and 'ordinary' Germans from Nazi Germans. Many morally sensitive people in Britain looked back with some chagrin at their own applause for some features of Britain's conduct of the war. That chagrin must have accounted for their government's drawing back from conspicuous congratulation of the leaders of Bomber Command who concocted the destructions of Hamburg and Dresden. But ordinary Britons did not directly concoct them.

In politics all dividing lines between those who did, and those who did not, concoct an evil are likely to be fluid. Somewhere down the bureaucratic chain of command from Hitler and Eichmann the Nuremburg judges drew their lines; but they did not do so with moral precision. Beyond the lines lay Germans who participated – as the mass of citizens usually do – in one level or another of collaboration in the German regime of 1933–45. With political evil *in particular* it is likely to be true that 'there is none innocent, no not one'.[23] Thus, in the decision of a human court not to prosecute, nor imprison, nor otherwise to punish a great indistinct mass of collaborators, there is an element of forgiveness, an element of 'letting go', which is the literal meaning of the Greek word used in the New Testament.

For both individual and collective behaviour, from far back in the Hebrew and Christian traditions, the letting-go of evil *behaviour*, or repentance, is the complement of forgiveness, the letting-go of revenge-in-kind. *Readiness* to forgive wrongdoers, so frequently illustrated in the lives of remarkable individuals in these chapters, is one thing; actual forgiveness, in the absence of actual repentance, is questionable – is really a contradiction in terms. Among the unjust slurs upon the reputation of forgiveness as morally justified, one of the most unjust has been the double-accusation that forgiveness flouts justice and ignores repentance, remedy, and other change in the forgiven. The Bible knows of no consummated forgiveness in the absence of repentance, a principle with collective as well as individual relevance. We have every reason to think that contemporary Germans have foresworn Nazism by a huge majority. If they have not, the rest of the world has reason to 'keep the jury out' on the Germans' right to have this part of their past considered genuinely past.

3. FORGIVENESS AND JUSTICE

With an imprecision that could only have annoyed rationalists like Immanuel Kant the biblical names for the norms of human life overlap, imply, include, exclude and modify each other. Over the centuries biblically tutored moralists have used the term 'justice' to mean many different kinds of divine and human action, for the Bible itself uses the term in many contexts and with diverse meanings.

Over against many a rational system of ethics from the Greek to Kantian, biblical moral norms are chiefly directed at the preservation, correction, and restoration of relationships between God and humans and among humans themselves. Not moral knowledge but *capacity for renewed society* is the object of many of these norms. One thinks of the provisions for the 'cities of refuge' in the Hebrew Bible, where people guilty of inadvertent violence ('manslaughter') could flee to avoid the retaliation which they might suffer at the hands of private or public avengers; the 'law of gleaning' which sought to provide economic justice for the poor having no land of their own, and thus to preserve their lives against the inertias of greed and contempt from the rich. And then, there was the most ambitious and least implemented of the social-justice laws of Israel, the Jubilee Year, which mandated a reshuffling of property every fifty years for cutting down the power of the rich to exploit the poor.[24] These specifications of social justice are a long way from the individualistic ethics of 'duty' which Kant and much historic Protestantism have promoted in the past few centuries. This is law addressed not to self-consciousness but to selves-in-relation, selves alienated, and selves restorable to each other.

In the final analysis does forgiveness contradict justice? The answer all depends on what sort of justice one thinks is just, and how forgiveness incorporates justice. In his study of the Hebrew word for 'justice' (*tsedeq*), Norman Snaith says that it means 'more than sound ethical conduct, and shows a persistent tendency to topple over into benevolence, and easily to have a special reference to those who stand in dire need of a Helper'.[25] The author of Psalm 51 was counting on this version of divine justice. As author of justice, God loves justice but, even more, he loves human beings and their restoration to just relationships.

Insofar as forgiveness requires the identification and condemnation of behaviour that has alienated two or more parties to a conflict, it meets Kantian requirements for safeguarding the 'majesty of the law'. But, like Dostoyevsky's Ivan Karamazov, Kant was so outraged at the reality of willed evil in human affairs that he is outraged also at the thought of forgiving that evil. Better, says Ivan, to protest forever against the cruel murder of children than ever to make peace with murderers. Murder, especially, is one crime for which there is no real restitution; and not even capital punishment is a sufficiently 'just' punishment for murder. But punishment is not at the centre of this argument. The question is how to safeguard the authority of the moral. Must we simply make a choice between the moral law and society among sinners? Can we have both? That is the question which Kant and Ivan manage to keep on the intellectual agenda of thoughtful people inside and outside of Christian churches.

In the politics of the twentieth century our collectively devised murders have been many. In a just world could there ever be forgiveness for the perpetrators of some of these atrocities? Whatever criminals we forgive, says Hannah Arendt, we must also be able to punish; and a criminal whose crimes transcend all conceivable restitution and punishment we cannot forgive.[26] But here Christian theology of the divine–human atonement in the cross of Jesus rescues the hope of every moral descendent of David the King: there *is* a depth of forgiveness possible in the mercy of God which is impossible to humans or their institutions. But if Christian theology and ethics take *refuge* in the unique powers of God to combine justice and love, they will have lost touch with the teachings of the very person who went to that cross to save us from our sins. In the power he demonstrated there to forgive, something happened in human form to empower other humans to participate in that form.[27] We Christians insult and diminish what has been revealed in Jesus crucified if we allocate forgiveness again, as in most of the Hebrew scripture, to the recesses of God's unique power. Do we not fall into a version of the docetic heresy when we fail to recognize the correspondence between the truth of Jesus' death and the truth of his teachings? And what are we to make of the resurrection of Jesus if it is not a declaration of present, powerful divine victory over all the powers of evil which pull us away from God and one another? William Temple used to call the ecumenical movement among Christians 'the great new fact of our time'. He was the first to assert the continuity of every reconciliation between Christians with the work of the Spirit who raised Jesus from the dead. But there are other, less ecclesiastical, great new facts. Who are we Christians to deny that this Spirit works in the politics of the great human community? That, perhaps, is the most daring theological assertion that can be made, from the viewpoint of the Christian faith, about the reality of forgiveness in politics or in any other human affair. Here, perhaps, we Western Christians need assistance from the theology of Eastern Orthodoxy: Christ rules the world. He has 'other sheep not of this fold'[28] and other brokenness he means to heal besides our own.

The appeal and difficulty of the Kantian ethic, with its high regard for the moral right, and of the biblical ethic of forgiveness, with its hope for the turning of moral tragedy into moral restoration, came to poignant expression in the novel by Herman Melville, *Billy Budd*. Captain Vere is caught by the unyielding maritime law that exacts capital punishment for murder, regardless of extenuating circumstances. In vain he searches for a way to uphold the majesty of that law (and the future of law and order on his ship) while preserving the life of Billy. Vere's dilemma is analogous to that of any politician who wants to maintain the civil relations of the community and to expunge the uncivil. Again punishment is not the issue here but respect for community survival in face of threat. Yet if *that* is the essence of justice on Vere's ship and in any society, then the greatest triumph of justice is not in actions that preserve the purity of law but in actions that preserve the integrity of the community. Preserving the place of offenders as part of that integrity is the essential work of forgiveness as it initiates healing, offers chances for repentance, and opens up the possibility of future recovery from the tragedies of the past. Revenge, retribution, and even justified punishment, can deepen tragedy in human communities. Forgiveness alleviates tragedy with unexpected blessing. And this is the implication of the very end of Billy Budd's life. As he jumps from the yardarm, he cries, 'God bless Captain Vere!' Readers of the story are left to wonder whose ethic is the more suited to the human condition, to true morality and true tragedy – the law-abider or the merciful? In the final analysis of the Hebrew–Christian view of the world, broken human beings are more valuable than the laws that they break or that break them. Most valuable of all is an act which restores law's authority while also healing the human brokenness. Forgiveness is that act.

Some of the politicians quoted in this book understand these complexities out of repeated experience of them. Kenneth Kaunda, as astute a theologian as politician, put the key issue of forgiveness, justice and political responsibility precisely: 'To claim forgiveness whilst perpetrating injustice is to live a fiction; to fight for justice without also being prepared to offer forgiveness is to render your struggle null and void.' For what is more null than a letter of law that kills, and what is more void than a society 'saved' at the price of destroying it?

4. FORGIVENESS AND THE POWER TO 'CHANGE OUR MINDS AND START AGAIN'

Experienced politicians like Kaunda will never expect from their own or others' theology exact guidance for effecting the justice, compromise and reconciliation proper to particular social conflicts. Nor will wise theologians ever expect to offer such precise guidance to politicians. Indeed, it is likely that much of the reason for beginning to ask about forgiveness as a political virtue comes from the testimony of political leaders and ordinary citizens, not from those who specialize in ethical theory. As the preceding chapters of this book demonstrate many times, humans, in their political communities, stumble and search after new relations with each other. They may have little or no inclination to give these relations high-sounding names like justice, love, community and forgiveness. But this does not mean that such terms are irrelevant or inaccurate descriptions of how in fact we act politically. When Oliver Tambo, President of the African National Congress, says simply, 'We all belong to South Africa and South Africa belongs to us all,' he is stating the intention of the ANC to include white people as well as black people in the new South Africa of the future. In that intention live some strong elements of forgiveness, for the acid test of the presence of forgiveness in politics is the willingness of offended parties to go on living as neighbours to those who have offended them.[29]

All argument over the role of forgiveness in the repairing of the damaged political community turns on the question of what human society requires in order to recover from past evils suffered and to reach toward new shared good in the future. Hannah Arendt was clear about two of the primary requirements: one is the ability of citizens to make covenants or agreements to live reciprocally in new ways that contrast to some of the old ways of the past. But the social freedom to enter with integrity into such new covenants requires a like freedom to set aside, not the memory, but the continuing hostility and thirst for retribution associated with the memory of past evils. This setting-aside Arendt names forgiveness; and, secular Jewish political philosopher that she was, she believed that:

> The discoverer of the role of forgiveness in the realm of human affairs was Jesus of Nazareth. The fact that he made this discovery in a religious context and articulated it in religious language is no reason to take it any less seriously in a strictly secular sense.[30]

These words have the ring of *honest* secularism in them. They share in the ironic appreciation that sometimes comes to religion in an increasingly secular Western culture whose leaders find themselves apologizing for truth that comes dressed in religious clothing. 'Whatever the clothing, it is still true,' they say. People of faith should be allowed their smile and their gratitude at such statements. Even we on occasion drift into that practical agnosticism which does not expect to see anything vividly connected with the Bible or our theology or our church language in the world of everyday. Forgiveness is what we need for that agnosticism!

But the point is that Hannah Arendt, like many people who played roles in the histories recorded in this book, was concerned with the human world of every day. Every day, she observed, humans are either the agents or the victims of wrongdoing or both, and that introduces great division into society. We may not call it that, we may try *not* calling it that, but the

most efficient way out of such division is the way of repentance
(a new covenant) and forgiveness (a new letting-go of the past).

> Only through this constant mutual release from what they
> do can humans remain free agents, only by constant willing-
> ness to change their minds and start again can they be
> trusted with so great a power as that to begin something
> new . . .
> . . . Forgiving, in other words, is the only reaction which
> does not merely re-act but acts anew and unexpectedly,
> unconditioned by the act which provoked it and therefore
> freeing from its consequences both the one who forgives
> and one who is forgiven.[31]

Forgiveness in this view, like governmental policy arrived at by
covenanted popular consent, is *eminently political* and fundamentally facilitative of *social change.* Arendt's claim here is the more
remarkable because most social scientists would discern the
function of forgiveness in the maintenance of social integration
but would not think to assign it a role in social change.

Equally remarkable is the fact that Arendt derives her political
morality here not from some static ideal, as Plato and Kant
might sanction, but from the requirements of everyday communal life. The precepts of political morality arise

> . . . on the contrary, directly out of the will to live together
> with others in the mode of acting and speaking, and thus
> they are like control mechanisms built into the very faculty
> to start new and unending processes . . . Without the fac-
> ulty to undo what we have done and to control at least
> partially the processes we have let loose, we would be
> victims of an automatic necessity bearing all the marks of
> inexorable laws.[32]

Such is the law of gravity or the Hindu *karma.* But such is not
the law of societies whose members want to be free to change
and free for each other after estrangement. Small or large, such
a society must learn some version of forgiveness if it is to *be* a
society for long.

A morally perfect society would have no occasion for forgiveness to hold it together. But we know of no morally perfect
societies, and so we know of none that can dispense with forgive-

ness for their own continuing integrity. The American poet Robert Frost put the matter with stark, accurate simplicity: 'To be social is to be forgiving.'[33] To be political is to be forgiving. In urging forgiveness as an indispensable political virtue Christians speak from within their experience of the exigencies of political life. Theirs is not the only experience of that life nor the only truth about it. We, too, may be surprised when we glimpse that truth, when the reality of what we believe about God resonates so exactly with something we see in the ordinary world. We have to be patient and open towards those of our fellows who do not describe the world as we describe it. But when we perceive a truth about our life and perceive it as a blessing, we are thankful that the blessing is there, in the real world, for us and all our neighbours.

NOTES

1 THE THREAD OF FORGIVENESS

1. Doris Donnelly, *Putting Forgiveness into Practice* (Argus Communications, USA, 1982), pp.ix–x.
2. Hannah Arendt, *The Human Condition* (University of Chicago Press, 1958), pp.237–8.
3. Reinhold Niebuhr, *Moral Man and Immoral Society* (Scribner, New York, 1932), p.268.
4. Reinhold Niebuhr, *Justice and Mercy* (Harper and Row, New York, 1974).
5. Paul Lehmann, *The Transfiguration of Politics* (SCM Press, 1975), p.69.
6. Alan Falconer, 'The Relation of Human Rights to Confidence Building and Detente', *Crucible*, 21 April 1982, p.168.
7. The Rt Revd David Jenkins, in a letter to the author in 1976.
8. Heinz-Horst Schrey, Hans Hermann Walz and W.A. Whitehouse, *The Biblical Doctrine of Justice and Law* (SCM Press, 1955), p. 183.
9. Charles C. West, in a letter to the author on 8 February 1985.
10. Dr Haddon Willmer, 'Forgiveness and Politics', *Crucible*, July–September 1979, p.105.
11. Dietrich Bonhoeffer, *The Cost of Discipleship* (SCM Press, 1959), p.259.
12. M.M. Thomas, 'The Political Message of the Cross', *Towards a Theology of Contemporary Ecumenism* (Christian Literature Society, India, 1978), p.5.
13. Nathan A. Scott Jr (ed.), *The Legacy of Reinhold Niebuhr* (University of Chicago Press, 1975), p.54.
14. Dietrich Bonhoeffer, *Letters and Papers from Prison* (SCM Press, 1953), p.167.

2 THE SOVIET UNION AND HER NEIGHBOURS

1. Henri Troyat, *Tolstoy* (Penguin, 1967), pp.558–63.
2. Nicolas Zernov, *Three Russian Prophets* (SCM Press, 1944), p.124.
3. Troyat, *Tolstoy*, p.562.
4. Edmund Wilson, *To The Finland Station* (Macmillan, 1972), p.250.
5. Ibid., p.316.
6. Ibid., p.316.
7. Wright Miller, *Who Are The Russians?* (Faber, 1973), pp.93–4.
8. Mikhail Gorbachev on Russian television, reported in *The Independent*, 3 Nov. 1987.
9. Report in *The Independent*, 22 Jan. 1988.
10. See report in *The Independent*, 25 Feb. 1988, p.12.
11. Edward Rogers, in a letter to the author in February 1985.
12. Lesek Kolakowski, in a letter to the author in September 1984.
13. Edward Rogers, in a letter to the author in February 1985.
14. Y. Karyakin, *Re-Reading Dostoyevsky* (Moscow, no date), p.132.
15. Paul Tillich, *The Courage to Be* (Collins, 1962), p.104.
16. Letter in *The Guardian*, 6 July 1985.
17. Miller, *Who Are The Russians?*, p.177.
18. George Konrad, *Anti-politics* (Harcourt Brace Jovanovich, New York), pp.76–7.
19. See 'Hungarians try to exorcise the terror of Stalin's era', *The Independent*, 24 Dec. 1988.
20. William Shawcross, *Dubcek* (Weidenfeld and Nicolson, 1970), p.52.
21. *New York Times Magazine*, 12 Jan. 1969, quoted in Shawcross, *Dubcek*, p.149.
22. Z.A.B. Zeman, *Prague Spring*, A report on Czechoslovakia, 1968 (Penguin, 1969).
23. Ibid., p.129.
24. See report in *The Times*, 5 Nov. 1987.
25. Yevgeny Yevtushenko, *The Independent*, 28 Jan. 1991, p.21.
26. Reported in *The Listener*, 25 Oct. 1990, pp.8–9.
27. Alexander Solzhenitsyn, 'Repentance and Self-Limitation of Nations', *From Under the Rubble* (Collins, 1975), p.106.
28. Ibid., p.115.
29. Ibid., p.117.
30. Ibid., p.121.
31. Ibid., p.129.
32. Ibid., p.133.
33. Ibid., p.134.

34. Yevgeny Yevtushenko, *A Precocious Autobiography* (Collins, 1963), pp.24–5.
35. Archbishop Pitrim, quoted by Jim Forest in *Christianity and Crisis*, April 1985.
36. Taken from a letter by Henry Metelmann in *British-Soviet Friendship* (February 1985), p.10.
37. Klaus Krance, 'The Real Russia', *Peace by Peace*, 10 Nov. 1984, pp.4–5. (*Peace by Peace* is the magazine of the Peace People in Northern Ireland.)
38. Jim Forest, *The Tablet*, 25 July 1987, p.800.
39. Gunter Krusche, 'Freedom of Religion under the Helsinki Final Act 1981', a paper presented at a consultation on 'Christianity, Human Rights and Confidence Building', Croydon, 3–8 October 1981.
40. Quoted in Charles W. West, *Communism and the Theologians* (SCM Press, 1958), pp.55–6. The extract is taken from 'I Was Liberated' in *Five Years of Hungarian Protestantism* (Budapest 1950), reprinted in the Hungarian Church Press, 1 April 1950.
41. *The British Weekly*, 25 Jan. 1951.
42. Charles W. West, *Communism and the Theologians* (SCM Press, 1958), p.75.
43. *Index on Censorship* 4, 1973, p.51. (Translated from Norwegian and Russian by Brit Thornberry and Michael Scammell.)
44. Interview with Mikhail Gorbachev in *Time Magazine*, 9 Sept. 1985.
45. Milovan Djilas, *The Unperfect Society* (Allen and Unwin, 1969), p.2.
46. Nicolas Berdyaev, *The Meaning of History* (Geoffrey Bles, 1936), p.224.
47. Fyodor Dostoyevsky, *The Brothers Karamazov* (Heinemann, 1912), p.252.
48. Fyodor Dostoyevsky, *The Journal of An Author*, quoted in E.H. Carr, *Dostoyevsky* 1821–1881 (Allen and Unwin, 1931), p.228.
49. Dostoyevsky, *The Brothers Karamazov*, p.337.
50. Petru Dumitriu, *Incognito* (Collins, 1964), p.353.

3 GERMANY'S ROLE IN EUROPE

1. *The Times*, 24 Oct. 1984.
2. Alan Wilkinson, *The Church of England and the First World War* (SPCK, 1978), p.72.
3. Ibid., p.97.
4. Ibid., p.264.

5. Peter Green, *The Manchester Guardian*, 21 Nov. 1918.
6. Stewart Herman, *The Re-Birth of the German Church* (SCM Press, 1946), Introduction.
7. Ibid., p.126.
8. Ibid., pp.130–1.
9. Ibid., pp.138–9.
10. Harvey Cox, 'The Statute of Limitations on Nazi Crimes – A Theological and Ethical Analysis', *On Not Leaving It to the Snake* (SCM Press, 1968), p.152.
11. Willi Brandt when Chancellor, October 1969, in Peter Lane, *Europe Since 1945: An Introduction* (Batsford, 1985).
12. Gola Mann, *The History of Germany Since 1789* (Chatto and Windus/Hogarth Press, 1984), p.512.
13. *New York Times*, 21 March 1965.
14. Cox, *On Not Leaving It to the Snake*, p.170.
15. *The Daily Mail*, 22 April 1985.
16. Extracts from a speech by President Richard von Weizsäcker in the Bundestag on 8 May 1985, during the ceremony commemorating the 40th anniversary of the end of the war in Europe and of National Socialist tyranny (translation from the advanced text supplied by the West German Embassy in London).
17. Willi Brandt, speech at Mannesmann Steel Plant, Mulheim, 30 April 1970, quoted in Terence Prittie, *Willi Brandt – Portrait of a Statesman* (Weidenfeld and Nicolson, 1974), p.253.
18. Stanislaw Markiewicz, 'A Correspondence of Cardinals', *Polish Perspectives, Summer Quarterly Review* (vol.XXVIII, Warsaw 1985), p.10.
19. Ibid., p.12.
20. Ibid., p.14.
21. Siegfried Buschshluter, *The Guardian*, 21 Sept. 1978.
22. Diocesan Gazette, fourth anniversary of the beginning of the war, quoted in Ronald Jasper, *George Bell, Bishop of Chichester* (OUP, 1967), p.276.
23. Ibid., p.297.
24. Ibid., p.299.
25. Ibid., p.307.
26. See Nikolai Tolstoy, *Victims of Yalta* (Corgi, 1979).
27. Letter in *The Times*, 26 July 1978.
28. H.C.N. Williams (Provost Emeritus of Coventry Cathedral), *The Latter Glory* (The Whitehorn Press, Manchester, no date).
29. *The Independent*, London, 15 Nov. 1990.
30. Gabriel Marcel, *Fresh Hope for the World* (Longmans, 1960), p.24.

For the story of Irene Laure see also the film *For the Love of Tomorrow*.

31. Corrie ten Boom (with John and Elizabeth Sherrill), *The Hiding Place* (Hodder and Stoughton, 1976).
32. BBC Television News, 6.00 p.m., 2 July 1986.
33. *The Daily Mail*, 29 Oct. 1984.
34. Nigel Hamilton, *Monty the Field Marshal, 1944–1976* (Hamish Hamilton, 1986), quoted in *The Observer Review*, 29 June 1986.
35. *The Times*, London, 16 March 1990.

4   ISRAEL

1. Golda Meir, *My Life* (Weidenfeld and Nicolson, 1975), p.290.
2. See Canon Anthony Phillip's article in *The Times*, 8 June 1985, which raised the issue of forgiveness and Judaism, and his subsequent article 'Forgiveness Reconsidered' in *Christian-Jewish Relations*, vol. 19–1, March 1986. In the latter article he argued that 'holocaust theology must be directed at a universal healing of experience for mankind, but it can only do that if it embraces forgiveness'.
3. Rabbi A. Friedlander in *The Times*, May 1985.
4. *Jerusalem Post*, 7 May 1985, p.2.
5. *Jerusalem Post*, 24 May 1985, p.2.
6. *The Independent*, 13 April 1990, p.2.
7. Martin Buber, 'Genuine Dialogue and the Possibilities of Peace', in *Pointing the Way*, collected essays translated from the German and edited by Maurice Friedman (Routledge and Kegan Paul, 1957), p.232. Buber received the prize in the Paulskirche, Frankfurt-am-Main, 27 September 1953.
8. *The Guardian*, 26 June 1985.
9. Ibid.
10. *The Sunday Times*, 2 Oct. 1966.
11. *Jewish Chronicle*, 28 Aug. 1968.
12. Victor Gollancz, *Shall our Children Live or Die?* (Gollancz, 1942), p.64; quoted in Victor Gollancz, *Above All Nations* (Gollancz, 1945).
13. Elie Wiesel, *Night* (Pyramid Books, New York, 1961), p.78.
14. Golda Meir, *My Life* (Weidenfeld and Nicolson, 1975), p.342.
15. Emil Fakenheim, *Quest for Past and Future* (Beacon Press, Boston, 1968), p.23.
16. F.E. Cartus (pseudonym), 'Vatican II and the Jews', *Commentary*, January 1985, p.21.

17. Irving Greenberg, 'Judaism and Christianity after the Holocaust', in *Dialogue*, vol.12, no.4, autumn 1975.
18. Charlotte Klein, 'Guidelines – A Preliminary Balance Sheet', *Christian-Jewish Relations*, vol.17, no.1, 1984, pp.33–4.
19. Ibid., p.35.
20. *The Times*, 1 July 1985.
21. Rosemary Ruether, *Faith and Fratricide* (Search Press, 1975), pp.227–8.
22. Quoted by Dr Paul M. Van Buren in 'Jesus Christ as Shalom between Jews and Christians?', *Dialogue Toward Inter-Faith Understanding*, Ecumenical Institute for Theological Research Yearbook 1984–1985 (Tantur, Jerusalem), p.129.
23. Ibid., p.130 and 137.
24. Geza Vermes, *Jesus the Jew* (A Historian's Reading of the Gospels), (Collins, 1973), p.225.
25. Terezin was an assembly station for Auschwitz, but painted by Nazi propaganda as a 'paradise ghetto', a Jewish 'spa'.
26. Anwar el-Sadat, *In Search of Identity* (Collins, 1978).
27. David Hirst and Irene Beeson, *Sadat* (Faber, 1981).
28. Jonathan Dimbleby, *The Palestinians* (Quarter Books, New York, 1979), p.86.
29. Hirst and Beeson, *Sadat*.
30. Michael Adams, *The Guardian*, 27 Sept. 1984.
31. Sister Emmanuelle, *Sister with the Ragpickers*, translated by Kathryn Spink (Triangle-SPCK, 1982), pp.158–9.
32. Elias Chacour, *Blood Brothers* (Kingsway Publications, Eastbourne, 1984), p.146.
33. Ibid., p.207.
34. Ibid., pp.170–2.
35. Amos Kenan, 'Between Gaza and Tel Aviv, De Facto, We Already Live in a Bi-National State', in *Zionism the Dream and Reality*, a Jewish critique edited by Gary V. Smith (David and Charles, Newton Abbot, 1974), p.192.
36. 'A Father's Prayer upon the Murder of his Son' is taken from *Bahram William Denqani Tafti, 1955–1980* (Church Missionary Society, 1981).
37. Michael Goldberg, *Namesake* (New Haven and London, 1980), p.87.

5   JAPAN AND THE WEST

1. Kyatoro Deguchi, letter to the author, 29 May 1985.
2. Ibid.
3. Kosuke Koyama, *Mount Fuji and Mount Sinai: a Pilgrimage in Theology* (SCM Press, 1984), p.26.
4. Ibid., p.27.
5. Ibid., p.29.
6. Garth Lean, *Frank Buchman* (Constable, 1985), p.388.
7. Ibid., p.387.
8. Ibid., p.389.
9. Ibid., p.389.
10. Ibid., p.390.
11. Ibid., p.390–1.
12. *The Guardian*, 20 Jan. 1986, p.6.
13. Charles W. West, *Communism and the Theologians* (SCM Press, 1958), p.43.
14. *The Statesman*, 15 Sept. 1952.
15. Martin E. Weinstein, *Japan's Post-War Defence Policy 1947–1968* (New York, 1971).
16. *Washington Evening Star*, 18 Dec. 1957.
17. *The Guardian*, 7 Sept. 1984.
18. David Watts, *The Times*, 7 Aug. 1985.
19. Laurens van der Post, *The Night of the New Moon* (Hogarth Press, 1970), p.154.
20. Ernest Gordon, *The Miracle of the River Kwai* (Fontana/Collins, 1962), pp. 157–8.
21. Ibid., p.162–4.
22. Ibid., p.168.
23. Roy McKay, *John Leonard Wilson: Confessor for the Faith* (Hodder, 1973), pp.31–2.
24. Ibid., p.37.
25. Ibid., p.178.
26. *The Daily Mail*, 13 June 1984.
27. BBC Television News, 6.00 p.m., 28 Feb. 1985.
28. 'Japanese War Veteran Plans River Kwai Temple', *Bangkok Post*, 19 Aug. 1976, and *Japan Times*, 13 Oct. 1976.
29. Toyohiko Kagawa, 'Naimida to Katuru' (A Conversation with Tears) written and published in English in *The Christian Century*, 5 Jan. 1938. The poem was written shortly after the outbreak of the second Sino-Japanese war.
30. Funiko Amano, 'Peace for the Children of the World', Christian Peace Conference 83–4, 3–4 (Prague, 1985), p.36.

31. D.J. Enright, review of Peter Townsend's *The Postman of Nagasaki* (Collins, 1984), in *The Observer*, 1 Aug. 1984.
32. Nichidatsu Fujii, speech on 9 July 1978 in Washington DC, translated by Yumiko Miyazaki and published in *Buddhism for World Peace* (Japan-Bharat Sarvodaya Mitrata Sangha, 1980), p.178.
33. Ibid., p.119.
34. Albert Bigelow, 'Why I am Sailing this Boat into the Bomb-Test Area', *Civil Disobedience*, Feb. 1958, pp.4–6 (reprinted from *Liberation*).
35. Kyatoro Deguchi, letter to the author 29 May 1985.
36. Nichidatsu Fujii, *Buddhism for World Peace*, p.270.
37. Ibid., p.323.
38. Kazoh Kitamori, *Theology of the Pain of God* (SCM Press, 1966), p.150 (trans. of *Kami no Itami No*, Tokyo, 1946).

6 CHINA'S REVOLUTION

1. From a *Daily Telegraph* article, quoted in Roger Garside, *Coming Alive, China after Mao* (André Deutsch, 1981), p.426.
2. Quoted in *Time Magazine*, 23 September 1985.
3. Donald J. Munro, *Concept of Man in Contemporary China* (University of Michigan Press, 1977), p.184.
4. For the wisdom of Confucius see *The Analects of Confucius*, translated and annotated by Arthur Waley (Allen and Unwin, 1938).
5. For an introduction to Confucianism see D. Howard Smith, *Confucius and Confucianism* (Paladin, 1974).
6. For background to China's rulers this century see Sterling Seagrave, *The Soong Dynasty* (Sidgwick and Jackson, 1985).
7. *Mao Zedong* (Bantam Books, New York, 1967), p.76.
8. See *Selected Works of Mao Zedong (S.W.)* (Peking–Foreign Languages Press, vol.4, 1961; vols.1–3, 1965). The specific point can be found in *S.W.* III, p.73.
9. Raymond L. Whitehead, *Love and Struggle in Mao's Thought* (Orbis Books, 1977), p.69. Whitehead quotes as his source, 'The Correct Attitude towards Oneself' (8 March 1967, SCMP no.3901, 17 March 1967, p.19.), although he says he has made some changes in translation after a comparison with the original Chinese.
10. *S.W.* III (pp.90–1), quoted in Whitehead, p.128.
11. For Mao Zedong's view of fraternity see *S.W.* III (p.178) and *S.W.* IV (p.429), Whitehead, p.131.

12. Benjamin Schwartz, quoted in Dick Wilson, *Mao Zedong in the Scales of History* (CUP, 1977), p.34.
13. R.H. Tawney, *Land and Labour in China* (Allen and Unwin, 1932). The book is Tawney's account of his study of Chinese peasant communities in the 1920s.
14. William Hinton, 'Fanshen, a Documentary of Revolution in a Chinese Village', *Monthly Review Press* (New York, 1966), p.332f.
15. See Percy Jucheng and Lucy Guinong J. Fang, *Zhou Enlai: a Profile* (Foreign Languages Press, Beijing, 1986).
16. Reported in *Now*, 12 October 1979.
17. See Fox Butterfield, *China Alive in a Bitter Sea* (Hodder and Stoughton, 1982), p.348.
18. *Selected Works of Deng Xiaoping, 1975–1982*, p.100. Translated by the Bureau for the Compilation and Translation of Works of Marx, Engels, Lenin and Stalin under the Central Committee of the Communist Party of China (Foreign Languages Press, Beijing, 1984).
19. Ibid., p.159.
20. Ibid., p.259. The speech was made at the Third Meeting of the Fifth Plenary Session of the Eleventh Central Committee of the Communist Party of China.
21. Ibid., p.262–3.
22. Ibid., p.281.
23. FE 6764/C7. (The reference is to the Far East section of the School of Oriental and African Studies in London, which files the English translations of Chinese broadcasts in Chinese, and also the text of broadcasts by China in English.)
24. FE/Xinhua, 30 June 1976.
25. FE/Xinhua, 8 Feb. 1979.
26. Philip Short, *The Dragon and the Bear* (Hodder and Stoughton, 1976), p.300.
27. *The Independent*, 26 January 1989, p.12.
28. FE/NCNA in Chinese, 28 May 1980.
29. FE 6430, 28 May 1980.
30. FE 7813, 29 Nov. 1984 (Xinhua in English, 27 Nov. 1984).
31. *Beijing Review*, no.47, 22 Nov. 1982.
32. His Holiness the Dalai Lama, *Collected Statements, Interviews and Articles* (Dharamsala, India, 1982).
33. Ibid., p.71.
34. *The Independent*, 16 June 1988.
35. Deputy Secretary Dangzin, reported on Lhasa Radio 11 Dec. 1985 (FE 8135, 16 Dec. 1985).
36. FE 7980, 18 June 1985.

37. *China Study Project Bulletin* (28 Nov. 1985), p.21.
38. Chen Zemin, *Chinese Christians Speak Out*, Addresses and Sermons (New World Press, Beijing, 1984), p.44. Chen Zemin is a Professor of Systematic Theology and Vice-Principal of Nanjing Union Theological Seminary.
39. K.H. Ting, 'Fourteen Points from Christians in the People's Republic of China to Christians Abroad', ibid., p.52.
40. Ibid., p.114.
41. Ibid., p.50.
42. *Beijing Review*, no.41, 8 Oct. 1984.
43. Editorial in *Beijing Review*, 8 Oct. 1984.
44. Jonathan D. Spence, *The Gate of Heavenly Peace: The Chinese and Their Revolution 1885–1980* (Faber and Faber, 1982), pp.349–50.
45. *Beijing Review*, vol.25, no.11, 15 March 1982.
46. *A KMT War Criminal in New China*, written by She Zui with the assistance of Shen Meijuan, translated by Liang Xintu and Sun Binghe, Hunan People's Publishing (Foreign Languages Press, Beijing, 1984), p.122. In all, eleven senior military personnel were given special pardons.
47. Ibid., p.129.
48. Dai Houying, *Stones of the Wall*, translated by Frances Wood (Michael Joseph, 1985).
49. His Holiness Tenzin Gyatso, the fourteenth Dalai Lama, *Kindness, Clarity and Insight* (Lion Publications, New York, 1984).
50. *Ta Chuan*, chapter 5, p.3, quoted in Da Liu, *The Tao and Chinese Culture* (Routledge and Kegan Paul, 1981).
51. 'An Interview with Ba Jin' by Jang Yi, included in Ba Jin, *Autumn in Spring and other stories* (Panda Books, Beijing, 1981), p.147.

7 INDIA'S STRUGGLE FOR INDEPENDENCE

1. C.F. Andrews (ed.), *Mahatma Gandhi, His Own Story* (Allen and Unwin, 1930), p.44.
2. Ibid., p.45 (*ahimsā* means non-injury).
3. Ibid., p.121.
4. Ibid., p.121.
5. See M.K. Gandhi, *The Story of My Experiments with Truth* (Phoenix Press, 1949), p.320.
6. Mahadev Desai, *The Gospel of Selfless Action – The Gita According to Gandhi* (Navajivan Publishing House, Ahmedabad, 1946), quoted in Louis Fischer, *Life of Gandhi*, part 1, ch.4, pp.32–5.
7. M.K. Gandhi, *Satyagraha in South Africa* (Madras, 1928), p.32.

8. M.K. Gandhi, *Hind Swaraj*, 1921, Introduction by Louis Fischer.
9. Andrews (ed.), *Mahatma Gandhi*, p.164.
10. Mahatma Gandhi, *Collected Works*, vol.v, p.299; taken from Dhamamjay Keer, *M. Gandhi: Political Saint v. Unarmed Prophet* (Bombay Popular Prakshan).
11. Louis Fischer, *Life of Gandhi*, part 1 (Cape, 1951), p.117.
12. Ami ya Chakravarty (ed.), *A Tagore Reader* (Macmillan, 1961), p.24.
13. Ibid., p.203.
14. Report of the Committee appointed by the Government of India to investigate the disturbances in the Punjab (HMSO, 1920), Command 681.
15. *Young India*, 11 Aug. 1920.
16. *Young India*, 8 Dec. 1920.
17. *Young India*, 23 March 1921.
18. *Young India*, 23 Feb. 1922.
19. Chakravarty (ed.), *A Tagore Reader*. Tagore's letter to C.F. Andrews from London was sent in 1928 and can be found in the section 'Letters to a Friend'.
20. Verbatim proceedings of the 1922 Trial of Gandhi – M.K. Gandhi, *Speeches and Writings of M. Gandhi* (G.A. Nateson, Madras, 1933).
21. *Young India*, 2 Oct. 1924.
22. *Young India*, 9 July 1925.
23. *Young India*, 5 March 1925.
24. *Young India*, 5 Jan. 1922.
25. Fischer, *Life of Gandhi* pp.280–1.
26. Ibid., p.266.
27. Ved Mehta, *Mahatma Gandhi and His Apostles* (Andre Deutsch, 1977), p.147.
28. Ibid., p.148, quoting a report by Webb Miller, a United Press correspondent.
29. Fischer, *Life of Gandhi*, pp.274–7.
30. Mahadev Desai, *Gandhiji in Indian Villages* (Triphicane Madras, S. Ganeson, 1927), p.166.
31. Fischer, *Life of Gandhi*, p.267.
32. *Young India*, 2 April 1931.
33. *Harijan* (formerly *Young India*), 18 Feb. 1939.
34. *Harijan*, 13 April 1940.
35. *Harijan*, reprinted in *Tribune*, 23 Oct. 1942.
36. *Harijan*, 22 June 1940.
37. *Harijan*, 6 July 1940.

38. Sibnarayan May (ed.), *Gandhi, India and the World* (Philadelphia Temple University Press, 1970), Introduction.
39. M.K. Gandhi, *Satyagraha* (Ahmedabad, India, 1955), p.103.
40. S.N. Das Gupta, *History of Indian Philosophy*, vol.1 (Cambridge, 1957), p.270.
41. *Bombay Statesman*, 8 Aug. 1942.
42. *Young India*, 16 March 1922.
43. Interview reported by Associated Press in *Bombay Chronicle*, 22 Nov. 1946.
44. See Eknath Easwaran, *A Man to Match his Mountains: Badshah Khan, Non-violent Soldier of Islam* (Nilgiri Press, Blue Mountain Centre of Meditation, USA), p.174.
45. Quoted in Ved Mehta, *Mahatma Gandhi and His Apostles* (André Deutsch, 1977), p.171.
46. Speech in New Delhi, *Delhi Diary*, vol.2 (1947), p.101.
47. *Harijan*, 15 Feb. 1948.
48. Pandit Nehru in Foreword to *Mahatma* (D.G. Tenchulkar, 1951).
49. Taken from N.B. Sen (ed.), *The Wit and Wisdom of Gandhi, Nehru and Tagore* (New Book Society of India, New Delhi), p.170.
50. Thomas Merton, 'Gandhi and the One-Eyed Giant', *Gandhi and Non-Violence* (New Directions, New York, 1964), p.20.

8 BRITAIN AND IRELAND

1. Cecil Woodham-Smith, *The Great Hunger: Ireland 1845–9* (Hamish Hamilton, 1962), p.410.
2. Thomas Jones (ed. Keith Middlemas), *Whitehall Diary*, vol.III: Ireland 1918–1925 (OUP, 1971), p.78.
3. Ibid., p.88.
4. Ibid., p.93.
5. Ibid., p.93.
6. Ibid., p.193 (quoted from *Victory of Sinn Fein*, pp.83–4).
7. See W.B. Yeats' poem 'Easter 1916', *The New Oxford Book of Christian Verse* (OUP, 1972), p.820.
8. See W.B. Yeats' poem 'The Second Coming', ibid.
9. Jones, *Whitehall Diary*, vol.III, p.193.
10. See Terence De Vere White, *Kevin O'Higgins* (Methuen, 1948).
11. It was only in the 1980s that it became clear who performed this act.
12. From a letter sent by Revd Fr Michael O'Carroll to Mrs Una O'Higgins O'Malley, one of Kevin O'Higgins' daughters.
13. Lord Hylton, in a letter to the Rt Hon. Margaret Thatcher, 12

May 1981; published in *Forgiveness and Politics Study Pack 1984*, 'Britain and Ireland – a Test Case?' (out of print).

14. For Britain's responsibility to Ireland see a sermon preached in Westminster Abbey, 14 October 1979, by the Sub-Dean (now the Rt Revd J.A. Baker, Bishop of Salisbury); *Forgiveness and Politics Study Pack 1984* (as note 13).

15. Ibid.

16. Denis Barritt, *Northern Ireland – a Problem to Every Solution* (Quaker Peace and Service/Northern Friends Peace Board, 1972).

17. David Bleakley, *Saidie Patterson – Irish Peacemaker* (Blackstaff Press, 1980), p.89.

18. Liam McLoskey, from an article privately circulated.

19. Stephen Cummins, report in *The Liverpool Daily Post*, 10 March 1989.

20. Denis Faul, *The Guardian*, 28 Dec. 1982.

21. Desmond Wilson, *The Listener*, Easter, 1979. This article was the printed version of a Lent talk on the BBC Northern Ireland service, 20 March 1979.

22. Rt Revd J.A. Baker (see note 14 above).

23. *Guardian Weekly*, 14 Dec. 1980.

24. *The Guardian*, 14 May, 1979, editorial.

25. Philip Donnellan in *The Observer*, 1 Dec. 1985.

26. *Derry Journal*, 12 April 1985.

27. *New Testament*, 1 Peter 7:2–7.

9 THE NORTH AMERICAN EXPERIENCE

1. Christmas broadcast by Her Majesty Queen Elizabeth II, 1976.

2. Billy Graham, address to South African Congress on Mission and Evangelism, Durban 1973, in *I Will Heal Their Land* (African Enterprise, Maseru, Lesotho, 1974), p.329.

3. From notes quoted by Gustavo Gutierrez in *Telegia desde el Reversode la Historia Lima*, February 1977, p. 59.

4. Dee Brown, *Bury My Heart at Wounded Knee* (Bantam Books, 1970), p.418.

5. See James Wilson, 'The Original Americans: US Indians', *Minority Rights Report*, no.31 (new edn, June 1980), p.8.

6. Professor Francis Paul Prucha SJ, in a letter to the author, 15 April 1986. Professor Prucha is the author of a two-volume study *The Great Father: The United States Government and the American Indians* (Lincoln and London, University of Nebraska Press, 1984).

7. Francis Paul Prucha, *The Indians in American Society – From the Revolutionary War to the Present* (University of California Press, 1985), p.94.

8. Wilson, 'The Original Americans', p.22.

9. Ibid., p.23.

10. *The Guardian*, 30 Aug. 1988.

11. Prucha, *The Indians in American Society*, p.90.

12. Paul Radin, *God Struck Me Dead* (Fisk University, USA), Introduction, p.8.

13. James H. Cone, *The Spiritual and the Blues* (Seabury Press, New York, 1972).

14. Eugene D. Genevese, *Roll, Jordan, Roll* (André Deutsch, 1975), p.284.

15. James Baldwin, *The Fire Next Time* (Dial Press, New York, 1963); *Nobody Knows My Name* (Michael Joseph, 1964); *Go, Tell It on the Mountain* (Dell, New York, 1952).

16. Martin Luther King, Junior, *Where Do We Go from Here? – Chaos or Community* (Harper and Row, New York, 1967); taken from James M. Washington (ed.), *A Testament of Hope* (Harper and Row, 1986), p.583.

17. Martin Luther King, *Stride Toward Freedom: the Montgomery Story* (New York, 1958); quoted in Stephen B. Oates, *Let the Trumpet Sound* (Search Press, 1982), pp.70–1. The text of the speech is in the Harry Watchel Papers, New York City.

18. Ibid., p.90.

19. Martin Luther King, 'A Conversation in Ghana' (an interview by Homer A. Jack), *The Christian Century*, 10 April 1957, pp.446–7; quoted in Oates, *Let the Trumpet Sound*, pp.116–17.

20. Martin Luther King, in Washington (ed.), *A Testament of Hope*, p.198. The speech can be found in typescript in Martin Luther King Archives at Boston University.

21. Martin Luther King, *Why We Can't Wait*, paperback edn (New York, 1964); quoted in Oates, *Let The Trumpet Sound*, p.142. The material was originally published in *Ebony*, July 1959, in an article called 'My Trip to the Land of Gandhi'.

22. Martin Luther King Junior, *Why We Can't Wait* (Harper and Row, New York, 1963); quoted in Washington (ed.), *A Testament of Hope*, p.290.

23. Martin Luther King, taken from Washington (ed.), *A Testament of Hope*, pp.217–20. The speech 'I Have A Dream' was published in *Negro History Bulletin*, no.21, May 1968, pp.16–17. It was given on 28 August 1963.

24. Ibid., pp.217–20.

25. Peter Ackroyd, *The Sunday Times*, 29 Dec. 1985, in a review of *The Price of the Ticket – Collected Non-Fiction of James Baldwin* (Michael Joseph, 1985).
26. Martin Luther King, *Strength to Love* (Hodder, 1964), p.52.
27. From reports in *Time Magazine*, 13 Aug. 1965.
28. Coretta Scott King (ed.), *The Words of Martin Luther King* (Collins/Fount, 1984), p.23.
29. *New York Times*, 22 June 1966.
30. The Black Power debate is spelt out in Martin Luther King, *Where Do We Go from Here? – Chaos or Community* (New York, 1968), pp.35–7.
31. Stokely Carmichael was reported in *The New York Times*, 5 Aug. 1966.
32. Fritz Fanon, *Wretched of the Earth* (Grove Press, New York, 1966).
33. See Martin Luther King, *Where Do We Go from Here? – Chaos or Community*.
34. Martin Luther King, 'The Casualties of the War in Vietnam', address to the National Institute, Los Angeles, 25 February 1967.
35. Martin Luther King, from a series of lectures given for the Canadian Broadcasting Corporation; quoted in Oates, *Let the Trumpet Sound*, p.452.
36. Flip Schulke (ed.), *Martin Luther King Junior, A Documentary . . . Montgomery to Memphis* (New York and London, 1976), p.236.
37. *The Evening Standard*, 12 Nov. 1984.
38. Lord George Brown (ed.), *The Voice of History* (Sidgwick and Jackson, 1979).
39. *The Daily Express*, 5 Feb. 1977.
40. *Presidential Proclamation of Pardon* (Public Papers of the Presidents), Proclamation 4483, 21 January 1977, granting pardon for violations of the Selective Service Act, 4 August 1964 to 28 March 1973. *Executive Order Relating to Proclamation of Pardon* – Executive Order 11967, 21 January 1977.
41. John Howard Griffin, *Black Like Me* (Collins, 1962).
42. See *The Readers' Digest*, British edn, Nov. 1968, pp. 163–70.
43. Simon Hoggart, *The Observer*, 19 January 1986.
44. Ibid.
45. Vincent Harding, 'The Challenge of Martin Luther King Junior', given at a conference 'The Black Church and the Third World', Atlanta, Georgia, and reproduced in the magazine *Sojourners*, October 1984, p.21.

10   LATIN AMERICAN RESPONSES

1. Estella Horning, 'Reflexions on the death of a friend', in *Risk*, vol.9, no.1, 1973, World Council of Churches, Geneva; reproduced from the *Brethren Messenger*.
2. See *Cambridge Encyclopaedia of Latin America and the Caribbean* (OUP, 1985).
3. Paulo Freire, *Pedagogy of the Oppressed* (Penguin, 1972), p.30.
4. *Amnesty International*, Special Report, February–March, 1985.
5. Gustavo Gutierrez, *The Power of the Poor in History* (SCM Press, 1983), p.48.
6. *The Guardian* 20 July 1979, p.6.
7. Charles Elliott, 'Nicaragua's Spirit of Forgiveness', *Christian Aid Bulletin*, 1983.
8. Jim Forest, 'Paradigm for a Political Culture of Peace', 1984.
9. BBC television interview, Channel 4 Series on Nicaragua, 28 Oct. 1985.
10. Oxfam Report, 'Nicaragua – The Threat of a Good Example', 1985.
11. Henri Nouwen, 'Christ of the Americas' in *America*, 21 April 1984, pp.298ff. (*America* is the weekly magazine of the Jesuits of the USA.)
12. Ibid., p.299.
13. Amnesty International, *Nicaragua – The Human Rights Record*, published in March 1986.
14. Simon Hoggart in *The Observer*, 29 June 1986.
15. José Miguez Bonino, *Toward a Christian Political Ethics* (SCM Press, 1983), p.112.
16. Giulio Girardi, *Amor Christiano y Lucha de Clases* (Salamanca Editions Siguemes, 1971); quoted in José Miguez Bonino, *Revolutionary Theology Comes of Age* (SPCK, 1975), p.57.
17. Cardinal Arns, speaking in Jack Pizzey's BBC 2 Series 'Sweat of the Sun, Tears of the Moon' – no.6: 'A Continent Crucified', 13 August, 1986.
18. Vamos Caminando, *A Peruvian Catechism* (SCM Press, 1985), p.354.
19. Ibid., p.355.
20. Jon Sobrino, *The True Church and the Poor* (SCM Press, 1985), p.170.
21. Archbishop Romero, Sermon in Divine Providence Hospital Chapel, 24 March 1980.
22. See Rubem A. Alves, *A Theology of Human Hope* (Abbey Press, USA, 1969) for a theology of human hope in Latin America.

23. *The Guardian*, 8 Nov. 1985.
24. *Responsibility of the Common Good*, Declaration of the Uruguayan Bishops, 8 May 1984, no.2179, 23 June 1984, translated by Valerie Dee.
25. *To Contribute to Reconciliation*, Declaration of the Permanent Committee of Bishops, 11 April 1984, translated by Valerie Dee.
26. *The Church and the National Community*, Final considerations, 8 May 1981, Argentine Episcopal Conference, from *Documentos del Episcopado Argentino*, 1965–1984, translated by Valerie Dee.
27. *The Road to Reconciliation*, Permanent Commission of the Argentine Episcopal Conference, 10 August 1982, Buenos Aires, translated by Valerie Dee.
28. Reinhold Niebuhr, *The Irony of American History* (Scribner, New York, 1952), p.63.
29. Gustavo Gutierrez, *The Power of the Poor in History* (SCM Press, 1983), p.76.
30. Donald Campbell, letter to the author, 23 July 1986.

11 AFRICAN IDENTITIES

1. Trevor Huddleston, in his introduction to Olive Schreiner, *Trooper Peter Halket* (Ernest Benn, 1959).
2. Aimé Césaire, quoted in Adeolu Adegbola, 'From Tribalism to Nationhood', in John C. Bennett (ed.), *Christian Ethics in a Changing World* (SCM Press, 1966), pp.194–5.
3. Albert Schweitzer, *Civilization and Ethics* (A. and C. Black, 1923), p.9.
4. Bill Stallybrass in a letter to Lord Hylton, 27 June 1984, used with permission.
5. Lesslie Newbigin, *Unfinished Agenda* (SPCK, 1984), p.242.
6. *Africa*, January 1974.
7. Bishop Festo Kivengere, *I Love Idi Amin* (New Life Ventures, Fleming H. Revell, New Jersey, USA), p.62.
8. See Turi Muhammadu and Mohammed Haruna, 'The Civil War', in Oyeleye Oyedirai (ed.), *Nigerian Government and Politics under Military Rule* (Macmillan, 1979), p.38.
9. A.A. Ayida and H.M.A. Onitiri (eds.), *Reconstruction and Development in Nigeria*. Proceedings of a conference on national reconstruction and development held at the University of Ibadan, 24–29 March 1969) (NISER, Ibadan, 1971), p.46.
10. Okion Ojigbo, *Nigeria Returns to Civil Rule* (Tokion–Nigeria, Lagos, Nigeria), p.45.

11. *Complete Speeches of Ojukwu and some comments of General Gowon 1966–70* (J.C. Brothers Bookshop, 20–26 New Market Road, Onitsha, Nigeria, 1984), pp.62–3.

12. General Gowon, interview in *DRUM* magazine, April 1970. See also Zdenek Cervenka, *A History of the Nigerian War, 1967–70* (Onibonje Press, Ibadan, 1972), pp.149–150.

13. Ntieyong U. Akpan, *The Struggle for Secession 1966–1970* (Frank Cass, 1972), p.xl.

14. Chinua Achebe, *The Trouble with Nigeria* (Heinemann, 1983), pp.45–6.

15. E.A.A. Adegbola, 'Blessed Are the Peacemakers' in *Christian Concern in the Nigerian Civil War* – a collection of articles which have appeared in issues of the *Nigerian Christian*, April 1967–April 1969 (Daystar Press, Ibadan, 1969), p.7.

16. Ibid., p.9.

17. Ibid., p.15.

18. James Macmanus, 'Black Africa's Richest Nation Ruined by Splits', in *The Daily Telegraph*, 28 Aug. 1985.

19. Jomo Kenyatta, *Suffering without Bitterness* (East African Publishing House, 1968), pp.29 and 54.

20. Ibid., p.123.

21. 'Face to Face', BBC TV, 24 August 1961.

22. Kenyatta, *Suffering without Bitterness*, p.188.

23. Ibid., p.189.

24. Ibid., p.201. The article appeared on 24 April 1963.

25. Ibid., p.214.

26. The Rt Hon. Malcolm MacDonald, Introduction to *Harambee! the Prime Minister of Kenya's speeches 1963–64* (OUP, 1964), p.x.

27. Elspeth Huxley, *Out in the Midday Sun* (Chatto and Windus, 1985), p.202. The author was quoting from a speech she heard made by Jomo Kenyatta in May 1963.

28. Jeremy Murray-Brown, *Kenyatta* (Allen and Unwin, 2nd edn, 1979), p.313.

29. Kenyatta, *Suffering without Bitterness*, p.vi.

30. Robert Gabriel Mugabe, *Our War of Liberation*, Speeches, Articles, Interviews 1969–1979 (Mambo Press, Zimbabwe, 1983), p.90.

31. David Smith and Colin Sampson with Ian Davies, *Mugabe* (Pioneer Head, Salisbury, Zimbabwe), p.121 (also Sphere Books, UK, 1981).

32. 'How Rhodesia Almost Stayed White', *The Times*, 1 July 1985.

33. Robert Mugabe, 'Address to the United Nations, 26 August 1980' (Ministry of Information and Tourism, Zimbabwe), pp.12 and 14.

34. David Smith et al., *Mugabe*, p.205.
35. Alec Smith with Rebecca de Saintonge, *Now I Call Him Brother*, (Marshalls, 1984).
36. Quoted in *The International Herald Tribune*, 9 April 1983.
37. *The Times*, 1 July 1985.
38. See Stephen Ndlovu, 'Church Aids Zimbabwe's Search for Peace' in *Church and Peace*, vol.18, no.4, 1988, p.31. *Church and Peace* is a magazine of the Peace Churches in Europe and is published in West Germany.
39. 'Treatment for Traitors', a film produced by Dutch television. The narrative here is a digest of the English dubbing in the film taken down by the author.
40. Kenneth Kaunda, *Kaunda on Violence*, ed. Colin Morris (Collins, 1980).
41. *Zambia: Independence and Beyond*, the speeches of Kenneth Kaunda, edited with an introduction by Colin Legum (Nelson, 1967), p.ix.
42. Ibid., p.192.
43. Ibid., p.138.
44. Kaunda, *Violence*, p.179.
45. Ibid., pp.181–3.
46. Angolan Bishops' Statement, Luanda, 17 February 1984.

12   SOUTH AFRICAN POSSIBILITIES

1. Emily Hobhouse, quoted in John Fisher, *That Miss Hobhouse* (Secker and Warburg, 1971), p.206.
2. Rudyard Kipling, 'The Settler' (1903), in *Rudyard Kipling's Verse 1885–1918* (Hodder and Stoughton, 1917).
3. William Plomer, *Collected Poems* (Jonathan Cape, 1977).
4. Fisher, *That Miss Hobhouse*, pp.269–70.
5. J.C. Smuts, *Jan Christian Smuts* (Cassell, 1952), p.32.
6. Brian Willan, *Sol Plaatje, South African Nationalist 1876–1932* (Heinemann, 1984).
7. Tom Lodge, *Black Politics in South Africa* (Longman, 1983), pp.23–4.
8. Eugene D. Genovese, *Roll, Jordan Roll* (Andre Deutsch, 1975).
9. Albert Luthuli, *Let My People Go* (Collins, 1962).
10. J.H.P. Serfontein, *Ecunews*, March 1985, published by the South African Council of Churches.
11. Alan Paton, *Cry the Beloved Country* (Penguin, 1948).
12. Lodge, *Black Politics in South Africa*, p.6.

13. Dr C.F. Beyers Naudé, 'For the Sake of True Peace', Dom Helder Camara lecture, read for Dr Naudé on 1 June 1983 at the Free University in Amsterdam.
14. Ibid.
15. Steve Biko, *I Write What I Like*, a selection of his writings edited with a personal Memoir by Aelred Stubbs CR (Bowerdean, 1978), p.32.
16. Ibid., p.86.
17. Ibid., pp.120–1.
18. Ibid.
19. Ibid., p.136.
20. Ibid., pp.214–5.
21. For an account of this see Ellen Kuzwavo, *Call Me Woman* (Women's Press, 1985), pp.48–9.
22. Desmond Tutu, interview in *The Observer*, 18 Nov. 1984.
23. BBC television, *Face the Press*, 6 October 1985.
24. Desmond Tutu, 'Enthronement Sermon', published in *South African Council of Churches News*, no.1, March 1985.
25. Desmond Tutu, *Hope and Suffering* (Fount/Collins, 1983), p.99.
26. Ibid., p.131.
27. Nelson Mandela in *Ecunews*, March 1985. Address read by Zinzi Mandela on 10 February 1985 at Jabulani Amphitheatre.
28. Osward Mtshali, 'Ride Upon the Death Chariot', in *Sounds of a Cowhide Drum* (Renoster Books, 1971), p.64.
29. Memorial Service, 16 June 1985, p.24. The service was published after its adoption by the Executive of the South African Council of Churches, 16 April 1985.
30. Charles Kadhikwa, unpublished narrative in the hands of G.W. Cleaver, Selly Oak Colleges, Birmingham (used with permission).
31. 'Last Supper in Hortsley Street', People to People series, Channel 4 television, 16 June 1985.
32. *Mission to South Africa*, The Commonwealth Report (Penguin, 1986), p.73.
33. Ibid., p.137.
34. 'Amandla', Riverside Theatre, London, September 1985.
35. Dennis Brutus, 'A Letter to Basil' in *A Simple Lust* (Heinemann Educational Books, 1973).
36. *The Independent*, 4 Feb. 1991.
37. Report in *The Independent*, 23 Feb. 1991, p.10, of Donald Woods' BBC television programme 'Assignment', 13 February 1991.
38. CCSA Analysis no.19 (undated).
39. *The Independent*, 23 Feb. 1991, p.10.

40. National Conference of Church Leaders in South Africa, Hunters Rest, Rustenberg, Transvaal, 5–9 November 1990.
41. Ibid., p.5.
42. Ibid.
43. Ibid.
44. John Carlin, *The Independent*, 23 Feb. 1991, p.10.

THEOLOGICAL REFLECTIONS

1. From a 1973 newspaper report. In her novels O'Connor practised what she preaches here, especially in her discernment of numinous evil in the human world.
2. The Greek word *metanoia*, literally 'change of mind', has New Testament connotations of repentance affecting the whole self, and mind-changing as a moral imperative for learning to *see* the world in new ways. It has an arresting modern quality, especially as echoing one of the impressive intellectual virtues of science which submits its best theories to constant re-evaluation and new experiment.
3. Cf. Dietrich Bonhoeffer, *Letters and Papers from Prison*, enlarged edn, ed. Eberhard Bethge (Macmillan, New York, 1971), p.282.
4. Hebrews 13:8.
5. Ephesians 3:20.
6. Psalm 8:3–4.
7. Psalm 133:1.
8. Exodus 20:2 (cf. Exodus 20:12).
9. 2 Samuel 12:1–7.
10. Psalm 51:4, 10–11.
11. Romans 12:19, Paul's adaptation of Deuteronomy 32:25.
12. Cf. Charles N. Cochrane, *Christianity and Classical Culture* (Oxford University Press, 1957).
13. Ephesians 2:8. For a discussion of this issue, see Donald W. Shriver, *The Lord's Prayer: A Way of Life* (John Knox Press, Atlanta, 1983), pp.72–6.
14. Mark 2:7. (cf. Matthew 9:3 and Luke 5:21).
15. Cf. Matthew 18:15–35.
16. Luke 23:34 and Acts 7:60. Luke's is the only one of the gospels to attribute this saying from the cross to Jesus. Textual scholars doubt that the saying belonged in the original manuscript. If so, the later text reflects the sense of the early Church that such words would have been profoundly compatible with Jesus' own teachings and the meaning of his death to the Church.

17. H. Richard Niebuhr, *Christ and Culture* (Harper, New York, 1951).

18. Hannah Arendt, *The Human Condition* (Doubleday, New York, 1959), p.215.

19. See Susan Jacoby, *Wild Justice: The Evolution of Revenge* (Harper and Row, New York, 1983), for a thorough exploration of this theme in relation to the expectation, ancient in human society, that wrongdoing will be avenged either by the victims or victims' kin, if not by an institutionalized representative. Jacoby regards the 'domestication of revenge' as a significant social-institutional achievement, because it tames the random lawless vengeance of offended individuals and their families.

20. Hosea 11:8–9.

21. Cf. 2 Corinthians 5:19. Theologians who stress the unique power of atonement and forgiveness achieved in the cross of Jesus, to the exclusion of the kinship of this mysterious divine remission of sin to human forgiveness, are close to the doctrine of the Hebrew Bible that refers the forgiveness of human sin to God alone. In the history of the Church this tendency has gone hand in hand with a certain individualism in doctrines of salvation, to the detriment of the horizontal, communal significance of the crucifixion. Some eucharistic liturgies, on the other hand, are careful to signify the birth of the 'new community', the Church, in this mystery. Perhaps, when in the middle of the second century, Christians in Rome put together the so-called Apostles' Creed, they knew from experience why it was appropriate to follow a confession of belief in 'the Holy Catholic Church' and 'the communion of saints' with 'the forgiveness of sins'.

22. Ezekiel 18:2.

23. See Romans 3:10; Psalms 14:1, 53:1.

24. On cities of refuge, cf. Numbers 35; for the law of gleaning, Leviticus 19:10 and Deuteronomy 24:21; and the law of Jubilee, Leviticus 25 and 27.

25. Norman H. Snaith, *The Distinctive Ideas of the Old Testament* (Schocken Books, New York, 1964), p.77; Epworth Press 1944 and 1983.

26. Arendt, *The Human Condition*, p.217.

27. Cf. Philippians 2:5.

28. John 10:16.

29. Cf. Donald W. Shriver, Jr, 'Forgiveness and Politics: The Case of the American Black Civil Rights Movement', Case study 1. Forgiveness and Politics Study Project (New World Publications, London, 1987), p.53.

30. Arendt, *The Human Condition*, pp.214–5.
31. Ibid., p.216.
32. Ibid., p.221.
33. Robert Frost, 'The Star-Gazer' in *The Poetry of Robert Frost*, ed. Edward Connery Lathem (Holt, Rinehart and Winston, New York, 1979).